58.00
5-2013

✓

D0207885

The Rising Costs of Higher Education

Recent Titles in the
CONTEMPORARY WORLD ISSUES
Series

Child Soldiers: A Reference Handbook
David M. Rosen

Medical Tourism: A Reference Handbook
Kathy Stolley and Stephanie Watson

Women and Crime: A Reference Handbook
Judith A. Warner

World Sports: A Reference Handbook
Maylon Hanold

Entertainment Industry: A Reference Handbook
Michael J. Haupert

World Energy Crisis: A Reference Handbook
David E. Newton

Military Robots and Drones: A Reference Handbook
Paul J. Springer

Marijuana: A Reference Handbook
David E. Newton

Religious Nationalism: A Reference Handbook
Atalia Omer and Jason A. Springs

Rising Costs of Higher Education, The: A Reference Handbook
John R. Thelin

Vaccination Controversies: A Reference Handbook
David E. Newton

The Animal Experimentation Debate: A Reference Handbook
David E. Newton

Books in the **Contemporary World Issues** series address vital issues in today's society such as genetic engineering, pollution, and biodiversity. Written by professional writers, scholars, and nonacademic experts, these books are authoritative, clearly written, up-to-date, and objective. They provide a good starting point for research by high school and college students, scholars, and general readers as well as by legislators, business-people, activists, and others.

Each book, carefully organized and easy to use, contains an overview of the subject, a detailed chronology, biographical sketches, facts and data and/or documents and other primary source material, a forum of authoritative perspective essays, annotated lists of print and nonprint resources, and an index.

Readers of books in the **Contemporary World Issues** series will find the information they need in order to have a better understanding of the social, political, environmental, and economic issues facing the world today.

CONTEMPORARY WORLD ISSUES

Science, Technology, and Medicine

The Rising Costs of Higher Education

A REFERENCE HANDBOOK

John R. Thelin

KARL E. MUNDT LIBRARY
Dakota State University
Madison, SD 57042-1799

 ABC-CLIO

Santa Barbara, California • Denver, Colorado • Oxford, England

Copyright 2013 by ABC-CLIO, LLC

All rights reserved. No part of this publication may be reproduced, stored in a retrieval system, or transmitted, in any form or by any means, electronic, mechanical, photocopying, recording, or otherwise, except for the inclusion of brief quotations in a review, without prior permission in writing from the publisher.

Library of Congress Cataloging-in-Publication Data

Thelin, J. R. (John R.)

  The rising costs of higher education : a reference handbook / John R. Thelin.

    pages cm. — (Contemporary world issues)

  Includes bibliographical references and index.

  ISBN 978–1–61069–171–0 (hardback) — ISBN 978–1–61069–172–7 (ebook)

  1. College costs—United States. 2. Education—United States—Finance. 3. Education, Higher—Economic aspects—United States. I. Title.

LB2342.T45   2013

378.3'8—dc23   2012036136

ISBN: 978–1–61069–171–0

EISBN: 978–1–61069–172–7

17 16 15 14 13   1 2 3 4 5

This book is also available on the World Wide Web as an eBook. Visit www.abc-clio.com for details.

ABC-CLIO, LLC
130 Cremona Drive, P.O. Box 1911
Santa Barbara, California 93116-1911

This book is printed on acid-free paper ∞

Manufactured in the United States of America

In Honor of Howard R. Bowen (1908–1989)
Professor and President
An Economist of Higher Education
who showed how academic values
should define the budgets of colleges and universities

Preface

On February 4, 2012 the *New York Times* featured an editorial, "Reining in College Tuition," noting that "A national discussion on how to make public colleges more affordable is long overdue" (*New York Times,* 2012). This attention by the press to the college costs topic came in response to a White House conference of experts convened by the president of the United States in December 2011 and was testimony to the importance of higher education in our national forum of public affairs. Indeed, the rising costs of higher education have coincided with the rising stature of American colleges and universities. But this coincidence is no simple direct cause-effect relationship. It is, rather, a complex story over time. Higher education in the United States now stands out as a success story—an enterprise that commands both prestige and power worldwide (Jencks and Riesman, 1968). This prominence is relatively new and was hardly inevitable. A century ago, American colleges and universities were defensive, often apologetic, about the quality of their PhD programs, medical colleges, scientific laboratories, research libraries, faculty credentials, and undergraduate admissions standards (Slosson, 1910). A bachelor's degree from a college in the United States often was considered suspect when a student applied for advanced studies at a European university. Even as late as 1930, American colleges and universities did not fare well in international rankings and ratings of higher education institutions (Flexner, 1930).

But at the start of the twenty-first century, it is universally acknowledged that these rankings and ratings have undergone a profound reversal of fortunes (Geiger, 1986). Gradually yet persistently since the end of World War II there has been no less than a complete inversion such that American higher education underwent what has been called the Great Transformation that came to full fruition between 1960 and 1980 (Kerr, 1991). The result is that the United States now sets the standard for university-based research and development, for excellence in PhD programs, and the interesting combination of quality and quantity in a diverse configuration that includes more than 2,000 academic degree–granting institutions (Geiger, 1993; Graham and Diamond, 1997; Wildavsky, 2009).

The significant development since the end of World War II is that American higher education has enjoyed expansion and support, which has led it to become, according to some economists, a Knowledge Industry representing as much as 4 percent of the national gross domestic product (GDP) (Machlup, 1975). Starting about 1960, presidents of major research universities unabashedly described their elite institutions as Knowledge Factories, using such metaphors as "economic engines" of state and national development (Kerr, 1963). Along with the rise of the American research university, one finds a concurrent growth and prestige among all categories of postsecondary education, especially its residential liberal arts colleges (Clark, 1970; Koblik and Graubard, 2000). The trend of growth and prosperity extended to community colleges and state comprehensive universities. It also has included the presence of a dynamic, enterprising sector of for-profit academic institutions (Breneman, Pusser, and Turner, 2006).

This profile justifiably warrants national pride but not complacence. At the same time that we celebrate the achievements of colleges and universities, there is a need also to consider critically unresolved issues that have fostered growing concern (Altbach, Berdahl, and Gumport, 1999). According to a *New York Times* article in 2011, a federal government report on student loan default rates plus record levels of student indebtedness indicates multiple questions about the effectiveness and efficiency of the American system of postsecondary education (Lewin, 2011). There also are signs that the structures put into place over the last half-century are creaking and groaning, leading advocates for prestigious colleges and universities to remind the American public why the now-great American universities must be protected and maintained (Cole, 2009). State university presidents routinely complain that their state governments are no longer providing the requisite state funding to ensure institutional vitality.

The alleged financial crisis is complicated by the finding that the allocation of resources within our colleges and universities is not necessarily aligned appropriately with essential missions. For example, a 2010 report from the Knight Foundation Commission presented the alarming news that most university presidents acknowledge they have little control over extravagant spending on commercialized big-time intercollegiate athletics programs. Most troubling in terms of rising costs of higher education was the datum that "Median athletics spending per athlete at institutions in each major athletics conference ranges from 4 to nearly 11 times more than the median spending on education-related activities per student" (Kirwan and Turner, 2010, 5). Overemphasis on big-time college sports has been cited for having inordinate influence that is seen by some articulate analysts as setting the tone of "beer and circus" on the American campus, which is "crippling undergraduate education" (Sperber, 2000).

Alarms about the deteriorating condition of undergraduate education were not confined to the excesses of such extracurricular activities as commercialized college sports. A 2009 study sponsored by the Mellon Foundation drew from comprehensive statistical databases that covered more than 30 years of student records to show that the retention and degree completion rates for undergraduates, especially at state universities, was low and was still in descent (Bowen, McPherson, and Chingos, 2009). By 2010, allegations about the decline in critical thinking and general education as part of the undergraduate experience were widespread in national media, even becoming a source of jokes and caricatures in comic strips and op-ed pieces (see, for example, Trudeau, 2011). The common thread was that students were depicted as spending increased time on socializing, with less time devoted to academic studies. Most troubling was the inference that neither parents nor college officials seemed especially worried about the combination of grade inflation and declining achievement.

Beyond the humor and hyperbole, these cumulative commentaries suggest a serious malaise indicating that higher education in the United States early in the twenty-first century faces crises of confidence. Systematic studies of the civic education of American college students suggest severe deficiencies in the most essential aspects of knowledge about the U.S. Constitution and the respective roles of the legislative, executive, and judicial branches of the federal government, that is, the grounding one would expect to find in citizens and voters are college educated (Bauerlein, 2011, 161–170). This combination of mixed messages conveying both celebration and doubt signal that the rising costs of college as part of the economics of higher education is a significant topic whose complexity justifies a guide to the references and resources for an informed citizenry to follow the fortunes—and try to make sense out of—higher education in the United States as a high-stakes enterprise.

This work presents readers with information, summaries, and sources. And for the topic of rising costs of higher education, it adds another distinctive feature: an emphasis on introducing readers to the logic and analytic processes associated with its scholarly discussions of college costs. This is a reference handbook that considers inquiry to be an active venture, not a spectator sport. The historical and social science sources are most informative when they are animated by drawing from such memorable works as *Judgment Calls in Research* (McGrath et al., 1982) and *Unobtrusive Measures* (Webb et al., 1966). The blend of quantitative and qualitative data that readers can use for following the discussions of the costs of higher education draws from such social and behavioral sciences as economics, political science, history, and sociology. And it also gains some insights from Hollywood. Readers of this book who become involved in the discussions and disputes about rising college costs are advised to consider Bette Davis's warning in the 1950 movie *All About Eve*: "Fasten your seat belts! It's going to be a bumpy night!"

Acknowledgements

I owe special thanks to the contributing authors who wrote timely original essays about the costs of higher education for Chapter 3. Ronald Ehrenberg of Cornell University, Jane V. Wellman of the Delta Cost Project, Terry Hartle of the American Council on Education, Bruce Johnstone of the International Comparative Higher Education Finance and Accessibility Project, James Hearn of the Institute of Higher Education at the University of Georgia, Kristine Dillon of the Consortium on Financing Higher Education, Andrew Kelly of the American Enterprise Institute, Jorge Klor DeAlva of Nexus, Alisa Federico Cunningham and Brian Sponsler of the Institute of Higher Education Policy, and Robert Archibald and David Feldman of the College of William & Mary took time from their own writing and work to provide state-of-the-art analyses of policies and practices in higher education. Douglas Lederman, editor of *Inside Higher Ed,* gave me a good forum to present my analyses and arguments about policies and practices in the economics of higher education. Discussions and presentations at the American Enterprise Institute's periodic gatherings of the working group on the future of higher education, led by Frederick Hess, brought higher education policies to life.

Historical documents in Chapter 5 connect the past and present. My thanks go to Dr. Rita Kirshstein of the Delta Cost Project of the Association of Institutes for Research for permission to reproduce the Delta Cost Project's reports and news releases. Charlotte Bruce Harvey, managing editor of the *Brown Alumni*

Magazine, made possible the inclusion of Debra Shore's 1981 article, "What Price Egalitarianism?" Jessica Steytler, archivist for the Congregational Library of the Congregational Christian Historical Society in Boston, assisted me in tracking down the 1816 charter of the American Educational Society. At the University of Kentucky, Government Documents librarian Roxanna Jones located several landmark documents and transcripts for me. Barry Saturday provided research assistance in obtaining original copies of federal documents dealing with student financial aid programs. Tara Baas, PhD candidate in higher education studies at the University of Kentucky, contributed exemplary research and reviews for the chapters on key people and organizations.

ABC-CLIO publishers have made this project both possible and enjoyable. I wish to thank acquisitions editor Mim Vasan for inviting me to write this book. Beth Ptalis helped me get set up for the project and its author's center. Media editor Melissa Corbett selected excellent illustrations to convey chapter themes. Senior production editor Vicki Moran gave oversight to the project and put me in touch with Suba Ramya Nambiaruran, project manager for PreMedia Global, for overseeing the entire production process. And I am especially appreciative of the expertise and patience of editor Robin Tutt, who provided editorial oversight and commentary for the entire manuscript.

A. Sharon Thelin provided thoughtful commentary, editorial assistance, and a keen eye that makes writing memorable and enjoyable.

References

Altbach, Philip G., Berdahl, Robert O., and Gumport, Patricia J., eds. *American Higher Education in the Twenty-First Century: Social, Political, and Economic Challenges.* Baltimore and London: Johns Hopkins University Press, 1999.

Anonymous. "Reining in College Tuition," *New York Times,* February 4, 2012, A18.

Bauerlein, Mark. "Don't Believe the Hype: Young Voters Are Still Disengaged and Universities Have Few Incentives to Fix It," in David Feith, ed., *Teaching America: The Case for Civic Education*. New York: Rowman & Littlefield, 2011, 161–170.

Bowen, William G., Chingos, Matthew M., and McPherson, Michael S. *Crossing the Finish Line: Completing College at America's Public Universities*. Princeton, NJ: Princeton University Press, 2009.

Breneman, David W., Pusser, Brian, and Turner, Sally E. *Earnings from Learning: The Rise of For-Profit Universities*. Albany: State University of New York Press, 2006.

Clark, Burton R. *The Distinctive College: Antioch, Reed & Swarthmore*. Chicago: Aldine, 1970.

Cole, Jonathan R. *The Great American University: Its Rise to Preeminence, Its Indispensable National Role, Why It Must Be Protected*. New York: Public Affairs of the Perseus Books Group, 2009.

Flexner, Abraham. *Universities: American, English, German*. New York, London, Toronto: Oxford University Press, 1930.

Geiger, Roger L. *To Advance Knowledge: The Growth of American Research Universities, 1900–1940*. New York and Oxford: Oxford University Press, 1986.

Geiger, Roger L. *Research and Relevant Knowledge: American Research Universities Since World War II*. New York and London: Oxford University Press, 1993.

Graham, Hugh Davis and Diamond, Nancy. *The Rise of American Research Universities: Elites and Challengers in the Postwar Era*. Baltimore and London: Johns Hopkins University Press, 1997.

Jencks, Christopher, and Riesman, David. *The Academic Revolution*. Garden City, NY: Doubleday Anchor, 1968.

Kerr, Clark. *The Uses of the University*. Cambridge, MA: Harvard University Press, 1963.

Kerr, Clark. *The Great Transformation in Higher Education*. Albany: State University of New York Press, 1991.

Kirwan, William E., and Turner, Gerald R. *Restoring the Balance: Dollars, Values, and the Future of College Sports*. Miami, FL: Knight Commission on Intercollegiate Athletics, 2010.

Koblik, Steven, and Graubard, Stephen R., eds. *Distinctively American: The Residential Liberal Arts College*. New Brunswick, NJ: Transaction Press, 2000.

Lewin, Tamar, "Student Loan Default Rates Rise Sharply in Past Year," *New York Times,* September 13, 2011, A14.

McGrath, Joseph, Martin, Joanne, and Kulka, Richard. *Judgment Calls in Research*. Beverly Hills, London, New Delhi: Sage Publications, 1982.

Machlup, Fritz. *Education and Economic Growth*. New York: New York University Press, 1975.

Slosson, Edwin E. *Great American Universities*. New York: MacMillan, 1910.

Sperber, Murray. *Beer and Circus: How Big-Time College Sports is Crippling Undergraduate Education*. New York: Henry Holt, 2000.

Trudeau, Gary. *Doonesbury*. Lexington (Kentucky) *Herald-Leader,* August 14, 2011, D2.

Webb, Eugene, Campbell, Donald T., Schwartz, Richard D., and Sechrest, Lee. *Unobtrusive Measures: Nonreactive Research in the Social Sciences*. New York: Rand McNally, 1966.

Wildavsky, Ben. *The Great Brain Race: How Global Universities Are Reshaping the World*. Princeton, NJ: Princeton University Press, 2009.

The Rising Costs of
Higher Education

WILLIAM AND MARY COLLEGE,

WILLIAMSBURG, VIRGINIA.

--->✦<---

Session Begins First Thursday in October, Closes June 28th.

The Oldest and Cheapest College in the South.

Provides a thorough Normal and Academic Training. Historical Surroundings. Healthy climate. Forty-eight miles from Richmond. on the C. & O. Railroad.

--->✦<---

—EXPENSES—

FOR STUDENTS PLEDGED TO TEACH AS REQUIRED

--->✦ BY LAW. ✦<---

(Tuition, board, fuel, lights and washing) . . . . $10 per month,
Other Students, from . . . . $12 to $14 per month
Tuition fee chargeable against pay Students $17.50 half session.

SEND FOR CATALOGUE.

LYON G. TYLER, President.

Introduction: College Costs in the National News Media

The rising costs of higher education is not a topic that evokes the drama associated with news headlines and photographs reporting a tsunami that hits Japan. However, concern over rising college costs does endure as a continual source of news and national discussion in American society. Rather than bringing to mind a catastrophic wave or a disastrous "perfect storm," it conjures the maritime image of a tide that is problematic because it gradually yet persistently reaches new heights each year. Most troubling is that there appears to be no relief in sight. Consider, for example, the range of national media coverage that college costs attracted during the summer of 2011 and then continued to escalate in 2012:

- At a White House briefing for personal finance writers, President Barack Obama emphasized his concern over high college costs, noting that both the First Lady and he had acquired substantial student loan debts so that they could attend law school. This personal matter had policy implications because his experience (and debt) shaped his thinking on federal student financial aid legislation (Novack, 2011).

1892 Admissions Poster for The College of William & Mary. (John Thelin)

- The *AARP Bulletin* presented senior citizens with suggestions for "99 Great Ways to Save." Marbled in with predictable hints on how to reduce utility bills, to lower health care premiums, and to shop frugally at the grocery store was a strategy not usually associated with the lifestyle of older retirees—"Item 14: Cut college costs: Make direct subsidized federal loans your first choice; they're easier to get, tend to be cheaper, and there's no interest while your in school at least half-time" (AARP, 2011, 24).

- The CNN evening television show *In the Arena* featured commentator Eliot Spitzer's report "The High Cost of College." His concluding message to viewers was, "As states are increasingly financially stressed, raising tuition at public universities is becoming more and more common. While still a bargain compared to private universities, public higher ed is no longer the cost-free avenue to education it once was" (Spitzer, 2011).

- A *Washington Post* editorial, "Don't Gut Pell Grants," stated that "Debate is intensifying over the federal Pell Grant program. Some see runaway spending that can't be sustained in the face of mounting national debt; others believe no one with skill and determination should be denied a college education for lack of financial resources . . . We think it's shortsighted to try to save money by denying [people] the chance to better themselves, but there is merit in making the program more cost-effective" (*Washington Post*, 2011, A23).

- High-tech entrepreneur Peter Thiel announced the first recipients of a fellowship that "Pays 24 Talented Students $100,000 Not to Attend College." His rationale for the fellowship program was that "some entrepreneurial students may be better off leaving college" in order to "develop their ideas more quickly than they would at a traditional university. Its broader aim goes beyond helping the 24 winners, by raising big questions about the state of higher education" (Wieder, 2011).

- The College Savings Foundation held a press conference announcing that its national survey showed that "A Quarter of Parents Want the Government to Regulate College Costs" (*Chronicle of Higher Education*, 2011).

- The U.S. Department of Education announced a new federal regulation that required colleges to provide student consumer information for a "net price" calculator. The legislation includes provisions for a website on which consumers can find out which colleges are most expensive, and which are least expensive. This "college navigator" feature is part of the Higher Education Opportunity Act Information on College Costs (Lewin, June 30, 2011, A13).

- The *New York Times* Sunday Review section featured a "Room for Debate" forum on the topic, "College: Is It Worth The Cost?" (*New York Times*, August 28, 2011, SR 12).

- National Public Radio's *Here and No*w talk show focused on the question, "Will Today's Generation Be Less Educated Than Their Parents?" One implication was that rising college costs in the United States have become unbearable for many students and are lowering graduation rates (Young, 2011).

- The lead story on NBC's *Evening News* on Friday, September 16, 2011, was, "Is College Still a Good Investment?" The report noted that "since 1980 the price of college tuition had gone up 800% more than the rate of inflation and that student loan debt is projected to pass the $1 trillion mark this year." The news broadcast noted that according to reporter Rehema Ellis, there was "more student loan debt than credit card debt." More than 250,000 recent college graduates were unemployed and there was widespread discontent about whether the expense of going to college was warranted given dismal job prospects (Ellis, 2011).

- Rising college costs reached high tide in national political news in January 2012 when the president of the United States mentioned the topic in his State of the Union Address. Then two days later, on January 27 in an address in Ann Arbor on the campus of the University of Michigan, he called for linking federal aid to tuition costs. According to the Associated Press coverage, "President Barack Obama fired a warning at the nation's colleges and universities on Friday, threatening to strip their federal aid if they 'jack up tuition' every year and to give the money instead to schools showing restraint and value" (Kuhnhenn and Heffling, 2012, A15).

The sound bites and headlines in the samples of press coverage that appeared in 2011 and 2012 are alluring and, in some cases, alarming. But their brevity and a tendency to slant toward sensationalism in order to attract viewers, readers, and voters also call for the caveat that they are not the whole story. Therefore, the role of this work is less to provide simple answers, and more to help readers and researchers progress toward significant questions and thoughtful explorations.

From Popular Press to Public Policies

To make the transition from popular press coverage to public policy analysis, it is useful to have a guide to the concepts, context, and contents of the college costs discussions. This includes providing a systematic and logical strategy by which to respond to the kinds of claims and issues raised in the news media. For example, CNN commentator Eliot Spitzer's 2011 *In the Arena* broadcast began with the startling statement, "Today's number of the day is 38%. That's the percentage that Arizona State University—the nation's largest public university—raised its tuition between the 2007–2008 school year and this year. From \$4,971 to \$6,844." Spitzer then went on to report, "One of the most expensive places to send your kids—Bates College in Maine at \$51,300 a year. On the school's website President Elaine Tuttle Hansen makes this promise: 'You will be changed by Bates forever.'" But, Spitzer, cautioned, "Change can mean many things—being deeply in debt to being one of the many well-educated-but still-unemployed college grads searching for that good entry-level job. It is tough out there these days for recent college grads, especially with big debts to pay off" (Spitzer, 2011).

This provocative and often polemical material hardly exhausts the topic. Selected statistical fragments in the news coverage raise more questions than they answer. Consider, for example, the inference that $6,844 for state university tuition is expensive—or that a 38 percent annual increase in tuition is high. Perhaps so, but compared to what and when? The initial response is to compile a list of reasonable questions about the claims that are integral to the news broadcast:

- How do states other than Arizona provide for higher education? Is the Arizona State University tuition charge relatively high or low among state universities?

- Why is 38 percent a call for alarm? Is the annual percentage increase announced by officials at Arizona State University relatively high or low among its counterpart state universities elsewhere?

- Is Bates College gouging the student market with its $51,300 charges per year? Does it include room, board, and books as well as tuition and fees?

- How does one reconcile the significant differences between the two colleges Spitzer has mentioned in the same paragraph? In other words, is there some readily available explanation for the fact that Arizona State University charges $6,844 per year and Bates College charges $51,300? Are the respective charges referring to the same services?

- What are the connotations of "public" and "private" institutions for understanding differences in calculating college costs?

- What is the historical perspective on Spitzer's snapshots? Have higher education costs gone up more than other major purchases, such as health care, real estate, household utilities, or automobile fuel? Are there sources and tools that allow a reader to take into account changes in inflation rates over the years?

- How do trends in the costs of higher education compare to taxation for other public spending categories such as prisons or highway construction?

The news coverage underscores the need to find access to—and then read about—the context, content, and concepts that must accompany the statistical fragments and editorials. Beneath and beyond the headlines of daily news coverage, rising college costs is a topic that has attracted—and maintained—the serious, systematic analysis of numerous academic disciplines. We now have access to an abundance of interesting statistical and financial databases compiled by a mix of state and federal agencies, private foundations, and university-based researchers.

Furthermore, the topic includes informed analyses from a variety of perspectives, ranging from economists (Bowen, 1977; Bowen, 1980; McPherson, Schapiro, and Winston, 1993; Ehrenberg, 2000; Vedder, 2004; Archibald and Feldman, 2010) and public policy researchers to sociologists, historians, anthropologists, organizational theorists, and philosophers. The result is a formidable information base that has generated an ongoing series of interesting debates.

So an initial query—perhaps sparked by the curiosity of prospective college students and their parents and teachers—about why college costs so much leads to the need for a work that enables concerned readers to be able to learn about how colleges and universities operate. This work then can proceed to the broad, complex topic of the economics and finances of higher education. The availability of excellent databases, articles, reports, and books on the topic does not mean that reference librarians and researchers now have obvious answers to questions. Rather, thoughtful consideration and use of these resources will promote better and more informed questions and discussions about a topic that permeates the life of our culture, our national economy, and academic institutions.

Context: Access and Affordability
in American Higher Education

One explanation for the persistent newsworthiness of rising costs of higher education is that "going to college" is serious business for Americans, and it is inseparable from paying for college. So although making college accessible and affordable is widely praised as part of the American Dream, this national commitment quickly leads to serious questions about what is reasonable and what has gotten out of hand in determining college costs. It is a volatile topic that usually generates more heat than light. To reverse the trend—away from heat and toward illumination—one needs to consider essential issues about college costs from a variety of perspectives so as to provide students, parents, taxpayers, and other citizens—along with college and university leaders, state and national legislators—with clarity about the implications of various higher education practices and policies.

Why is this clarification of terms and issues important? Since the end of World War II, we as a nation have aspired to provide mass and even universal access to postsecondary education (Zook, 1947; Gardner, 1961). In 2010, for example, more than 2,000 accredited colleges and universities in the United States enrolled more than 17 million students—of which about 70 percent were undergraduates. This represents a dramatic change over the past century. In 1910, for example, less than 5 percent of late adolescents between the ages of 18 and 22 attended college. Since about 1970, more than 60 percent in that age cohort enroll in a college, university, or institute—an achievement that has fulfilled projections made by sociologists in 1970 (Trow, 1970). Furthermore, college enrollments now include a significant, growing number and percentage of adults older than 25.

Yet these consistent gains in college enrollment kindle rather than temper heated debates about who should pay for college— and how much. To speak of higher education as an "investment in learning" underscores that for most American families, it (along with buying a house) is one of the largest expenses one faces over a lifetime. All this converges to indicate that the topic of college costs has endured and grown as a perennial source of concern for students as college consumers. At the same time, academic institutions—colleges and universities—grapple with what to offer students, how much such services and facilities will cost, and how much to charge each student for tuition and fees. At the level of national policies and pride, there has been recurrent concern that inordinate increases in the costs of higher education have contributed to the United States' decline in worldwide standings related to the percentage of college graduates in the general population (*Hechinger Report*, 2011; Johnstone and Marcucci, 2010).

College Costs: A Tradition of College Consumerism

One source of continuity in the analysis of the rising costs of higher education is a tradition of *student consumerism* that has extended from the 17th to the 21st century. For example, at Harvard College in the 18th century, students rebelled against the administration, demanding that the Board of Overseers dismiss the president when they discovered that the president's wife—who was in charge of dining commons—was acting in a bizarre, spiteful manner by putting mackerel guts and lamb's dung in the hasty pudding (*Harvard Crimson*, 1933; Sack, 1949, 3).

In contrast to this infamous episode of "food for thought" consumer protest, there are many positive examples of college students in America being quick to appreciate a college bargain. For example, in 1876, an undergraduate explained to Professor Henry Adams that he had journeyed from the Midwest to Boston to enroll at Harvard because, after all, said the student, "A degree from Harvard College is worth money to me in Chicago" (Veysey, 1964, 270). Then as now, aspiring and ambitious young Americans have viewed an investment in college as an option both for their immediate advanced studies and their long-term future prospects.

Students' keen awareness about what they perceive to be the costs and benefits of colleges has, in turn, prompted American colleges and universities to be perpetually vigilant about tuition charges and balanced budgets while at the same time making certain to provide programs and features that college officials think (or, rather, hope) will be attractive. These simultaneous demands have created an institutional behavior animated by the realization that each college has to compete vigorously to enroll students—especially, students who can pay their bills. An illustration of this dependence on paying students is a 2011 a survey reported by the *New York Times* that noted that universities were "seeking out students of means," with the elaboration, "More than half the admissions officers at public research universities, and more than a third at four-year colleges, said that they had been working harder in the past year to recruit students who need no financial aid and can pay full price, according to the survey of 462 admissions directors and enrollment managers conducted in August and early September" (Lewin, September 21, 2011, A18). The result is a living history, that is, a tradition of consumerism marked by a reciprocal process in which students and colleges each year go through an elaborate ritual of application, acceptance, and rejection.

This pattern of admission and enrollment in American colleges and universities seems so obvious to students and parents in the United States today that often it is erroneously taken for granted as a universal, typical feature of higher education worldwide and for all times. But it is not. It is the result of a distinctive American arrangement of social, economic, and political features. One determinant is that the United States has been a nation of enthusiastic college builders. Hence, the number and diversity of colleges and universities give prospective students a large selection from which to choose. Each college, in turn, has the challenge of positioning itself in terms of market appeal, including such variables as tuition, curricular offerings, extracurricular activities, and alumni success. The strong consumerism tradition is paradoxical in that it can at times drive up college costs, whereas in other instances it drives college costs down.

Charters and College Building in America

Consumerism and competition for college admissions, then, are at the heart of understanding the costs of higher education. A second defining characteristic that has greatly influenced college costs is that higher education in the United States over the past three centuries often has been an *overbuilt enterprise*. This is a bold claim, especially since it seems to be counterintuitive to news media coverage about how difficult it is today for high school students to gain admission to college—and, once admitted, to pay for college. Despite these questions and concerns today about how to gain admission to college, the historical record indicates that with the exception of a few periods, there have been an adequate number of colleges to accommodate students who have sought to go to college.

The genesis of this distinctive consumerism that shapes American higher education tradition dates back to political and legal changes the American colonies underwent in becoming the new United States. The importance of this transition was that colonial colleges under the auspices of the British Empire were defined and operated by specific legal resources and restraints. In England and, hence, in its colonies, it was difficult for a group to obtain a college charter, that is, an official document that allowed an institution to confer academic degrees. However, if a colony did gain approval, it usually meant that the host government honored an obligation to provide the chartered college with adequate and sometimes generous funding. A colonial legislature often dedicated taxes from tobacco sales, toll roads, and bridges and ferries, for example, to provide direct support to the colony's chartered college. This American arrangement in the New World was analogous to the supervision and support the monarchy bestowed on the historic English universities Oxford and Cambridge.

Elsewhere in Europe, monarchies, or sometimes popes and bishops, tended to protect and provide for their favored elite universities to which they had granted a charter. In the American colonies, there was typically one chartered college per colony, which tended to make an established college a protected entity. A good illustration of this is that Princeton University was originally named The College of New Jersey. Brown University was founded as The College of Rhode Island and Providence Plantations. The University of Pennsylvania was—and still is—the University of Pennsylvania. A college charter was serious business and a rare commodity. When settlers in western Massachusetts petitioned the colonial governor for a charter to establish a new college, Harvard College officials protested to maintain their exclusive academic franchise in Massachusetts. A college charter was valuable as a crucial arrow in the quiver of ambitious entrepreneurs in their political maneuvering. For example, the president of Dartmouth College, located in New Hampshire, held out the promise of transporting the college's charter to western Massachusetts on the condition that the citizens there would then declare this region as a new "state" and then appoint him as governor of this proposed new political entity (Curti and Nash, 1965, 34–35).

College Costs and Competition in the 19th Century

These customs of college charters and their funding changed drastically with the creation of the United States (Whitehead, 1973). This was because the new nation had a limited national government. Power tended to be vested in the member states of the union, especially in the area of education. Unlike England, France, or Germany, the United States had no central ministry of education. There were no royal or national charters for a college in the United States. Each state reserved the right to charter such essential institutions as banks and colleges. And, unlike universities in England or France, in the early 19th century, state governments in the United States were eager to grant collegiate charters—often as a convenient, cheap way of repaying political debts and providing patronage to voters and donors. But the same state governors and legislatures were frugal when it came to subsidies. So unlike the royal or colonial governments, the states were reluctant to provide much in the way of regular funding for the chartered colleges. The result was that a college president who had the good fortune to obtain a state charter then had to face the career-long prospect of having to work persistently to attract donors and paying students for the stark reason that the state legislature was unlikely to be either stable or generous in year-to-year college subsidies.

The colleges' quest to enroll and retain paying students in the young United States also meant that starting in the early 1800s, there was a boom in founding colleges (Burke, 1982). Numerous new towns, especially in the South and Midwest, founded local colleges, often with religious denominational affiliation, as part of their community-building and civic pride. This continued well into the 20th century. This building boom meant that around 1890, compared to England's three universities with charters that allowed them to grant bachelor's degrees, the United States had more than 300, with the state of Ohio hosting more than 50 colleges.

All the more peculiar about this abundance of American colleges was that outside major metropolitan areas, provisions for a *bona fide* public school system ranging from elementary school through high school were uncertain and in many cases absent. What this meant was that a large number of colleges were competing to enroll a small number of students. The competition was especially fierce if a college wished to enroll a student who had a high school diploma and could afford to pay tuition. Not surprisingly, there was a relatively high institutional closure rate among colleges. Or, in numerous cases, a college with dwindling enrollments and bleak demographic prospects might merge with another college as a survival strategy.

The enterprising spirit among colleges included numerous curricular experiments intended to make courses of study relevant and attractive to prospective students. A typical form of academic consumerism at many medical colleges was for students to purchase tickets for each medical lecture. Professors also charged students fees for examinations that were required to receive the medical degree. Both students and faculty were aware of costs and benefits of professional degree programs. At some medical schools, students were required to purchase a cadaver for use in anatomy classes. One reason the medical colleges were attractive was that they were expedient and inexpensive. This was so because they had few admissions requirements and the course of study was relatively quick—usually two years of full-time enrollment at most.

Perhaps the extreme example of institutional efficiency was a flourishing medical college in Indiana in the 1830s (Smith, 1994). It was able to keep instructional expenses low simply because it did not have any classroom, laboratories, libraries, or dormitories. The medical college president also kept faculty salaries to a minimum because there were no professors or instructors so that students just paid a fee and received a diploma. He was the only personnel on the payroll in his dual roles of founder and president. The main expense was to purchase high-quality sheepskin diplomas. Students paid a fee to receive the MD degree (and high-quality diploma). This was a marvel of saving time, money, and trouble. Both the new MD students and the college president went away happy. This case illustrates yet another tradition in American higher education—the diploma mill. In an unregulated industry, the message to patients who went to a medical doctor was *caveat emptor*, "let the buyer beware!"

Many college presidents in the 19th century experimented with adding new courses parallel to the traditional liberal arts curriculum. This included such programs as a "scientific school," a "commercial course," a "normal school" for teacher education, a law school, a seminary, and an agricultural college. Enterprising colleges often offered special courses to provide secondary school instruction—a strategy that allowed a college to collect tuition payments for these precollege courses and, later, to enroll the same student who had eliminated admissions deficiencies and was ready to begin freshman studies.

American colleges over the course of the 19th century also provided students as consumers with another set of options, suggesting a differentiated market: namely, gearing a college to a particular demographic constituency. Although middle class young white men constituted the core of the college-going populace, there was a steady addition of new, specialized colleges such as women's colleges, colleges for particular religious denominations, and colleges for African Americans. Eventually coeducational colleges in which both women and men enrolled in the same course of study became available. On balance, colleges in the 19th century served a diverse American population, but usually did so with exclusive rather than wholly integrated student bodies.

Context: Student Financial Aid Precedents and Practices

Collegiate competition for students, and an impulse to combine both a service ethos to attract talented students as well as to ensure a flow of cash into the bursar's office, gave rise to a third significant feature of college (and college costs): offering student financial aid. The most enduring, historic tradition of student financial aid has been from college endowments and holdings. Even within the "elite" colonial colleges founded in the late 17th and 18th centuries, undergraduates typically were designated as "commoners" or "servitors." The former were those who could afford to pay "full freight" for tuition and dining. The latter were the equivalent of work-study recipients who had to defray their scholarship awards by working in the dining halls. Important to note is that not until years later—the late 1960s—did colleges and universities give large amounts of scholarship grants to a student. Rather, the institutional strategy, especially in the 19th and early 20th centuries, was to keep costs low (so that tuition was relatively low for all students). Students who were not able to afford tuition relied on loans that they had to repay.

Colleges in the nineteenth century were lean operations, with overhead expenses kept to a minimum. One exception was the practice of a well-paid president, who then hired a multipurpose administrator called the college agent whose job was to scour the adjacent region and counties for two kinds of prey: donors for even relatively small amounts and paying students who might also be able to read and do rudimentary mathematics. Most colleges existed on a year-to-year basis, seldom certain that they could meet their payroll. There were few full-time professors, and most instructors were paid low wages and had little job security. What a difference a century makes! Typical colleges and universities of the 21st century rely on multiple sources to acquire large amounts of money and then to spend these funds on a large, diverse array of projects that suggest a complex institution beyond the wildest dreams of college presidents and professors from an earlier era.

Even though most 19th-century colleges wanted to maintain control over their young and restless students, they were limited by a lack of money. It was expensive to build on-campus dormitories to house all students and then hire instructors to serve as proctors who supervised student conduct. In contrast to the typical campus today, colleges invested little in libraries or laboratories. There was no student union building, let alone a gymnasium, fitness club, drama theatre, or health center.

Outside the campus, there was a thriving private loan industry whose participating institutions included regional and national church groups, private foundations, and private enterprises (Wilkinson, 2005; Horowitz, 1987). By our standards and expectation today, what is most surprising about paying for college until after World War II was that there was little participation by the federal government as a source of scholarship grants or student loans until the late 1960s—and not really in any substantive way until 1972. The consequences of these practices was that even at prestigious, established colleges, tuition charges were low, seldom surpassing more than $130 per year between about 1890 and 1920.

Attracting Students by Discounts and Low Prices

Most puzzling to our contemporary notions of going to college and paying for college is that in the late 19th century, many American colleges behaved in a peculiar bidding war for students. A full tuition charge in April might be $110. However, if a college had not filled its entering class with paying students by August, the president and bursar would arrange to lower the tuition charge, for example, to $75. The rationale was that low price at the last minute was better than having an empty seat in the lecture hall. One flaw in this strategy was that college trustees often either were ignorant or indifferent to the social fact that for most American families, a charge of zero for tuition would not have turned the tide to allow a son or daughter go to college. Price and cost were not the issue since most families depended on earned income or free labor from children working on the family farm or help out with the family business.

Well into the late 19th century, there was another phenomenon that lessened the appeal of colleges: most work in the American economy did not require a college degree. Even if a young adult could afford to pay for college, more often than not, the idea of spending four years on campus meant a delay in making one's fortune. This was obviously true if one were a gold prospector, a store clerk, a farmer, or a traveling salesman. Less obvious is that even such professions as law, medicine, journalism, engineering, and clergy seldom required a bachelor's degree. Little wonder, then, that college presidents often supplemented the traditional liberal arts college course of studies with some innovations.

In the South, where state economies and family incomes had been decimated by the Civil War, historic colleges made some valiant marketing efforts to persuade prospective students that enrollment was both prestigious and affordable. The College of William & Mary in Virginia, founded in 1692, promoted itself as the Oldest and Cheapest College in the South. To further enhance the college's attractiveness, Virginia's state legislature provided full scholarships to William & Mary students who pledged to teach in the state's public schools.

Prosperity and Prestige from 1880 to 1910

Along with such marketing and student recruitment efforts, American colleges and universities survived and then flourished between 1870 and 1910 due to two fortuitous turns of events. First, they became the favorite object of large-scale philanthropy, generously bestowed by a new generation of industrialists who had made unprecedented fortunes in oil refining, coal, steel, shipbuilding, railroads, and commerce. The most visible manifestation of this largesse was the construction of large, ornate historic revival-style campus buildings. The second simultaneous development was that going to college unexpectedly became fashionable, especially among the new wealthy American families, with diffusion to the middle classes. And, for the American working class, even if sending their children to college was unaffordable, the college campus and its student life acquired an aura of prestige and mystique. These combined trends gave colleges in the United States new, unprecedented leverage in attracting donors, students, and political supporters.

Despite this new popularity and prestige, for the first two decades of the 20th century, there is little evidence of "selective admissions" in the statistical sense that a college had a surplus of qualified applicants over admissions slots. If a student could pass a college's entrance examination and pay tuition, he or she was admitted. When the number of new students increased substantially, a college simply allowed the size of the student body to continue to grow. After World War I, however, there are some signs that selected colleges started to limit growth. Selective admissions sometimes included screening out applicants on the basis of low grades but also was symptomatic of exclusion and discrimination based on such nonacademic factors as race, religion, ethnicity, and gender (Synnott, 1979; Karabel, 2005).

One reason that enrollments started to grow nationwide was more public high schools in all regions. This steady growth of both compulsory education and well-funded, tax-supported high schools provided the necessary academic preparation for a student both to receive a high school diploma and then to qualify for admission to the state university or to numerous private colleges. It also allowed colleges to reduce the amount of time and resources they had to devote to preparatory and remedial studies for entering freshmen. Indeed, in many states in the West, Midwest, and South, the flagship state university took on the role of being the center of a statewide comprehensive educational system.

Most college-related press coverage between 1890 and 1910 focused on the emergence of potentially "great American universities," with particular attention to such innovations as PhD programs, research libraries, advanced scientific laboratories, university presses, and publication of scholarly journals (Veysey, 1964). And one of the foremost and most publicized examples of this model was the Johns Hopkins University, founded in Baltimore in 1873. On closer inspection, however, by 1910, Johns Hopkins University provided a stern lesson that university builders and their advocates often overlooked: namely, no American university no matter how impressive its advanced programs might be, could afford to neglect the multiple benefits of having a base of undergraduate studies. The traditional four-year college within the university structure provided the necessary source of institutional revenues along with a potential supply of future students for master's and doctorate programs. Between 1900 and 1910, Johns Hopkins University made a daring move to reduce both the size and priority of its undergraduate college, a strategy that put the entire university at financial risk by 1910 (Slosson, 1910). Elsewhere, undergraduate life and enrollments thrived at both colleges and universities nationwide.

Colleges between World War I and World War II

The two decades between World Wars I and II represented a period of aspiration and ambition, both for American colleges and for prospective students (Levine, 1986). Eventually, the popularity of going to college combined with the increased number of academically qualified applicants created a substantial market that allowed many colleges to persistently raise tuition charges after 1920. One development was that the tuition price differential between public and private institutions widened. According to economists Claudia Goldin and Lawrence F. Katz (1999), "The average (listed) in-state tuition plus fees for under-graduates at public sectors in 1933 was $61 ($753 in 1999 dollars), as compared with $265 ($3,272 in 1997 dollars) in the private sector" (50, 37–62). An early example of a dramatic change in the balancing of price and cost in a college education came about, ironically, during the Great Depression. A small number of socially elite (albeit not necessarily academically strong) colleges assessed their constituencies and marketing position, leading to the decision that they would raise tuition to an unprecedentedly high level simply because they were aiming to enroll students from exceptionally affluent families who were impervious to more typical circumstances of unemployment, limited income, and minimal discretionary wealth. According to a 1937 study published in the *Journal of Higher Education*, "Amherst, Williams, and Wesleyan all charge tuition fees of $400, while women's colleges of comparable type in the same geographical area charge $500. State universities, such as those in Wisconsin, Illinois, and Michigan charge from incidentals to $100 per annum, while large independent universities in the same area tend to charge $300" (Stoke, 1937, 297). Vasssar College's tuition was $1,200 in 1931. Bennington College in Vermont charged $1,650 for tuition in 1936. When one indexes for inflation, figures for 2011 are about $18,000 and $27,000, respectively.

The expansion of state colleges and universities often included, in some states, a commitment to taxpayer subsidy for tuition. For over a century in California, for example, public higher education maintained a policy of no tuition charges. State legislatures, governors, and taxpayers in the Midwest and on the Pacific Coast supported the argument made by university presidents: "You can't have a great state without a great state university." The result was that from about 1920 to 1970, public higher education enjoyed growth and a generous flow of state resources. By 1950, enrollments in public higher education were equal to those in private (i.e., independent) colleges and universities. This expansion continued such that by 1990, public higher education enrolled about 80 percent of college students.

Post–World War II Innovation: The GI Bill and Student Financial Aid

The crucial events in the complexities of college costs and college pricing came about after World War II. This included the GI Bill (Kiester, 1994, 128–139) along with the vision of student aid and college access provided by the 1947 Truman Commission Report on Higher Education in a Democracy (Zook, 1947). The GI Bill was notable in that it was portable, that is, a veteran who qualified for the scholarship was allowed to carry the financial aid to an accredited college of one's choice. The financial award attempted to acknowledge and cover a broad range of expenses, including living expenses, books and supplies, and tuition. In addition, this federal program was an *entitlement*, that is, a there was no cap on the number of recipients. If an applicant met the published eligibility requirements, the federal government was pledged to award the financial aid. Congressional discussions and drafting of the bill were forthright in noting that one aim was to show national gratitude for those who had served in the wartime military; a related aim was to make college feasible and affordable to a large number of young Americans who prior to World War II might not have considered going to college.

A distinct yet related document was the 1947 President's Commission Report, *Higher Education for American Democracy*, chaired by George Zook. The presidential commission's recommendations extended the spirit of the GI Bill into the peacetime economy with recommendations that state governments should increase their commitment to funding public higher education. A novel wrinkle was that the report encouraged the federal government to enter into partnership with colleges and universities as well as with state governments to become a major, enduring source of need-based student financial aid. Although the report was hailed by numerous national constituencies, the letter and spirit of its recommendations did not reach fruition for about two decades. Its significance was that it served as a blueprint for the pioneering federal student financial aid legislation that was approved starting in 1972.

Prestige and Popularity of Colleges, 1950 to 1970

The rapid increases in college enrollments nationwide due to the affordability made possible by the student financial aid of the GI Bill tapered some by 1952. Nonetheless, there was an indelible change in the American public's expectations about opportunities to go to college. Undergraduate enrollments continued to rise consistently over the next two decades, mainly because the number and percentage of high school graduates who sought advanced education continued to increase, culminating eventually with Baby Boomers reaching college age. Quantitative increases were accompanied by qualitative changes as colleges and universities acquired mystique and reputation for excellence and prestige.

A good example of the heightened awareness of college prestige—both by proud, upwardly mobile parents as well as by prospective students—is provided by novelist Philip Roth's memoir about his generation's experience in the era of the prototypical undergraduate world of Joe College and Betty Co-Ed. Roth's parents, reasonably prosperous after World War II but without prior experience in going to college, journeyed from their urban New Jersey neighborhood to take their academically oriented son on visits to various colleges during his senior year of high school. After visiting Bucknell University in Pennsylvania, both parents and son agreed that this was a special place that fulfilled their image of how an historic and traditional campus should look. Bucknell stood out to them as a "real college"—an idyllic residential campus with red brick neo-Colonial buildings, athletic fields, green lawns, and an impressive, lively student life. Roth, however, was worried about his family being able to pay the relatively high tuition at Bucknell, stating, "Yes, but how can we afford it if they won't give me a scholarship for September?"

His father put his son's fears to rest, exclaiming, "You like it, don't you? Forget the scholarship ... You want to go here, you're going" (Roth, 1987, 45). The revealing feature of this episode, which was played out numerous times nationwide, was that parental pride and the aspiration for their children to go to a prestigious college factored into decisions about college choice. Going to the "right" college meant that low price was not the sole or even main criterion in these deliberations. This was a social fact that gave selective colleges great leverage in the American preoccupation with college as a source of upward mobility and social prestige. The appeal of academic architecture and campus mystique was hardly confined to the historic private colleges, as the state universities had come of age and conveyed their own distinctive heritage. As historian Allan Nevins observed in 1962:

> One of the more difficult obligations of these new institutions has been the creation of an atmosphere, a tradition, a sense of the past which might play as important a part in the education of sensitive students as any other influence. This requires time, sustained attention to cultural values, and the special beauties of landscape and architecture ... This spiritual grace the state universities cannot quickly acquire, but they have been gaining it. (82)

State universities gained leverage thanks to some thoughtful legislation as well as generous appropriations from governors and legislatures. One helpful innovation was the practice of states' formulas for per capita student funding. This provided incentive and resources for the state universities to gain substantial funding by carrying out the state's commitment to educate an unprecedented number of high school graduates. In addition, universities enjoyed the benefit of what economists call "increasing returns to margin" in which the institution's expenditures for educating each additional student enrolled are less than the state's subsidy to the institution in return for enrolling that additional student.

During the high-inflation years immediately following World War II, private colleges were at a disadvantage in that they had little way to raise additional monies to absorb inflation. The competition for top students often was a matter of prestige versus price. Between 1950 and 1960 for the first time in American higher education, undergraduate enrollments in public colleges and universities surpassed the number of students enrolled in private institutions—a trend that would continue in an era of mass higher education (Trow, 1970).

Need-Blind Admissions and Need-Based Financial Aid, 1960 to 1980

The important sequel to the popularity of going to college as well as the related campus visits and family deliberations about college choices is that as late as 1960, even the most prestigious, affluent colleges did not give a great deal of student financial aid (Karabel, 2005). Families were expected to make their own arrangements by dipping into savings or borrowing from uncles or grandparents. Banks were reluctant to make loans for college, especially since a student's potential future earnings were not regarded as legitimate collateral. And most available student aid from a college or university financial aid office was in the form of loans.

Independent colleges and universities started to shed this parsimony after 1960 by taking initiative to provide need-based student financial aid in the form of scholarships. The terminology that came to be used was student financial aid "packaging," that is, a tier of scholarship, work study, and loans. The amount and type of award was calculated by college officials who relied on information that a student provided via a standardized form—the parent's confidential statement on income known as the *FAF* (Financial Aid Form)—administered through the College Entrance Examination Board's *CSS* (College Scholarship Service). Colleges that took the lead on such policies tended to be private and established, with a large endowment and a commitment to recruiting talented students from all income levels and geographic areas throughout the United States.

The effective, dramatic change in making academically prestigious private colleges affordable was the implementation of a two-step procedure. First, at Ivy League colleges and other academically strong institutions, admissions decisions were *need blind*. This meant that admissions officers read applications and made decisions about acceptance without regard to financial need. Admissions committees did not know whether an applicant could afford to pay the college's tuition. Second, student financial aid awarded by the college was *need based*. This meant that if an applicant were granted admission, the college guaranteed that the admission offer would be accompanied by a financial aid package—a combination of scholarships, loans, and work study—that met the student's financial need required to pay for attending the college. This was a bold move for colleges because it was expensive. It also showed that colleges were increasingly serious about casting their nets to attract academic talent regardless of family income. It signaled a genuine academic revolution in American life that sociologists hailed as the "partial triumph of the meritocracy" (Jencks and Riesman, 1968, 12).

The institutional initiatives to make college affordable were eventually assisted substantially by the eventual entrance of the federal government into major programs of student financial aid for higher education that were negotiated in the late 1960s and put into place in the early 1970s.

The Federal Government and Student
Financial Aid Initiatives, 1950 to 2010

The federal government's substantive role in student financial aid eventually gained some momentum with the National Defense Education Act of the 1958, which put forth a concerted effort to provide generous funding to promote advanced studies in the sciences and other fields—an impetus triggered by concerns that the nation's educational achievement was lagging behind the Soviet Union in the wake of its successful launching of Sputnik..

A broader base of federal support for student financial surfaced in the mid-1960s, gradually gaining appeal as part of extensions of civil rights legislation. Student financial aid reached fruition in 1972 with bipartisan congressional approval of and funding for *the Basic Educational Opportunity Grants (BEOG)*—later renamed Pell Grants—federal student loans, work-study programs, and the *Supplemental Educational Opportunity Grants (SEOG)*. These federal programs followed by a few years a massive change in campus commitment to providing need-based student financial aid that started around 1964. Pell Grants altered the dynamics of college choice because the scholarship grant award was designated to individual students, as distinguished from being allocated to colleges to award at their discretion. This meant that colleges had an incentive to compete for students who would bring with them the portable Pell Grant award to help pay tuition. One source of leverage was that a college's financial aid director could fold in a Pell Grant award as part of the packaging to supplement grants and other forms of aid provided by the college itself. The net result for students was increased access, choice, and affordability.

The growth of the Pell Grant program was impressive. In its first year, the program received an appropriation of $122 million and awarded grants to 176,000 full-time undergraduates. Two years later, appropriations jumped three-fold, to $475 million, with 567,000 student grant recipients. By 1990, the program served 3 million undergraduates, with an appropriation of $4 billion per year (worth about $6.5 billion in 2010 dollars). In 1997 and 1998, those figures had increased to 3.8 million students, with an average Pell Grant award of $1,923 each (about $2,600 in 2010 dollars) for a total funding of $3.8 billion (worth $5.1 billion in 2010 dollars).

Hard Times: The New Depression in Higher Education, 1973 to 1985

The launching of the new, large-scale federal student financial aid programs coincided with one of the most financially troubling period faced by colleges and universities in the 20th century. The unexpected bad news came about when the Carnegie Commission on Higher Education's report alerted the American public to "the New Depression in higher education" (Cheit, 1971). Despite the prestige and heritage of American campuses, economists' analyses of college and university budgets indicated serious erosion of revenues and endowments that put colleges at risk. The situation was sufficiently problematic that a number of books published in the mid-1970s and early 1980s provided college boards of trustees and presidents with advice on "how to survive the decade of the eighties" (Mayhew, 1979. One study warned that as many as a quarter to a third of colleges nationwide were at risk and might have to close down (Carnegie Council , 1980. Innovative books such as George Keller's *Academic Strategy* provided college administrators with a new blueprint for incorporating modern approaches to data collection to promote informed decision making about admissions, enrollments, financial aid, fundraising, endowment portfolio planning, course registrations, and myriad aspects of college operations to create a *managerial transformation* in American colleges and universities. These innovations, which were based on the warnings of various reports about academic crises, helped avert the catastrophic projections about failing colleges.

Between 1975 and 1985, most colleges and universities faced the unprecedented problem of "stagflation"—a puzzling combination of double-digit inflationary costs in operating expenses, combined with a decline in the productivity of the national economy. The initial response by most colleges was to tighten budgetary belts, reduce spending, and defer physical plant maintenance. Deans of admissions and directors of financial aid demonstrated new levels of expertise and energy in seeking out college applicants and simultaneously making good use of new federal student financial aid programs. The problem with these administrative short-term solutions was that they did not necessarily provide systemic solutions. For example, repair expenses compounded the longer they were delayed. Important to keep in mind was that for the mission and vitality of a campus, eventually neglected repairs and other maintenance tended to make a campus decline in attractiveness to prospective students and their parents. This was particularly problematic for most colleges at the time because of fewer high school graduates combined with a decline in the percentage of high school graduates opting to go on to college. In some states and regions, this meant a net decline in the number of qualified young adults who were applying to college— a dramatic and unexpected contrast to the overcrowding and high demand that had characterized American higher education since the end of World War II. The result was that college and university presidents had serious concerns about their institutions' abilities to attract and enroll academically qualified students.

A decade of financial constraints forced even academically prestigious institutions to rethink some of their historic priorities and commitments. Most precarious was the sanctity of the bold policy of need-blind admissions coupled with need-based financial aid. At Brown University, campus officials doubted whether the institution could continue indefinitely to fulfill its financial aid–admissions pledge. The situation facing an expensive, selective private college was that about 70 percent of admitted students were paying a high tuition price that enabled the financial aid office to provide scholarships for the remaining 30 percent of the entering class. Some students who were paying "full freight" objected to this redistribution strategy. Even admissions officers who were in favor of the need-based financial aid policy faced a dilemma: when considering applicants in a ranked order, for the final, remaining admissions slots, could the university afford not to consider how much was at stake for the university's costs in terms of a student's financial aid award? For example, if the applicant whose academic ranking was 800th in the applicant pool would require the financial aid office to award a scholarship of $10,000, and the 801st ranked applicant had no financial need, was the university justified in passing over the high-need applicant in favor of the next candidate, who had no financial aid need?

This prolonged adversity provided unexpected insights on the behavior of college applicants as consumers. One beleaguered college admissions dean seeking to attract good high school students in a competitive region discovered that offering low tuition was not an effective strategy. The surprise finding was that when the college raised tuition to a level higher than that of its traditional college rivals, the number and quality of its applicants increased.

The High Point of Student Consumerism

Since 1985, the rising price of tuition has had mixed, serious consequences for the academic marketplace. A first wave of reforms by colleges was to search for efficiency measures such as altering the academic calendar to reduce seasonal utility bills of heating in late December and air conditioning in June. A second wave was more proactive. By 1985, some colleges started to show signs of resilience and innovation in the face of financial adversity. Instead of keeping costs and price low, the new approach was to raise money to spend money, with the ultimate goal of increasing institutional appeal. This meant building elaborate facilities for career advising as well as recreation and fitness. It also necessitated dormitories with state-of-the-art wiring and amenities along with other features that appealed to upper middle class families. The logic was that failure to provide these amenities would deter applicants, especially academically strong students from affluent families.

A small number of academically selective private colleges and universities gained confidence through new levels of energetic, effective fundraising and admissions recruitment, so much so that they embarked on campaigns to "buy the best"—whether this meant offering high salaries to outstanding faculty recruits or providing generous scholarships to highly talented students at both the undergraduate and graduate levels (Clotfelter, 1995). These enterprising institutions initiated what would turn out to be an enduring pattern of *cost escalation* in American higher education. One salient example of this was an increased emphasis on *merit scholarships*, which are grants that were aimed to attract highly talented students, with no requirement that a student have demonstrated financial need.

In some cases, providing students with increased academic choices tended to undermine institutional efficiency. At the University of California–Berkeley, for example, a report released in 1980 identified a peculiar culture of student consumerism: at the start of each academic term, students "went shopping" for course—often enrolling in six courses during the first week then later dropping two courses. A second related phenomenon was that students, especially freshmen and sophomores, were making unwise course selections in which they chronically overrated their preparedness for, for example, calculus or organic chemistry. The result was a high incidence of either dropping such courses at mid-semester, or getting failing grades. The cumulative effect of these kinds of consumerism was to force the university to offer more repeat courses and absorb re-enrollments. Accommodations of student choice may have been endearing to students, but they were expensive for the university to absorb indefinitely (Schoch, 1980).

Student consumerism in American higher education included the popularity of annual ratings and rankings of colleges and universities published by *U.S. News and World Report*. Relying on selected and changing indices of quality education for undergraduates, the reports kindled competition among colleges and universities—and provided sophisticated college applicants and college counselors with added tools by which to compare and compete in the quest for admissions and financial aid. Numerous college and university presidents complained that the ratings often were unfair or based on dubious criteria. Yet the pressure on deans of admissions and presidents overall made the annual ratings undeniable if not irresistible. One consequence was that keeping pace with the ratings of benchmark and rival institutions prompted colleges and universities to increase their spending.

Cost Escalation and Tuition Price Fixing Allegations

The cost escalation was tolerable as long as there was an overall increase in national prosperity and academic endowments. However, starting around 1985, there were recurrent signs of complaints by the American public, by Congress, and by federal agencies that for many colleges, the annual tuition increases surpassed the inflationary rate as measured by the *Consumer Price Index (CPI)*. One allegation was that colleges were too often oblivious to the burden high tuition charges imposed on American families. In fact, long before outside critics raised the question, many academically selective and prestigious colleges and universities started as early as 1973 to initiate their own systematic studies on the effect of rising costs on college choice. The studies were not in response to external critics, but rather, long before even congressional criticisms surfaced, the self-analyses were prompted by concern that rising college costs eventually would be harmful by "pricing them out of the market" in an effort to attract the academically top students (Spies, 1973). This was a particularly urgent concern in what was called an "era of student consumerism" because many states' prestigious flagship universities had either low or no tuition charge (Riesman, 1981).

Government and public concerns over tuition charges and college policies came to a head between 1989 and 1993 in a case involving the Justice Department's investigation of 55 private colleges and universities (Associated Press, 1989). The concerns were two-fold: first, charges for tuition plus room and board were high, having surpassed $19,000 in 1989 (indexed for inflation, $35,000 in 2011 dollars) and had for over a decade increased at a rate that outpaced the Consumer Price Index; second, the Justice Department alleged that some colleges were banding together as a cartel to fix tuition prices.

Primary focus was on the Ivy League institutions whose presidents met each year to share information on financial aid, applications, and tuition. U.S. Attorney General Dick Thornburgh told reporters, "This collegiate cartel denied (students) the right to compare prices and discounts among schools just as they would in shopping for any service" (Associated Press, October 22, 1989). Under terms of a consent decree announced on May 23, 1991, the Ivy League presidents agreed to stop their "overlap" practice of sharing information. Princeton's vice president for public affairs, speaking for the Ivy Group presidents, defended the overlap as a means to ensure that optimal student financial aid was awarded to students with financial need and to curb the possibility of a student "shopping" and playing one college off against another.

Although the Ivy Group agreed to this settlement, the Massachusetts Institute of Technology (MIT)—an institution included in the initial suit—declined to go along. Two years later, the U.S. Court of Appeals for the Third Circuit in Philadelphia set aside the highly publicized ruling that held that MIT conspired with the colleges in the Ivy League to violate the Sherman Antitrust Act. MIT was exonerated from the accusation of "price fixing" because for many years, it had followed a common financial aid policy. Writing in the *Chronicle of Higher Education*, two attorneys (one of whom was general counsel for the American Council on Education) who had filed a friend-of-the-court brief on behalf of the private colleges argued that the flaw in the Justice Department's case was a reductionist fallacy in which a college education and student financial aid were cast as merely another business activity without regard for the noneconomic justifications of what is meant in being a college or a college student (Gulland and Steinbach,1993).

A legacy of this landmark case was that henceforth colleges and their critics would increasingly rely on the courts and the press to argue over the principles of paying for college. College and university presidents responded to criticisms about the rate of tuition increases by noting that the conventional inflationary measure—the Consumer Price Index (CPI)—was inappropriate because it was tilted toward certain kinds of daily and weekly purchases. As such, they argued, it was a poor choice by which to track changes in a major once-in-a-lifetime cost (e.g., a college education). The resolution was the creation of a new inflationary measure—*HEPI*, the Higher Education Price Index. Introducing the HEPI did not end the debates, as its net contribution was to complicate the allegations. These exchanges in the decades since the MIT ruling took place in a period of rising college costs and the increasing dominance of federal loans as a form of student financial aid.

The Rise of Loans in Federal Student Financial Aid Programs, 1978 to 2011

The Pell Grant program, which was started in 1972, gained foremost attention from college officials, prospective students and their families, and the press, especially due to its emphasis on scholarship grants that a student recipient did not have to repay. The constituency to whom the program was directed from the start was high school students with good academic grades and high financial need. This did not necessarily mean that recipients were from impoverished families. The calculations to determine need, for example, took into account how many children from a family were attending college at the same time—a kind of consideration that reasonably could allow a middle income family to qualify for a Pell Grant. Yet the intent was to serve those who had great financial need. The grant program fused federal financial aid with the initiative of social justice and civil rights. For other students, student loan programs apart from the Pell Grants were central to the strategy was for the federal government to act as broker in providing college financial aid in the form of attractive student loans.

Efforts by Congress to persuade banks to join in the partnership of federal agencies, students, colleges, and the private financial sector were in suspense in 1972, as they had been bogged down since the late 1960s. Bankers showed little interest in taking on the risk of lending to students. As a result, Congress continually revised the terms of lending proposals so that they were increasingly attractive to banks. The capstone of this initiative was creation of the *Student Loan Marketing Agency*, whose abbreviation of SLMA led to the popular nickname of *Sallie Mae*. The essential strategy was for Sallie Mae, as a federal agency, to provide a *GSL (Guaranteed Student Loan)*. It would do so by buying up student loans from banks, thus becoming the owner of the loans. Sallie Mae would lend money to banks, up to 80 percent of the face value of student loans, thus reducing substantially the bank's own money it otherwise would have to tie up in the student loan portfolio.

In 1978, Congress favored a shift in proportions and priorities of federal student financial aid programs, characterized by a new emphasis on attractive, easily available loans and a simultaneous lessening of attention to providing grants to students with financial need. The result was the *Middle Income Student Assistance Act (MISAA)*. According to a Brookings Institution analysis, it "brought college loans to the middle class by removing the income limit for participation in federal aid programs" (Light, 2002, 22).

By the late 1970s, the era of consensus for support of higher education started to weaken due to the weight of current and projected expenditures—both from Pell Grant and student loan programs. This coincided with a severe recession in the national economy, which was punctuated by groundswells of recovery but then dipped again. Colleges and universities, usually favored in policy deliberations, faced hard questions about their stewardship of resources. Some members of Congress claimed that colleges and universities had artificially driven up college costs as a strategy of institutional enrichment. Citing data showing that the amount of Pell Grant awards had not kept pace with rising college costs, college officials, in turn, raised concerns that Congress had retreated from its 1972 commitment to expanding college access and affordability.

Between 2000 and 2006, when Congress favored having banks, rather than a federal agency, as the primary lenders of student loans, a new generation of private agencies grew. Using internet technology and marketing directly to college students, such new entities as My Rich Uncle pursued students as loan customers in part by promising good service and fast replies on applications. The result was an escalation of student loan advertisements and marketing both by established banks as well as by new start-up lenders. The ease by which students gained access to application forms on the Internet combined with fast turn-around for approval on applications also meant that the number of college students taking out federally based loans reached new heights. By 2010, the average amount of loan indebtedness for recent college graduates was more than $17,000. This situation of increased student loan volume plus increased student indebtedness was the high-tension, high-stakes situation in which colleges and students found themselves—a situation characterized by unresolved debates and policy deliberations.

The Best of Times and the Worst of Times in Student Financial Aid, 2000 to 2011

By 2006, prospective college students enjoyed a cornucopia of advertisements and enticements for student financial aid.

Banks, once reluctant to advertise services and not interested in loaning to college students, orchestrated expensive campaigns. One flyer mailed out by a bank depicted a smiling, tanned student wearing sunglasses and driving a sporty car, with the caption, "You have choices!" Students also had toll-free numbers for an array of services, ranging from college loans to computer purchases and debt consolidation as part of the Education One Loans program. Either students or parents could borrow up to $25,000 per year for these loans that were based on credit, not need. Applying students could be either full-time or part-time enrollees. Drawing from this same bank's flyer and illustrative of the bank's attention to consumer appeal was its pledge that a check would be mailed within 24 hours after it received a qualified application. Student spending on loans was accompanied by increased student spending for various goods and services, as banks who were lenders to students also made credit cards easy for college students to obtain, prompting undergraduates to run up large bills—much to the belated displeasure of their parents.

The corollary to this good news about student loan choices was a growing concern by colleges and federal agencies that the shift from grants to loans had become dangerously lopsided. Furthermore, proposals in the reauthorization of the Higher Education Act included students henceforth being subject to a repayment rate of 6.8 percent on federal student loans, leading one major metropolitan newspaper to title an editorial, "Robbing Joe College to Pay Sallie Mae." The residual problem of these student aid issues was the indication that students from modest income families, even if academically strong, represented a small and declining proportion of undergraduate enrollments at prestigious private and public universities. Particularly alarming was a 2006 report sponsored by the Education Trust that characterized flagship state universities as "engines of inequality" as the earning gap separating students from low and modest income families from more affluent classmates increased (Gerald and Haycock, 2006). From the perspective of institutional differences among the nation's colleges and universities, there were disturbing signs of increasing disparities between rich and poor institutions in their respective spending levels for undergraduate education (Blumenstyk, 2011).

These concerns remained unresolved, subject to a continuing succession of volleys between constituencies and their advocates. Tensions were increased by congressional concern that universities with large endowments were not drawing out reasonable amounts for student financial aid and that, once again, the advantages accruing to the wealthiest colleges and universities were increasing (Arenson, 2008; Blumenstyk, 2007). Understanding rising college costs and prices requires knowledge of the diverse categories of colleges and universities as well as how these categorical differences influence the substance and pricing of their educational programs.

Context: Categories of College Costs and the Contemporary Campus

Most undergraduate students and their families characterize higher education costs based on an institution's undergraduate college—its facilities, curriculum, faculty, and staff. This is understandable since very few universities can survive without an undergraduate collegiate core. Parents may presume that their payment of tuition and fees correlates closely with the institution's paying for programs and personnel that their undergraduate child will use. This may be the case at a relatively small college dedicated exclusively to undergraduate liberal arts education. In a more complex institutional setting, however, a student's tuition dollars can be parsed and distributed in any number of ways. If one were to arrange the several thousand colleges and universities into categories of mission and scope, the taxonomy of institutions would be as follows:

- *Public two-year colleges*: Also known as community colleges. Typically these institutions offer the two-year associates degrees as well as numerous nondegree courses. Most community colleges are commuter institutions and have little if any provision for dormitories or a residential campus. In some states—for example, California and Florida—enrollment at a campus can be as high as 30,000, although most campuses are within the 2,000 to 10,000 range. Higher education researchers and academic leaders from the most prestigious institutions often overlook Community colleges because their attention tends to gravitate to historic, established four-year colleges and universities. In fact, community colleges are a distinctive American contribution to higher education and play a formidable role. In the 2011–2012 academic year, for example, public community colleges enrolled about 25 percent of all students in postsecondary education. More than half of the students who policy analysts designate as "freshmen" are enrolled in community colleges.

- *For-profit colleges:* Although there is great variation within this category, as a general rule, for-profit colleges tend not to offer a full range of student teams, activities, clubs, and other campus services and facilities. Some, such as the University of Phoenix, rely predominantly on online courses, instruction, and programs.

- *Undergraduate liberal arts institutions*: Usually these are private (i.e., independent), but this is not always so. Typically, a liberal arts college is relatively small in enrollment, varying from about 1,000 to 3,000 students, and is committed to providing on-campus housing and a residential experience. Liberal arts colleges are primarily if not exclusively devoted to undergraduate bachelor's degree programs.

- *Comprehensive universities*: These complex institutions are composed of multiple colleges (e.g., business, arts and sciences) and offer an array of undergraduate majors as well as several master's degree programs, often including entry-level professional degree and certification programs. Enrollment typically ranges from about 5,000 to 20,000 students.

- *Doctoral-granting universities*: This category refers to institutions whose bachelor's degree programs, master's degree programs are supplemented by a selected number of doctoral degree programs. A subtle difference separating this category from the subsequent discussion of *research universities* is that doctoral degree–granting universities are not committed to sponsored research and external grants at a level as high as the activity at the large research universities. This category includes numerous medium-sized institutions, both public and private, in which undergraduate programs still tend to be predominant in the overall operation of the institution.

- *Research universities*: This category refers to large, complex institutions with a wide, array of advanced degree programs, with resources and prestige concentrated in PhD programs, and a commitment to seeking large-scale sponsored research grants and projects, especially from such federal agencies as the National Science Foundation (NSF) and the National Institutes of Health (NIH). The category includes both public and private institutions, with enrollments typically spanning from about 5,000 to 50,000 students. Research universities that emphasize natural sciences often include on campus a coordinated structure that includes a college of medicine, a teaching hospital, and related research institutes, all of which is designated as an academic medical center (AMC).

- *Multicampus university systems headquarters*: This institutional type often is overlooked, especially by undergraduate students and their parents. It refers to the system-wide central administrative offices for a state university's structure of numerous campuses. Its role is primarily administrative and does not include offering courses or degrees, or enrolling students. Despite these absences, the system headquarters must be included in any discussion of college costs because it represents a distinctive organizational arrangement to accommodate growth and complexity that has characterized American public higher education since World War II. It employs many highly skilled, highly paid professional staff and administrators. For example, the California State University and College System headquarters has its own campus complex and employs 589 full-time staff. This is the headquarters for a system of 23 campuses with 12,063 full-time faculty; 21,000 full-time staff; and 12,030 part-time faculty to serve a total student enrollment of about 415,000 head-count students.

- *State coordinating councils*: Since 1972, more than 30 states have created or expanded some variation of a state coordinating council to serve as a mediator between the state legislature and the various public colleges and universities in the state. This entity differs from the aforementioned state university administrative system in that it is an umbrella organization over all public institutions and systems, and it also may include the state's independent colleges and universities in its deliberations. As is the case with state university headquarters, state coordinating councils employ a highly expert professional staff and either a president or director. In Kentucky, for example, statutes require that the president of the Council on Postsecondary Education receive a salary higher than that of any of the state's public college or university presidents—a real and symbolic demonstration of the stature (and expense) of the office. Names for these coordinating agencies are along the lines of Council on Postsecondary Education. They represent a relatively hidden expense because although they are part of the state's appropriations for higher education, they do not actually teach students, confer degrees, or do research. It represents one way in which administrative costs are increased as part of the "cost of doing business" in a complex, large higher education environment. The national organization for state coordinating council executive directors and presidents is *SHEEO* (State Higher Education Executive Officers).

These categories provide a good reference and reminder about the diversity of American higher education. They also provide a lens for at least a first glimpse of the differences among institutions related to the *costs* of educating a college student. For example, in 1993 and 1994 in California, the total taxpayer cost per student enrolled in public higher education was $5,000. Averages can be misleading because they gloss over significant per student cost differences among categories of institutions (Table 1.1). Therefore, when one disaggregates comprehensive statewide data into institutional categories, differences within public higher education are evident. The taxpayer cost per full-time student was distributed as follows (Douglass, 2000, 318–319):

Table 1.1   California Public Higher Education Taxpayer subsidies per student, 1993–94.

University of California	$12,000
California State University and Colleges	$7,800
California community colleges	$4,000

In other words, the taxpayer cost to educate a student at the flagship state university was three times the cost to educate an undergraduate at a public community college. A student at the state college system received almost double the state subsidy for a community college student. The inference is that a combination of prestige, advanced degree programs, and institutional mission contribute to a state funding formula that has a wide range. To understand the progression of size and complexity that influences costs of higher education, it is useful to start analysis by using a small liberal arts college devoted to undergraduate education as a base. Its structure and budget break out roughly as follows: academic departments and faculty, library, student affairs and extracurricular activities, art museum, performing arts center, intercollegiate athletics, administration, buildings and grounds.

What often complicates such discussions, especially for parents of prospective college students, is that even though undergraduate education may be the most conspicuous and even central part of an academic institution, it is not the complete story. One must consider also the following kinds of programs and services:

graduate programs and advanced degrees leading to master's degrees and PhD; advanced professional schools of medicine, law, and business; and auxiliary enterprises. If a university sees itself as a research university, it most likely has a vast constellation of research institutes and other special institutes scattered throughout the campus. Important at many universities is the medical campus—not only a college of medicine, but also a hospital, health center, and numerous other related offices and services, all of which are called an AMC (academic medical center).

A general rule of thumb for an academic institution is that more advanced courses and programs tend to be more labor intensive than, for example, lecture classes for freshmen and sophomores. A doctoral seminar taught by a senior professor with an enrollment of 10 PhD students is an expensive proposition. In contrast, an introductory psychology course may rely on one professor to lecture to a class of 200 undergraduates. Even within an undergraduate college, pedagogical choices determine costs. Does a calculus class enroll 10 students or 50? What differences are there in the expense and learning effectiveness between the two different classroom types

Costs Complexity: The Case of the Multipurpose University

In addition to surveying the structure and units of a typical university campus, it is also useful to consider a budget. At a medium-sized state flagship university with an enrollment of about 25,000 students, the annual operating budget is $2.7 billion. The projected *revenues* presented in millions of dollars and as a percentage of the total budget are shown in Table 1.2.

The summary data on expenditures tends to mask the presence of the medical and health sciences in the overall scheme of university activities. The line item of hospital services obviously shows the importance of the health sciences at 33 percent. Less obvious is that breaking down the large item of instructional services, would show that academic programs in medicine, nursing,

Table 1.2   Typical State University Revenues and Expenses for 2011

	% of budget	amount in millions of dollars
Student tuition and fees	12%	$314 million
Hospital operations	38%	$1,023
State support	11%	$304
Affiliated corporations	15%	$398
Gifts, grants, and contracts	9%	$235
Auxiliary enterprises	3%	$91
Other sources	12%	$311
Meanwhile, the estimated *expenditures* were allocated as follows:		
Instruction	13%	$354 million
Research	7%	$194
Academic support	4%	$103
Institutional support	4%	$110
Public service	12%	$311
Libraries	1%	$26
Student financial aid	5%	$116
Student services	2%	$37
Operations and maintenance	4%	$84
Auxiliary enterprises	6%	$165
Mandatory transfers	3%	$78
Hospital services	33%	$868
Other	6%	$160

pharmacy, and numerous bio-related PhD programs such as physiology and toxicology along with allied health curricula and public health graduate programs constitute more than half of the university's faculty positions and a large percentage of its total instructional budget. Another puzzle deals with intercollegiate athletics. Even though it is a highly visible university activity, its place within the budget summary is not evident.

Even though this budget snapshot lacks requisite details to probe thoroughly the flow of money, it does clearly document that large universities are complex and host numerous affiliated projects and organization. These various projects and their structures on campus could take the form of an ongoing service for state government, for example, the geologic survey center. If a university is designated as a land grant institution, most likely it has a substantial college of agriculture, whose responsibilities and funding include providing extension services in all counties of the state. Above all, it is an institution's identity and mission as a research university that drives priorities and spending in *R&D* (research and development) areas. As early as 1960, Clark Kerr, the president of the University of California, used the term *Federal Grant Universities* to designate a special category of about 20 major universities whose commitment to and excellence in research projects funded by federal agencies had become a large part of the university budget and mission (Kerr, 1963). This number has expanded so that a conservative estimate is that about 200 universities either see themselves in this category or are striving to acquire this identity.

Another significant consideration is that research universities in recent decades have become enterprising, which means they enter into such ventures as collaborative "research parks" or even "for-profit" research and development centers that focus on development of patents and commercial applications. The most difficult part of tracking these expansions and additions is deciphering whether a new institute, center, or research park brings in revenue to the university or if it drains resources. The question is clear, but the answers and explanations are not. These enterprising units may actually cost money.

Prices and Costs in Higher Education: Decentralized Academic Budgeting

How does a college or university track the costs of these myriad internal units and projects? Harvard is famous for having contributed to the lexicon of academic budgets the principle that "every tub floats on its own bottom," which is sometimes presented in the shorthand form of *ETOB* (Bethell, Hunt, and Shenton, 2004). This is an arrangement of decentralized funding in which each unit is expected to bring in sufficient revenues to pay its own way. This model of self-sufficiency suggests sound management and stewardship of wealth; however, more often than not, colleges and universities make numerous exceptions and allowances. In other words, each tub does not always float on its own bottom. What this means is that colleges and universities often rely on *cross subsidies* in which monies from one particular unit may be apportioned at the discretion of the president or the provost or, within a unit, by a dean or department chair.

The safeguard is that a college or university ought to have a gyroscope defined by its mission that provides proper guidance to ensure that the institution fulfills its priorities and is faithful to its essential values. How well a college or university adheres to this principle and the genuine spirit of its historic charter often is revealed by the priorities and allocations it shows in its detailed budget. These essential criteria then can guide more detailed questions on how this use of financial resources is reconciled within its respective institutional category and benchmarks in the ongoing consideration of problems, controversies, and solutions associated with its rising costs and prices in higher education.

References

American Association of Retired Persons (AARP). "Ninety-Nine Great Ways to Save." *AARP Bulletin* (July–August 2011): 23–28.

Anderson, Jenny. "For a Standout College Essay, Applicants fill Their Summers." *New York Times* (August 5, 2011), A1.

Anderson, Jenny. "With Admission Rates Tougher than Harvard's, Schools Reconsider Policies." *New York Times* (September 6, 2011), A22.

Anonymous. "The Yard: Puritan Pudding." *Harvard Crimson* (July 18, 1933), 3. "A Quarter of Parents Want the Government to Regulate College Costs, Survey Finds," *Chronicle of Higher Education* (August 16, 2011) http://chronicle.com/blogs/ticker/a-quarter-of-parents-want-the-government-to-regulate-college-costs-survey-finds/35381.

Archibald, Robert, and Feldman, David. *Why Does College Cost So Much?* New York: Oxford University Press, 2010.

Arenson, Karen W. "Soaring Endowments Widen a Higher Education Gap." *New York Times* (February 4, 2008), A14.

Associated Press. "College Tuition Survey Spurs Government Probe." *Newport News* (Virginia) *Daily Press* (October 22, 1989), A1.

Bartlett, Thomas. "Phoenix Risen: How a History Professor became the Pioneer of the For-Profit Revolution." *Chronicle of Higher Education* (July 10, 2009), A1, A10–A13.

Bethell, John T., Hunt, Richard M., and Shenton, Robert. "Harvard A to Z: From Aab to Zeph Greek: And Everything Crimson in Between." *Harvard Magazine* May–June 2004, 42–47.

Blumenstyk, Goldie. "Pressure Builds on Wealthy Colleges to Spend More of Their Assets." *Chronicle of Higher Education* 54 (10, November 2, 2007), A1–A20, A21.

Blumenstyk, Goldie. "Data Show Wider Gaps in Spending on Students." *Chronicle of Higher Education* (September 23, 2011), A1, A12.

Bowen, Howard R. et al. *Investment in Learning: The Individual and Social Value of American Higher Education*. San Francisco: Jossey-Bass, 1977.

Bowen, Howard. R. *The Costs of Higher Education: How Much Do Colleges and Universities Spend Per Student and How Much Should They Spend?* San Francisco: Jossey-Bass, 1980.

Breneman, David W., Leslie, Larry L., and Anderson, Richard E., eds. *ASHE Reader on Finance in Higher Education*. Needham Heights, MA: Simon and Schuster for the Association for the Study of Higher Education, 1996.

Burke, Colin B. *American Collegiate Populations: A Test of the Traditional View*. New York and London: New York University Press, 1982.

Callan, Patrick M., and Finney, Joni E., eds. *Public and Private Financing of Higher Education: Shaping Public Policy for the*

Future. Phoenix, AZ: American Council on Education and the Oryx Press, 1997.

Carnegie Council on Policy Studies in Higher Education. *Three Thousand Futures: The Next Twenty-Five Years for Higher Education*. San Francisco: Jossey-Bass, 1980.

Cheit, Earl F. *The New Depression in Higher Education: A Study of the Financial Condition of 41 Colleges and Universities*. New York: McGraw-Hill for the Carnegie Commission on Higher Education, 1971.

Clotfelter, Charles T. *Buying the Best: Cost Escalation in Elite Higher Education*. Princeton, NJ: National Bureau of Economic Research Monograph with Princeton University Press, 1996.

"College: Is It Worth The Cost?" *New York Times* Sunday Review (August 28, 2011), SR 12.

Curti, Merle, and Nash, Roderick. *Philanthropy in the Shaping of American Higher Education*. New Brunswick, NJ: Rutgers University Press, 1965.

"Don't Gut Pell Grants." *Washington Post*. July 16, 2011, A20.

Douglass, John Aubrey. *The California Idea and American Higher Education: 1850 to the 1960 Master Plan*. Stanford, CA: Stanford University Press, 2000.

Ehrenberg, Ronald. *Tuition Rising: Why College Costs So Much*. Cambridge, MA and London: Harvard University Press, 2000.

Ellis, Rehema, "Is College Still a Good Investment?," NBC Evening News (September 16, 2011).

Fain, Paul. "New Web Tool Helps Both Experts and Public Grasp Colleges' Costs." *Chronicle of Higher Education* (July 9, 2010) http://chronicle.com/article/New-Web-Tool -Helps-Experts-and/66222/.

Finn, Chester E., Jr. *Scholars, Dollars and Bureaucrats*. Washington, DC: The Brookings Institution, 1978.

Gardner, John W. *Excellence: Can We Be Equal and Excellent Too?* New York: Norton, 1961.

Gerald, Danette, and Haycock, Katie. *Engines of Inequality: Diminishing Equity in the Nation's Premier Public Universities.* Washington, DC: Education Trust, 2006.

Goldin, Claudia, and Katz, Lawrence F. "The Shaping of Higher Education: The Formative Years in the United States, 1890 to 1940." *Journal of Economic Perspectives* 13(Winter 1999), 37–62.

Gulland, Eugne D., and Steinbach, Sheldon E. "Antitrust Law and Financial Aid: The MIT Decision." *Chronicle of Higher Education* (October 6, 1993), B3.

Healy, Michelle. "Ivy League Settles Price-Fixing Suit on Aid." *USA Today* (May 23, 1991), 1A.

Horowitz, Helen Lefkowitz. *Campus Life: Undergraduate Cultures from the end of the Eighteenth Century to the Present.* New York: Alfred A. Knopf, 1987.

Jencks, Christopher, and Riesman, David. *The Academic Revolution.* Garden City, NY: Doubleday Anchor, 1968.

Johnstone, D. Bruce, and Marcucci, Pamela N. *Financing Higher Education Worldwide: Who Pays? Who Should Pay?* Baltimore: Johns Hopkins University Press, 2010.

Karabel, Jerome. *The Chosen: The Hidden History of Admission and Exclusion at Harvard, Yale, and Princeton.* Boston and New York: Houghton Mifflin, 2005.

Keller, George. *Academic Strategy: The Management Revolution in Higher Education.* Baltimore and London: Johns Hopkins University Press, 1983.

Kerr, Clark. *The Uses of the University.* Cambridge, MA: Harvard University Press, 1963.

Khalaf, Rhoula. "Customized Accounting." *Forbes* (May 25, 1992), 50.

Kiester, Edwin, Jr. "The G.I. Bill May Have Been the Best Deal Ever Made by Uncle Sam." *Smithsonian* 25 (November 1994), 128–139.

Kuhnhenn, Jim, and Heflinlg, Kimberly (Associated Press). "Obama Calls for Linking Federal Aid to Tuition Costs." *Lexington* (Kentucky) *Herald-Leader* (January 28, 2012), A15.

"Lessons from Abroad," *Hechinger Report* (August 24, 2011) http://hechingerreport.org/category/special_reports/lessonsfromabroad/.

Levine, David O. *The American College and the Culture of Aspiration, 1915–1940*. Ithaca, NY: Cornell University Press, 1986.

Lewin, Tamar. "What's the Most Expensive College? The Least? Education Department Puts It All Online." *New York Times* (June 30, 2011), A13.

Lewin, Tamar. "Universities Seeking Out Students of Means." *New York Times* (September 21, 2011), A18.

Light, Paul, "Increase Access to Post-Secondary Education," in *Government's 50 Greatest Achievevements: From Civil Rights to Homeland Security*, (Washington, DC: Brookings Institution, 2002).

McPherson, Michael, Schapiro, Morton Owen, and Winston, Gordon C. *Paying the Piper: Productivity, Incentives, and Financing in U.S. Higher Education*. Ann Arbor: University of Michigan Press, 1993.

Mayhew, Lewis B. *Surviving the Eighties*. San Francisco: Jossey-Bass, 1979.

Nevins, Allan. *The State Universities and Democracy*. Urbana: University of Illinois Press, 1962.

Novack, Janet. "Obama's Student Loans Paid Off, Will Yours?" *Forbes.com Personal Finance Blog* (June 14, 2011).

Paulsen, Michael B., and Smart, John C., eds. *The Finance of Higher Education: Theory, Research, Policy & Practice.* New York: Agathon Press, 2001.

Riesman, David. *On Higher Education: The Academic Enterprise in an Era of Student Consumerism.* San Francisco: Jossey Bass, 1981.

Roth, Philip, "Joe College: Memories of a Fifties Education," *Atlantic Monthly* (December 1987), 41–60.

Ruch, Richard S. *Higher Ed, Inc.: The Rise of the For-Profit University.* Baltimore: Johns Hopkins University Press, 2001.

Russell Schoch. "As Cal Enters the 1980s, There'll Be Some Changes Made." *California Monthly* 90(3, 1980), 1, 23.

Sack, Edward J. "College Has 300 Year Food Problem: Riots and Class Wars Mark History of Student Protests." *Harvard Crimson* (December 10, 1949), 3.

Shore, Debra. "What Price Egalitarianism?" *Brown Alumni Monthly* (February 1981), 12–19.

Slosson, Edwin F. *Great American Universities.* New York: MacMillan, 1910.

Smith, Andrew F. " 'The Diploma Pedlar': Dr. John Cook Bennett and the Christian College, New Albany, Indiana." *Indiana Magazine of History* 90(March 1994), 26–47.

Spies, Richard R. *The Future of Private Colleges: The Effect of Rising Costs on College Choice.* Princeton, NJ: Princeton University Industrial Relations Section, 1973.

Spitzer, Eliot. "Reporting the High Cost of College." *In the Arena* (CNN Broadcast, June 30, 2011).

St. John, Edward, and Parsons, Michael D., eds. *Public Funding of Higher Education: Changing Contexts and New Rationales.* Baltimore and London: Johns Hopkins University Press, 2004.

Stoke, Stuart M. "What Price Tuition?" *Journal of Higher Education* (June 1937), 297–303.

Synnott, Marcia Graham. *The Half-Opened Door: Discrimination and Admissions at Harvard, Yale, and Princeton, 1900–1970*. Westport, CT: Greenwood Press, 1979.

Trow, Martin. "Reflections on the Transition from Elite to Mass to Universal Higher Education." *Daedalus* 99 (Winter 1970), 1–42.

Vedder, Richard. *Going Broke by Degree: Why College Costs Too Much*. Washington, DC: American Enterprise Institute, 2004.

Veysey, Laurence. *The Emergence of the American University*. Chicago: University of Chicago Press, 1964, 270.

Whitehead, John. *The Separation of College and State*. New Haven, CT: Yale University Press, 1973.

Wieder, Ben. "Thiel Fellowships Pay 24 Talented Students $100,000 Not to Attend College." *Chronicle of Higher Education* (May 25, 2011) http://chronicle.com/article/Thiel-Fellowship-Pays-24/127622/.

Wilkinson, Rupert. *Attracting Students, Buying Students: Financial Aid in America*. Nashville, TN: Vanderbilt University Press, 2005.

Wilson, Robin. "Profit Colleges Change Higher Education's Landscape." *Chronicle of Higher Education* (February 12, 2010), A1, A16–A19.

Young, Robin. "Will Today's Generation Be Less Educated Than Parents?" *Here and Now* (NPR) (August 30, 2011).

Zook, George, chair. *Higher Education for American Democracy: A Report of the President's Commission*. New York: Harper and Brothers, 1947.

Connections: Past to Present

The question that animates most discussions about higher education is, "Why does college cost so much?" The concern is understandable, but the question is stilted because it *presumes* that a college education does cost a lot—and more than it should. It is echoed by many U.S. Senators and members of Congress, along with governors and state legislators (especially when they are seeking re-election). Their concern is warranted—and may well be true. However, it is a hunch that runs ahead of exploration or confirmation and then frequently relies on ambiguous, unclear terminology. In the preceding chapter, the historical narrative analyzed the continuity and changes in how students and colleges have dealt with rising costs and prices, sometimes with initiatives and responses that were not always predictable or even wise. This extensive historical overview needs to be accompanied by intensive consideration of how and why costs of higher education have tended to rise dramatically in recent years.

Sociologists Christopher Jencks and David Riesman observed in their 1968 classic work *The Academic Revolution* that for the children of education-minded American families, going to college is not a sprint, but a marathon. Some highly competitive families opt to start the preliminary heats of this race early by

---

(Tom Schmucker/iStockphoto.com)

investing a great deal of time and money in making certain that their children are accepted into highly regarded kindergartens and elementary schools. Prestigious private elementary schools in metropolitan areas are depicted as having so many applicants for a limited number of spaces that they have "admission rates tougher than Harvard's" (Anderson, September 6, 2011, A22).

The same dynamics of competitiveness may dictate a student's consideration of secondary schools as preparation to be an attractive college applicant. The early start in the college sweepstakes often can include going to summer camp to make influential friendships and learn skills, such as how to take the Scholastic Aptitude Test (SAT), that give a young person an edge in a highly competitive national educational culture (Singer, 2011, A1).

One implication of making informed decisions about college is to emphasize that it is important to identify and refine precisely the question one wishes to explore and answer. In other words, when one says, "How much does it cost to go to college?" this single query can be parsed into numerous specific subquestions, each with different inflections and emphases:

- How much does a college charge in tuition and mandatory fees?
- How much does a college spend in providing instruction and all services for a student?
- How much does a student have to pay for tuition and fees, plus room and board, plus books and other predictable expenses?
- How much does a family have to spend on special programs and preparations to make certain a child is competitive for admission and payment to a prestigious college?

A theme that connects the rising expenses of extra educational programs and the high costs of going to college as part of growing up in America was characterized about 40 years ago by John Gardner, in his 1961 book *Excellence,* in which he explored the question, "Can we be equal—and excellent, too?" Time and time again, discussion of college costs gravitates back to this essential question and its challenge for institutional practices and public policies, especially as a matter of social justice. Answering this question requires detailed consideration of the complex structure of the contemporary college and university.

Concepts Crucial to College Costs

To follow arguments from the past and present about the costs of higher education requires a few essential concepts and related analytic tools, which are presented in this section.

Distinguishing price from cost. The two terms often are used interchangeably. In fact, although they are related and interdependent, they are not synonymous (Finn, 1978, 47–50). Their different meanings are crucial. College *costs* refer to what a college or some other unit spends to *provide* a college education or some designated part of that whole. In other words, it is producing or providing services. In contrast, college *price* refers to what students and their parents are charged and then pay to the college or some other educational vendor. In a perfect or balanced world, it may well be that college price equals college costs. But that is seldom the case—and even if this equality were achieved, it still represents a calculation rather than a synonym.

Distinguishing tuition as a particular item. Among the items included in the costs and prices of a college education, *tuition* refers to the formal, official charges published by a college or university and to the course of study. Unless specified otherwise, it does not refer to such expenses as room and board, books, clothing, or incidentals.

Sometimes a college catalogue add on other academic charges, such as mandatory fees for campus library usage, student activities, laboratory breakage, room deposits, or student health insurance. Often colleges gloss over the distinction simply by noting a lump charge for "tuition and fees." This practice may be due to the benign act of merely compressing presentation of financial data.

It also can also be a deliberate act that is disingenuous because it allows a college to mask certain kinds of expenses being passed on to students as consumers. The category of "mandatory student fees," for example, can include the assessment by which a current generation of students is required to contribute to the repayment of construction projects that were bonded years ago. Or it could be mandatory payment to support some activity, such as intercollegiate athletics or the marching band, whether or not the student uses these services or activities. In fact, colleges and universities are required to break down the distinctions and categories into specific dollar amounts if asked to do so; but often some bank on the prospect that few if any students as consumers will raise the question.

In recent years, college admissions officers, high school counselors, parents, and reporters have used the vernacular term *sticker price*—drawing from the familiar practice of automobile dealers and salesmen—to refer to what the published, full tuition and fees charge is. The important inference is that a student as applicant may be eligible for "discounts" that reduce the actual required payment below the sticker price. These discounts can be related to any number of possibilities, such as financial aid in the form of a scholarship grant from the college, a waiver on some fee, or perhaps student aid from the federal government in the form of a Pell Grant or a Guaranteed Student Loan. To clarify this point, when researchers talk about all the accumulated expenses associated with going to college, they often use the term *COA* (*cost of attendance*). When making comparisons and calculations, it is important to know precisely what items are included—and excluded—when encountering these various terms.

Distinctions between public and private institutions. A rough, pervasive demarcation of colleges and universities in the United States is whether a particular institution is "public" or "private." More accurately, the proper categories are "state" or "independent." A state college or university usually has a statutory arrangement with its legislature in which the governor has substantial power in appointing university trustees, and the state provides funding that is reported both as a gross amount and as a per capita subsidy for each in-state student. Given this subsidy, most state universities tend to have a relatively low tuition charge passed on to students who qualify because they are residents of that state and their parents are taxpayers to that state. Thus a way to get a more complete approximation of the "cost" of tuition at a state university is to add the state subsidy plus the university's official tuition charge.

Depending on a particular state's traditions and tax code, the amount of student subsidy or the percentage of student subsidy varies greatly from state to state. California, for example, for well over a century, had a policy of "zero tuition charge" for state residents at its public institutions. In contrast, some states tend to view state university tuition charges as tantamount to a user's fee and less as a measure whose cost was shared by all citizens and taxpayers. In this latter category of states, the tuition charged to in-state residents is relatively high because the subsidy is relatively low.

As a general rule, private colleges and universities (more accurately known as independent colleges and universities) do *not* receive a state subsidy per student. Thus their tuition charges tend to be relatively high, that is, the *price* is a high percentage of the *cost* of a year of college education. The caution is that there are important exceptions to this generalization. Berea College in Kentucky charges no tuition. Rice University in Houston, Texas, for over 60 years since it opened in the early part of the century, did not charge tuition. Furthermore, many state legislatures have approved (and funded) a tuition assistance grant (TAG) that provides some amount of tuition scholarship for each state resident who attends an independent college or university within the home state.

A hypothetical yet plausible situation is that a state university charges an annual tuition of $5,000 and also receives a state subsidy per student of $10,000. Thus the "price" is $5,000 and the "cost" is $15,000. At the same time, a nearby private college that does not receive a state subsidy charges $15,000 for tuition yet has the same "cost" as the state university: $15,000. Since about 1980, researchers and analysts have used the term *tuition gap* to delineate the difference in price between a public and private institution due to the state subsidy for the public institution. In this case, then, the tuition gap is $10,000. The intent of this term and calculation is to remind taxpayers, consumers, legislators, and analysts that price does *not* equal cost, and that policy deliberations need to consider the distinction when making comparisons between public and private colleges related to efficiency or wastefulness.

Distinguishing nonprofit from for-profit institutions. In recent decades, the expansion and success of for-profit colleges such as the University of Phoenix means that this institutional category warrants inclusion in any analysis of college costs, Internet courses, and programs and related issues, including federal student financial aid, for-profit colleges have a long history in American higher education, and now they have a seat at the table in any related policy deliberations (Ruch, 2001). Today, more than 1.6 million undergraduates are involved with for-profit institutions, with the University of Phoenix enrolling 380,000 via its online campus. Furthermore, for college costs discussions, for-profit college students represent a major constituency for federal student financial aid awards, including grants and loans (Bartlett, 2009).

Distinguishing inflationary changes over time. Any comparison of tuition charges from one year to another requires that one acknowledge and, better yet, hold constant these inflationary changes in the larger economy. This perspective relies on the analytic strategy of *indexing for inflation*. It allows for comparisons of prices over time so as to include allowance for changes in annual inflation rates. The resultant adjustment is that one compares the dollars of one year with another year in terms of "real dollars," that is, with annual inflation neutralized. In other words, comparing Brown University's tuition in 2011 with its tuition in 1970 calls for some conversion so that the two years' amounts are expressed as 2011 dollars. Or one could go the other direction and express both years in terms of 1970 dollars by using the Internet to access such tools as an inflation calculator. One among many sources on the Internet is the *US Inflation Calculator* (http://www.usinflationcalculator.com). Indexing for inflation is not infallible and distinguishing inflationary changes over time eventually requires careful contextual analysis, but it is a useful step.

The perils of percentages. One of the biggest fallacies in statistical analyses trying to make sense of rising college costs is to rely on percentages in tuition changes over time without accompanying them with the corresponding ordinal dollars. For example, to say that the University of California–Berkeley raised its tuition by 30 percent between 1980 and 1981 may be accurate and sounds alarming. But what if that meant the tuition went from $100 to $130? Meanwhile, one could say that Vanderbilt increased its tuition by only 3 percent, with the inference that Vanderbilt has kept costs and price down. On closer inspection, one finds that Vanderbilt increased its tuition from $20,000 to $20,600—an increase of $600. Ironically, the University of California receives bad press for a $30 increase, whereas Vanderbilt is lauded even though it increased tuition by $600. Such is the danger of perception if one relies only on percentages.

Beware of budgets. Attempting to track prices and costs of higher education eventually and understandably bring one to analyze college and university budget documents. This is a necessary but precarious move because the annual budget reports of many institutions often are difficult to probe. Also, a *budget* usually is a proposal for revenues and expenditures, and may differ substantially from an after-the-fact statement of actual financial operations. In comparison to businesses and commercial corporations, colleges and universities are regarded as "loosely coupled" organizations, without commensurate accountability. A difficulty in making analyses over time is that not until the late 1960s with the introduction of such federal reporting systems as *HEGIS* (Higher Education General Information Systems) and its successor *IPEDS* (Integrated Postsecondary Education Data Systems) were there any nationwide annual surveys and compilations of institutional and national higher education financial data.

Caution must be exercised to not take budget reports at face value, even for academic institutions with relatively thorough financial accounting systems. In 1992, for example, Harvard University's public reports noted that despite an endowment of almost $5 billion (worth $8.1 billion in 2011 when indexed for inflation), its annual operating budget was $42 million in the red. One reason for this profile was the university's use of "fund-accounting" reports, suggesting that Harvard was "managing its bottom line in such a way as to appear poorer than it really is. The university is in the midst of a plan to reportedly raise $2.5 billion on top of what is already the world's largest private endowment. Harvard is a bit like the rich man who wears scuffed shoes and a frayed collar when he visits his doctor" (Khalaf, 1992, 50). Conversely, some universities present a deceptively glossy financial profile when doing so is expedient. This tactic reassures worried alumni, legislators, and donors that the president and board can balance the university's budget.

Endowments as part of college cost and price. Most colleges and universities in the United States have an accruing fund known as an *endowment.* This is an accumulation of monetary gifts made by donors—with each gift subject to conditions mutually agreed upon by the donor and the institution plus investment returns. In most cases, college endowments are *perpetual endowments,* a designation that means the institution is pledged to maintain and nurture the principle for perpetuity while drawing off some prudent amount of interest income (typically, about 4 percent to 5 percent per year) for annual operating expenses. The interest income can be used by the board of trustees and administration to cover some costs of existing educational services or, perhaps, to provide student financial aid—and thus lower the tuition price. Or it may be used in any number of discretionary, exploratory initiatives.

The relative health and wealth of a college or university can be estimated by the total amount of its endowment along with a snapshot of its *per capita* endowment. Harvard University reports the highest total endowment (about $27.5 billion in fiscal year 2010, which is down from its reported $36 billion four years earlier), with an endowment per student of $1.3 million. Princeton University's endowment of $14.4 billion is a little more than half the size of the Harvard endowment. Since Princeton has fewer students than Harvard, its per capita endowment is about $1.89 million. Both institutions are the envy of higher education because they personify the observation made in a 1963 Harvard brochure: "Age like wealth does not make a university great. But it helps."

The Complexity of the Modern Campus

The education and services provided as part of a college or university undergraduate program have been subjected to extraordinary cost increases beyond the general inflationary rate for expenses in what sociologists call systems maintenance—liability insurance; police force and security; compliance with local, state, and national safety and health regulations; and both the repairs of existing and construction of new, state-of-the-art facilities along with careful attention to the cosmetics of landscaping and repairs under the auspices of buildings and grounds.

Even a small college has diversified purposes and expensive permanent professional staffing that need to be continually monitored. Yet for years, these internal financial complexities of colleges and universities remained relatively unexamined. Cheit (1971) pioneered the financial analysis of over 40 institutions and presented the unexpected finding that most American colleges and universities were in precarious financial condition. Another influential work was published in 1987 when economist Michael O'Keefe relied on national databases to subject six colleges and universities to rigorous financial analysis to answer the question, "Where does the money really go?" O'Keefe's sample included the University of Chicago, the University of South Carolina, Lynchburg College, Western State College of

Colorado, Williams College, and Seattle University. Even though all colleges share some similarities, what O'Keefe found was great variance in spending—and in their respective responses to financial problems. Furthermore, increased spending at the diverse institutions demonstrated a commonality in both internal and external dimensions: each institution was seeking to improve quality within and at the same time trying to be competitive in its external environment of rival institutions (O'Keefe, 1987, 12–34). Rosovsky's *The University: An Owner's Manual* (1990) relies on the author's long experience as academic dean at Harvard to show the intricacies of decision making leading to resource allocation. Labor economist and former university vice president Ronald Ehrenberg's *Tuition Rising* (2000) uses an intensive case study of his home institution, Cornell University, to convincingly document the complexity of campus units and the residual difficulty of reducing university expenditures. The net contribution of these accumulated works is to provide models whereby one can scrutinize one's own institution, with at least partial context of other institutions and some national data.

Universities versus Business Corporations

Frustration about high college prices leads to the perennial, implicit question (and often a complaint), "Why can't a college be run more like a business?" The underlying argument is that many of the practices and policies associated with colleges and universities would be unacceptable in a business corporation. Furthermore, unbusiness-like practices mean that colleges and universities tend to accrue inefficiencies and expenses that could readily be eliminated, leading to substantial savings in the costs of higher education. Richard Vedder, an economist familiar with colleges and universities, has documented and advanced this argument in his influential book *Going Broke by Degrees* (2004).

Why have economist Vedder's well-reasoned reform suggestions been avoided and not led to substantive changes?

Institutional inertia, avoidance, complacence, and denial offer partial explanations. One additional limit to imposing the "business model" onto higher education is that its advocates may tend to gloss over the numerous examples where commercial businesses themselves do not make decisions that are cost-beneficial. For example, Thomas Watson, Jr., longtime chief executive officer (CEO) of IBM noted with a combination of good humor and lament, "Each year I give my legal staff an unlimited budget—and each year they over-spend it . . ."

If colleges and universities were to try to emulate business corporations as models of best practices in running a campus, it would leave unanswered the principles and examples that ought be heeded. Is the mark of a good business one that balances its budget and maintains strict accountability of its employees and their decisions? Or, at another extreme, is an exemplary business one that is bold and "enterprising"? Colleges and universities tend to have a good track record in terms of survival. It is unusual news to read that a college has closed its doors. Meanwhile, more than 75 percent of new businesses fold within a year or two of opening. So if one wants a university to be "run like a business," this probably requires the qualifier that it should *not* be run like General Motors of the 21st century.

Business and commercial corporations do not always ascribe to rational planning and thoughtful decision making, even as an ideal, let alone a practice. Consider in 2011, for example, the heralded start-up companies of Northern California's Silicon Valley—an unusual sector in the American economy that was optimistic and thriving. According to a *New York Times* article on August 21, 2011, one stock analyst commented, "In Silicon Valley, we are as a species wildly optimistic. But if we weren't, we wouldn't have so many entrepreneurs because no one who's being rational would ever found a company" (Miller, 2011, 1).

On balance, colleges and universities tend to behave more like the bureaucracies associated with government agencies (Wilson, 1989). Perhaps one of the major impediments facing colleges and universities that might wish to transform into a business is the problem of defining the missions and measurement of a college. As Bruce Vladek (1979) observed about colleges as nonprofit organizations: "The competition for students and faculty is closely interwoven with the general drive for institutional prestige. Like most people, administrators and trustees are generally eager to do a good job and to appear to be doing a good job. But in higher education, as in most nonprofit services, it is extremely difficult to tell what a good job is, since it is so extraordinarily difficult to evaluate the quality of the 'product' " (39).

Colleges and universities are, indeed, businesses in one important sense: they often are the largest employer and landowner in the local community. This certainly holds for large state universities in small, rural communities, for example, Indiana University in Bloomington or the University of Illinois in Champagne-Urbana. More surprising is that the same is also true of universities in large metropolitan areas. Johns Hopkins University is the largest employer and landowner in Baltimore. The same holds for Brown University and Providence; Harvard is the largest landowner in the greater Boston area and trails only the federal government in highest number of employees. Yet this does not mean that the modern research university does well in behaving or operating as if it were a business. To further complicate the puzzle, universities' efforts at emulating the enterprises and language of business and have seldom succeeded. American research universities have an uneven record in fulfilling their self-proclaimed role as a state's "economic engine."

Colleges are either prohibited or discouraged from some forms of business practice as a condition of their charter and Internal Revenue Service (IRS) status as nonprofit educational organizations. Failure to comply with these terms could jeopardize the tax exemption colleges and universities have received from state and local governments on real estate holdings and other activities.

Problems within the College and University

Given that few colleges and universities are either willing or able to run themselves as if they were businesses, what are the groups and actions within a campus that have tended to cause excessively high costs? This is a bit like the game of *Clue,* but instead of investigating whether it was Colonel Mustard in the drawing room who used the cognac bottle to commit the murder, we first shall look at the professors in the faculty club as the alleged culprits in the crime of escalating college expenses.

The Faculty as the Problem in Rising College Costs

Since colleges and universities are markedly different from business corporations, it makes sense to examine one of those distinguishing features: faculty. This is a large, highly educated, expert professional group that is paid well. And because full-time faculty has academic tenure, the professor has job security with few approximations in commerce or industry. Furthermore, a Supreme Court ruling has made law that professors cannot be subject to a mandatory retirement age. Perhaps faculty are a major problem?

Many university presidents agree. Robert M. Rosenzweig, former president of the Association of American Universities (AAU) and former vice president for government relations at Stanford, and Donald Kennedy, former president of Stanford, have emphasized this theme in their recent books (Rosenzweig, 1998; Kennedy, 1997). In addition, a 2011 survey of university presidents by the editors of *Inside Higher Ed* led to the finding that, indeed, presidents think that professors are a major problem. Even professors often agree with and reinforce this characterization, showcased with the apocryphal story about a dean who mentioned to a senior professor that there was a new, attractive plan in which the professor could retire immediately at half-salary. The infamous response by the professor was to decline the offer, "pointing out that, after all, he was already retired on full salary" (Rosovsky, 1990, 216).

Critics perennially complain about lack of teaching by faculty. Since 1960 as an increasing number of universities have pursued external research grants and simultaneously sought to increase the quality and prestige of their faculty. As part of the transformation, faculty have negotiated persistently to have their teaching course loads reduced, ostensibly so that they will have adequate or more time to devote to the research priorities and the other demands of the institution. As one historian of higher education characterized the extended changes in professional allocations of time toward research with less classroom teaching, it was no less than the story of "how scholars trumped teachers" (Cuban, 1999). This phenomenon has been most pronounced at the doctoral-granting research universities, followed by a halo effect that has diffused in varying degrees of imitation throughout all institutions. The result in the 21st century is that teaching loads for full-time faculty have been reduced, with great variance by institutional category. One might find a teaching load of four to five courses per semester at a public community college or a small, relatively unendowed private college. Conversely, prestigious research universities and liberal arts colleges may have typical teaching loads for tenured professors of one to two courses per semester.

Light or reduced teaching loads do not necessarily indicate faculty shirking that runs up institutional expenses and lowers productivity. Professors who receive federal research grants bring money to the university, including indirect costs and overhead worth about 47 percent of the principal amount of the research grant award. Also, a university tends to gain discretionary funds when a professor who is principal investigator for a grant "buys out" a regularly scheduled course teaching assignment—a situation in which the university's central administration often pockets a surplus because it charges the research grant fund more than the professor would have been paid as part of his or her regular salary. One of the more important complexities is that a university has at least a dozen different categories of faculty. As early as 1963, Clark Kerr commented on the appearance of the "un faculty," or "research faculty,"—professional research experts who may have titular faculty rank, but who are exclusively dedicated to research (Kerr, 1963).

Faculty salary and related personnel expenses such as benefits and paid sabbatical leaves are a major source of campus costs. That datum on campus costs calls for the context of numerous studies and research reports that have documented a steady decline in full-time, tenure track professors as a part of the entire faculty (Bowen and Schuster, 1986; Baldwin and Chronister, 2001; Hermanowicz, 2011; Ginsberg, 2011). Analyses of college and university budgets nationwide from 1999 through 2009 report a persistent rise in the percentage of institutional revenues from student tuition payments and state subsidies that has been dedicated to noninstructional costs (Desrochers and Wellman, 2010). Nor have salaries of tenure track, full-time faculty increased at the same rate as salaries of academic administrators.

The Administration as the Problem in Rising College Costs

Two allegations are at the core of the claim that administrative expenses represent a disproportionate part of rising college costs. First is administrative bloat, that is, the inordinate increase in the number of administrative positions over the past 25 years. Second is administrative salary escalation, characterized by an increasing gap between what presidents, provosts, vice presidents, and deans are paid compared to compensation for the heart of the institution, the faculty. On this matter, one observation is that university presidents have emulated businesses, at least in having the president as CEO enjoy raises in salaries and benefits, as well as buy-outs, that have far surpassed the comparable rates of increase for senior tenured professors.

Presidents and other senior academic administrators often enjoy added benefits not available to faculty, including enhanced institutional contributions into retirement funds, special health care and insurance plans, and funding for university-related travel, conferences, and entertainment. Ironically, some benefits such as sabbatical leave—which customarily were reserved for professors—are now frequently bestowed on academic administrators.

Nowhere is the inconsistency, perhaps hypocrisy, more pronounced than in the self-dealing of academic administrators in negotiating their own contracts. Often the same academic administrators who deplore the abuses of tenure for faculty take care to make certain their own appointment as, for example, a president, provost, or dean, includes a provision that upon leaving the administrative role, they become a tenured professor with a high salary, and a full year of paid leave before joining an academic department.

Students as the Problem in Rising College Costs

Students—as applicants and then as matriculants—continually "vote with their feet" to influence many aspects of college life, ranging from the administration's decisions about course offerings to dining hall menus and construction of dormitories. Although students potentially have the power to lower costs by their particular demands, in fact, student preferences tend to drive up costs—and prices. One of the major transformations of the American campus since 1985 has been institutional investment in student extracurricular facilities and programs, including recreation centers, career counseling offices, student unions, state-of-the-art residential complexes, and abundant parking lots. Colleges build these impressive facilities and staff them with professionals—and then pass the costs on to students via increased tuition and fees.

Naturally, students and especially their parents want costs to be low, usually because they believe (sometimes unfounded) that lower costs lead to lower price and lower tuition charges. But parents also want their children to have a safe, comfortable dorm room, laboratory, and library. They want a professionally staffed counseling center, student health service, varsity sports program, effective career center, and other services related to but distinct from the formal course of study. Above all, academically minded and professionally ambitious students want to attend a college that gives optimal signs of quality and prestige. Students also drive up institutional costs in their demand for financial aid, whether it be in the form of need-based grants or merit scholarships. This phenomenon has gained momentum since 1985 as part of the imperative of "buying the best" (Clotfelter, 1996).

The pressure for outstanding programs and services tends to be fueled by colleges' recruitment of a relatively affluent student body whose family values include both achievement and high expectations. According to an article in the *New York Review of Books*, the recent generation of college students, especially at prestigious and academically selective institutions, have personified the adage that in terms of goals and aspirations, "They'd much rather be rich" (Hacker, 2007). In addition to this consumerism characterized by expensive taste, numerous patterns of college student behavior have tended to drive up college costs. Applying to a large number of colleges, thanks to the electronic college application, has increased at least on paper the competitiveness of admission to prestigious colleges. Once enrolled, students drive up costs by dropping numerous classes, changing majors, and gradually pushing the college experience from four to six years in length. Recent studies of undergraduates at state universities show a low and declining retention rate, with an overall six-year degree completion rate of about 60% (Hess, Schneider, Carey, and Kelly, 2009; Bowen, Chingos, and McPherson, 2009).

Research and Development as a Problem in Rising College Costs

One of the most crucial decisions an academic institution makes is whether to seek to be a "research university," that is, to have its mission emphasize a large number of PhD programs accompanied by professors and graduate students who compete for sponsored research grants offered by federal agencies and private foundations. This venture gave rise to the terms *soft money* and *hard money* in the 1950s to distinguish between annual revenues derived from external grants whose lifespan was finite, versus permanent, recurring monies hard-wired into the annual operating budget. One attraction of pursuing soft money via grants was that it could be seen as an add-on and supplement with which a university could then do things otherwise unaffordable, a process known as bootlegging. The danger in that strategy was that external grants usually were tightly defined, with little allowance for deliberate deviation from the funding contract. In other words, the practice of bootlegging was both inappropriate and difficult if a foundation or federal agency had strict accountability systems in place. The research and development (R&D) enterprise was also risky and high stakes because the university had to draw from its own resources to construct and maintain an elaborate, expensive infrastructure associated with applying for and administering grants, including professional staff to tend to compliance with numerous federal regulations. Also, most federal agencies and foundations devote little to capital expenditures or construction of laboratories and facilities.

The costs and benefits of sponsored research and development were tenuous at best, and predicated on the track record (or wishful thinking) that a university's professors would over the long run be sufficiently successful in landing major grants that would warrant university investments in infrastructure. Even when external funding remains stable or increases, individual researchers and their projects are vulnerable because funding priorities of grant agencies change over time; a once vital research laboratory may find an abrupt halt to project support despite many successful years of abundant grant funding.

These uncertainties underscore university finance officers' vagueness about when soft money after several years of renewed funding comes to be regarded as hard money in budget planning. Given that federal agencies and foundations change priorities, if a particular research specialty funding is not renewed, how many years should a university subsidize the unfunded researchers? A problematic scenario is one in which a university's faculty has a weak or mediocre record in grant awards, thus forcing the university to find cross-subsidies from other parts of the budget, perhaps from some special offering in undergraduate education, such as an honors program. The institutions usually considered most successful in the research enterprise are the 62 members of the Association of American Universities (AAU). Estimates are that an additional 100 universities aspire to "research university" stature. Most likely, there will be a significant shake-out leading to a depletion in their ranks over the coming decade. As part of this deconstruction, provosts will discover that they lack comprehensive information on, let alone control over, the numerous research centers and institutes with high administrative costs that have sprouted throughout the campus without much coherent planning over several decades.

Academic Medical Centers as a Problem in Rising College Costs

One of the most interesting developments since about 1960 has been the rise of new, expanded fields of scientific research in which such traditional academic disciplines as chemistry, biology, psychology, physics, and engineering have been cross-fertilized to create new interdisciplinary departments such as biochemistry and biophysics that are accompanied by massive grant funding sponsored by the National Institutes of Health (NIH) and such private foundations as the Rockefeller Foundation and the Robert Wood Johnson Foundation. Often, the institutional homes of these new combinations are colleges of medicine or academic medical centers. The result of this transformation is that many, probably most, universities near the top of annual lists of top recipients of federal research grants have a research-oriented medical center intertwined with a teaching hospital and a college of medicine, and perhaps a college of pharmacy and a college of allied health. The abbreviation for such units include AMC (academic medical center) and GME (graduate medical education). At a research university with an AMC, it is not unusual to have more than half of all university-wide faculty appointments under the AMC auspices.

AMCs are expensive and, when running well, bring in a lot of revenue from federal agencies and, often overlooked, from the federal Medicare program. In 2011, for example, the 300 medical colleges designated as providing GME collectively received $9.5 billion. That is an average per institution award of about $264 million per year. According to one estimate from officials at Mount Sinai Hospital in New York City, this represents about 50 percent of a medical college's annual operating budget (Davis, 2011). One problem is persistent, growing discussions in Congress to reduce substantially and perhaps even eliminate this subsidy. The fragility of the AMCs is increased when one considers that funding from NIH and National Science Foundation (NSF) has tapered, and competition to receive medical- and other health-related grants has intensified to the point that numerous highly qualified academic researchers do not receive the funding they once anticipated.

Intercollegiate Athletics as a Problem in Rising College Costs

The paradox of college sports is that they often appear to be lucrative, yet often spend more than they bring in to their host university. In other words, despite the abundance of television contracts, product endorsements, and donations by alumni and boosters, big-time college sports programs have a voracious appetite that is insatiable. Intercollegiate athletics, especially the high-powered spectator-oriented sports of football and basketball, command a disproportionate amount of the press coverage given to higher education. Big-time college sports programs consume between 10 and 20 percent of a university president's time. The most recent estimates are that only about 20 universities have big-time athletics programs that consistently meet all their expenses with program revenues. Among the 1,000 four-year colleges and universities that offer varsity sports, 98 per cent of them rely on institutional subsidies to balance their annual operating budgets.

Reliance on institutional support is not surprising for programs that are not oriented toward commercial broadcasts and are defined as part of their institution's educational or student affairs activities. The justifiable alarm comes with big-time programs that, according to National Collegiate Athletic Association (NCAA) criteria, are expected to be self-supporting. Their drain on scarce institutional resources often is understated because many big-time programs enjoy rent-free use of university land and some services, even though the athletics program is under the auspices of a distinct incorporated unit, usually known as something similar to the University Athletic Association. To qualify for tax exemptions and to avoid jeopardizing the host university's receipt of federal funding for research and student financial aid, varsity sports programs must comply with the federal legislation known as Title IX to ensure equitable resources for women's varsity sports. Conferences and the NCAA also impose requirements on programs that fall into the area of compliance, which results in regulations that tend to run up costs without generating additional revenues.

Big-time intercollegiate athletics are a prime example of a higher education activity for which it is difficult to reduce expenses and almost impossible to avoid substantial annual increasing costs (Knight Commission, 2009; Knight Commission, 2010). Although many of the most successful big-time programs are annually able to generate a surplus of revenues over expenses, the drop-off in the number of programs that can do so each year is dramatic (Sperber, 1900; Suggs, 2002). The largest annual operating budget for an intercollegiate athletics program is slightly over $100 million, with about 100 programs in the range of $30 million to $100 million (Sperber, 1990; Suggs, 2006). Big-time programs, also known as NCAA Division IA, especially those that also are member of the Bowl

Champion Series category (BCS), according to the guidelines of the National Collegiate Athletic Association, are supposed to be self-supporting. However, even at universities at which big-time sports programs operate in the black, athletics usually still receives some income from elsewhere in the university. The University of Kentucky athletics department, for example, receives each year about $650,000 from the Student Government Association, money that came from a mandatory student fee.

Cost escalation is especially prevalent at the biggest, most successful programs, with salaries for head coaches of the nonrevenue sports such as volleyball surpassing $300,000 per year per coach (Gabriel, 2010). Among the NCAA BCS football programs, the average salary for a head football coach surpasses $1 million per year. Assistant football coaches at numerous universities received salaries in the range of $200,000 to $500,000 per year. In 1975, the coach of the NCAA championship basketball team at University of California–Los Angeles (UCLA) received a salary of $37,000. In 2012, the highest paid university head basketball coach received an annual compensation package of more than $4 million.

A good example of the institutional costs of a varsity sports program for men and women in a large number of sports that provides a large number of full athletics scholarship is the College of William & Mary in Virginia. According to the university catalogue, as a state institution, in 2011, William & Mary charged an in-state Virginia student about $13,132 for tuition and fees for the academic year. On closer inspection, one finds that the mandatory intercollegiate athletics fee is $1,485—about 11 percent of the total price for tuition and fees. The college sports burden on revenues can be even greater at a private college or university, where each full athletics grant-in-aid covers a tuition charge of about $30,000. Private universities playing NCAA Division IA sports, such as Vanderbilt and Tulane, provide an annual transfer of about $15 million from the education general fund into intercollegiate athletics to help cover athletic scholarship costs.

The peculiar relationship of prices and costs in higher education surfaces in the specific area of college sports. The NCAA, best known for its role in increasing revenues and commercial promotions, also serves at times to lower costs of intercollegiate athletics programs. It does so by placing limits on the number of athletics grants-in-aid per varsity sport a college is allowed to offer. In a comparable way, it places a ceiling on the number of assistant coaches per sport a program can hire. Without such mandates, prosperous programs with generous alumni donors would enter into an athletics arms race of personnel and student-athletes beyond the reach of most programs. The NCAA's restrictions on some categories of spending alleviate in part the financial pressures on colleges that wish to be competitive on the field, yet that cannot generate optimal revenues.

At colleges and universities outside the commercial sports orbit—usually in NCAA Division III—athletics are funded as part of student life or educational programs and are not expected to be self-supporting. Nor do these schools provide athletic scholarships. Despite these amateur ideals, college sports has an inordinate presence because sometimes anywhere from one-fourth to one-third of applicants offered admission to highly selective liberal arts colleges were recruited to play varsity sports (Bowen and Levin, 2003).

Policy Perspective: State Government and Higher Education

State government is the level of higher education support that tends to be under-appreciated. A review of state budgets indicates that education, including postsecondary education, consumes a large part of state budgets nationwide in terms of actual dollars and percentage of state revenues. There also is great variance from state to state in terms of higher education funding as part of state dollars and as a percentage of state appropriations. A dominant theme in the research literature is that public higher education has lost ground in state support, either in real or relative terms (Heller, 2001; Ehrenberg, 2006). This plays out with state universities responding to state parsimony with announcements of high annual percentage tuition increases, suggesting that state reductions in funding mean that costs are transferred to students and consumers as increased tuition prices.

Policy Perspective: The Federal Government and Higher Education

Thanks to the analysis by Chester Finn, Jr., in his 1978 classic *Scholars, Dollars and Bureaucrats*, we have a clear characterization of the federal government's role in higher education. The points of contact between federal agencies and colleges are numerous, but at the same time, limited and fragmented. There is no coherent, unified "federal policy" toward higher education. Rather, federal agencies enter into negotiations with institutions, sometimes with overlap and contradictions. Two major areas in which higher education gains federal resources are sponsored research (especially in the sciences) and student financial aid. The two areas are not integrated. Two federal agencies dominate sponsored research grants to universities—the National Institutes of Health (NIH) and the National Science Foundation (NSF). Other agencies with a strong research grant presence include the Department of Defense, the Department of Agriculture, and the Department of Education. Student financial aid, the other major source of federal funding to higher education, tends to be allocated to students who then carry their portable loans and grants to accredited institutions at which they are enrolled.

Federally sponsored research grants are substantial both in dollar amounts and in establishing the missions and character of institutions that opt to be what Clark Kerr called federal grant universities (Kerr, 1963, 46). In 2009, for example, each of 100 universities received $103 million or more in federal research funding for the sciences. Within this elite group, there was wide variance. Johns Hopkins University's total of $1.58 billion was the highest amount, more than double the second-ranked University of Michigan, which received an annual total of $636 million. Sponsored research is considered high stakes because of intense competition for grant awards combined with the major investment a university must make in research infrastructure to apply for and administer such grants.

Various federal regulatory agencies also influence higher education (Finn, 1978). The convergence of the federal roles is that these agencies give resources and regulations. In other words, it is the prospect of forfeiting federal dollars as a penalty if a college or university does not comply with federal regulations. This is an especially potent source of federal leverage because noncompliance by a single campus unit jeopardizes federal funds received by all units. Regulation and compliance include enforcement of legislation such as Title IX on nondiscrimination in educational programs. Also, if a university receives federal funding for research projects, then the entire university is subject to numerous regulations dealing with health and safety standards on campus. Colleges and universities advocate for increased federal funding in research support and student financial aid. Simultaneously, university presidents tend to object to the proliferation of regulations to which their institutions are subjected (Glazer, 1979; Bok, 1980; Carnegie Foundation, 1982). One dysfunction, the presidents claim, is that federal regulations significantly increase administrative costs as part of the academic operating budget.

Controversies over Policies: Problems of Rising College Costs

Having considered how various stakeholders are involved in rising college costs—both as part of the problem and part of the solution—one now can step away from probing the campus to consider issues as matters of policy discussions. Many of the questions and conflicts can be distilled to conceptual or philosophical discussions—and differences. Clarifying one's philosophical position or priority is both helpful and necessary before implementing reforms.

Price versus Cost

Price and *cost* were presented as key concepts in Chapter 1. Here the terms surface again, but with a difference: as end points of different approaches to reform. Does one prefer to lower college price? Or is the aim to lower cost? One may do both in some proportion, but it is essential to distinguish—at least as an intermediate step—one's particular focus.

Conventional wisdom is that if a college were to lower costs, it then would pass savings on to students as consumers by lowering tuition. In practice, however, colleges seldom do so. Rather, monies freed up by some savings measures typically are invested in new or existing programs. The observation reinforced by numerous economists is that the pursuit of academic quality and prestige tends to make tuition charges rise. Recall, for example, in Chapter 1, the CNN broadcast in which Eliot Spitzer singled out Bates College for its annual charges of $51,300. For context, it is useful to note that Bates College is hardly alone. In 2010 and 2011, ninety-nine academic institutions charged $50,000 or more per student; a year earlier, only 58 institutions charged prices that high (*Almanac of Higher Education*, 2012, 14).

Access versus Choice

In the United States, we are good at providing a spot somewhere for almost any student who wishes to go to college (Finn, 1978). But not everyone can go to Harvard, Stanford, Amherst, or the University of Michigan. So there is a trade-off that includes some consideration of providing each student with some reasonable choices that are compatible with their academic record and college application. A sound policy monitors for signs of tracking or slotting in which students are assigned to an institution, by administrators, either with favoritism or with some unexpected consequence that is dysfunctional.

Admissions versus Affordability

Consider a situation in which a student has been accepted to the college her or his choice, but the parents decide that this excellent college is too expensive. On second thought, perhaps one might argue that the student cannot afford *not* to go, because a bachelor's degree from this academically selective college will be a great springboard to graduate school and future professional success (perhaps!).

Efficiency versus Effectiveness

In most states, educating a college student at a community college is efficient, that is, it costs less than, for example, the University of California–Berkeley. But what about graduation rates, prestige, and leverage? Or, within a university campus, what is the educational trade-off if you take an on-campus online course for Economics 101 (along with 600 classmates) versus a seminar with 15 fellow undergrads, taught by a distinguished professor who probably will receive the Nobel Prize in a few years? To cut the consumer issues to a fine gradation, what are the pros and cons on a campus if some programs (e.g., engineering or business) charge a higher tuition for students opting to major in that field than do programs for history or English? What is right? What is fair? What is gained, and what is lost by one particular policy versus another?

Student Financial Aid: "Need-Based" versus "Merit" Scholarships

On what basis should a college award scholarship monies? Is the primary aim to make a college affordable to qualified applicants whose academic record warrants an offer of admission? Or is it to use scholarships as a magnet to attract talent, regardless of the potential student's family income? How does the policy vacillate depending on a student's particular situation? And what is the consequence for an institution depending on the particular niche or position of the college in recruiting students?

Student Financial Aid: Packaging and Layers

Should there be some priority for emphasizing among the major types of aid, that is, grants versus loans versus work study? What are the consequences in terms of how one sequences the different kinds of financial aid awards? How do the different layers or sources of student financial aid mesh? Typically today, this would be a college's resources that are used for student aid, state grants and loans, federal grants and loans, and private foundations' awards. According to James Hearn (2001), these kinds of discussions on the philosophy and aim of student aid have been lacking even though federal funding for student financial aid has increased over the years. Economist Robert Archibald (2002) argued that a sound policy of reform would be to switch the roles of federal financial aid and a college's financial aid. The redesigned financial aid system would then have colleges shifting from grants to loans, whereas the federal government would go from an emphasis on loans to grants. It is an intriguing, consequential proposal that, reinforcing Hearn's concern, has unfortunately received little serious consideration.

Public Good versus Private Good

Why does (or should) some larger body such as the taxpayers of a state or of the nation devote resources to invest in higher education? Is a college education a "public good" that benefits the entire society? Is it a "private good" by and for the individual? Or, perhaps, is it a mix of both? How one resolves this question will be the philosophical driving force in then shaping state and federal student financial aid policies.

The "Tuition Gap"

The price differential between public and private institutions in tuition charges persists as a peculiarity of higher education access in the United States. If the aim of various subsidies and supports for higher education is to maximize student access and opportunity, how might programs and policies deal with the difference between tuition charges at an independent (private) college versus those at a state university? More essential, why might there be a gap or differential? How did that come about?

An interesting dimension of this question is that when one looks at costs, the gap between the two sectors shrinks substantially. One underappreciated item in college pricing has been the ability of numerous small, independent colleges to keep tuition charges relatively low while also providing generous student financial aid (Sanoff, 2006; Koblik and Graubard, 2000).

Controversy: Explanations on College Costs

In addition to relying on economic analysis to answer *where* the money goes, comprehensive policy formulation ultimately gains when economists edge toward explaining organizational behavior, researching the question of *why* colleges and universities get and spend monies the way they do. Among numerous theories, two warrant particular consideration and comparison: the revenue theory of college spending and the disease theory.

Revenue Theory

According to economist and university president Howard Bowen (1980), colleges tend to raise all the money they can and then spend all the money they raise. The press for educational quality and services creates an approach to budgets that makes it difficult and unlikely to reduce costs. Rather, the inclination is to continually seek, through diverse sources, to maximize revenues.

Disease Theory

According to economists Robert Archibald and David Feldman (2006, 2010), the disease theory of rising costs first advanced by economist and former Princeton president William Bowen and by economist William Baumol is especially compelling to explain why higher education costs rise at a relatively high rate. One part of the theory is that in those parts of the national economy that rely heavily on advanced expertise and highly skilled professionals, there have been rising costs—far higher than manufacturing of products—that habitually outpace the annual inflation rate. This has been documented for performing arts (Baumol and Bowen, 1996) and, furthermore, appears to hold for professional athletes and for lawyers, for medical doctors as well as other health care professionals.

Reconciling the Theories

Evidently a source of tension between the revenue theory of costs in higher education and the disease theory is that Howard R. Bowen has cited higher education as a unique entity in the economy, whereas Baumol and William Bowen see the organizational behavior as extending to numerous organizations dependent on highly paid professionals. Archibald and Feldman, in contrast, favor the more widespread disease theory advanced by William Baumol and William G. Bowen, noting that the phenomenon extends to many fields. Perhaps a partial resolution or reconciliation that joins the two theories is to depict higher education as an enterprise that is distinctive, although not unique. Furthermore, most of the professions and fields that experience the disease theory have high rates of cost increase for educated, advanced experts probably have relied on university-based educational programs and certification—a feature that reinforces the significance of colleges and universities in the cost escalation phenomenon. Both theories overlap in agreement that high cost increases in these special fields are unlikely to subside.

Solutions to the Problems of Rising College Costs

Given the numerous problems and controversies associated with rising college costs, proposed solutions have surfaced in which both new and familiar strategies target the major constituencies within higher education—faculty, administration, and students. A commonality in the proposed solutions is an emphasis on reducing costs by means of accountability and efficiency measures.

Solution: Faculty Accountability

Ineffective and indifferent teaching by professors can be monitored and then tied to decisions on salaries, promotion, retention, and termination if a college or university implements a comprehensive faculty performance data collection system. One of many such plans was developed by Richard O'Donnell in his role as an advisor to the University of Texas system. O'Donnell conducted a study of faculty productivity that was intended to be implemented at Texas A&M University and the University of Texas in 2011 as the university regents sought to make public higher education accountable (O'Donnell, 2011; O'Donnell, 2011, July 20). In one phase of the initiative, the university released published reports that listed each faculty member in terms of a profit-or-loss statement. The subsequent criticism was that the accountability template tended to be simplistic in that it did not include faculty roles in advising, sponsoring research, chairing master's and doctoral degree programs, or supervising PhD dissertations.

An added complication is that long-term national studies conducted by university administrators elsewhere, such as the Delaware Study (formally, the National Study of Instructional Costs & Productivity), have led to the finding that "faculty pay is not part of academe's cost crisis." Michael Middaugh, assistant vice president for institutional research and planning at the University of Delaware, told reporters in 2006, "Faculty instruction has been managed and managed well," and that it had been spikes in the costs of health care, energy, and complying with federal laws constituted the "other stuff that's killing us" (Middaugh as quoted in Fain, 2006; see also Middaugh, 2001).

Solution: Eliminate Faculty Tenure

If professors with tenure are seen by the president and provost as a liability in keeping a college or university vital in its hiring and teaching, eliminating tenure is an attractive option. Yet changing faculty handbooks and then dealing with such external groups as the American Association of University Professors (AAUP) is arduous. Rather than eliminate a tenure policy, what already has happened at many institutions is for the president to evade tenure appointments. This is done by offering contracts to new faculty hires that have term limits and are not tenure eligible. Increased reliance on adjuncts and part-time instructors along with graduate teaching assistants and lecturers means that in 2011 professors who had tenure or were eligible for tenure constituted a shrinking proportion of the teaching faculty (Hermanowicz, 2011).

Eliminating—or avoiding—tenure track faculty appointments may cause problems for the long-term operation and character of an academically strong college or university in that fewer permanent, full-time professors would then be available for customary roles in advising undergraduate and graduate students as well as serving on the numerous university committees that constitute shared governance in numerous aspects of institutional decisions and operations. Implicit in these concerns is that faculty—and their various contributions to teaching, research, and service—are central to the academic mission and campus community.

Solution: High Tuition, High Need-Based Aid

This solution was proposed by Thomas Wallace in 1992 as an antidote to a problem of declining state support for public higher education. The rationale was that if state legislatures were reducing per student subsidies and simultaneously prohibiting state universities from raising tuition to offset the differential, public higher education was on a collision course on which students would ultimately suffer because curriculum would be leeched. The strategy was to step beyond the funding formula that had served public higher education well from about 1946 to 1990 but, due to inflation and rising costs, was no longer feasible. Why not charge a reasonable tuition that provided an excellent collegiate education?

To anticipate critics who feared that high tuition at public institutions would deter modest and low income students from applying, Wallace responded with the important addendum that state universities then could offset this repelling of modest income applicants by offering increased need-based student financial aid. In sum, public colleges and universities were to edge gradually toward the model of costs and prices long in place at academically strong private colleges and universities. Such innovation responds to a recurrent question about business as usual: Is it sound public policy to have a state university charge zero or low tuition?"

In California, for example, the long established tradition of not charging tuition to state residents who attended California public colleges and universities was considered by some analysts to be counterproductive in terms of promoting widespread higher education access and affordability. Was it sound public policy for a student from a family whose annual income was, for example, $500,000 per year, to not be expected to pay any tuition charge? The subtext of this question was that a noor low tuition policy was made possibly by a regressive tax policy. In other words, taxes paid by citizens, many of whom were from low and modest income categories and did not attend college, were paying a disproportionate amount to make the state subsidy for students possible.

Solution: Clarity of Purpose

Many colleges and universities offer a diverse range of concentrations and fields of study. This can suggest an admirable sensitivity to demands for new curricula, either by students or other external constituencies. Alternatively, it can lead to the proliferation of programs that ultimately lack coherence or a clear institutional mission. Gordon Davies, longtime director of the State Council of Higher Education in Virginia, spoke to this lack of clear institutional purpose and a proclivity for mission creep, noting that most colleges and universities were deliberately vague about their purposes and courses of study (Davies, 1986).

Not all mission statements are ambiguous or vague, but as a general rule, American colleges and universities were susceptible to the "omnibus syndrome" of trying to be all things to all people. What stands out in bold contrast to this curricular sprawl is the infrequent and refreshingly clear statement of purpose. A good example is the prospectus directed at potential applicants from the 1982 "view book" of the U.S. Naval Academy, titled "Why the Naval Academy? Time Hasn't Changed Our Mission":

> Service to the Country: We should be frank about this from the beginning. The purpose of the Naval Academy is to prepare young men and women to become professional line officers in the Navy or Marine Corps. Nothing else. But no one asks that you come to Annapolis with your mind made up that you want to be a career officer in the naval service. This commitment, if it is to come, develops in due time. It is considered necessary, however, that you arrive here free of preconceived goals toward some entirely different area of endeavor. If your primary interest lies in such fields as law, education, nursing, the ministry, ecology, etc., the Naval Academy is simply not the place for you ... Before deciding to come to Annapolis you should clear understand and accept that you will be educated and trained here for service to your nation. (U.S. Naval Academy, 1982, 9)

This institutional stance is exceptional. Most colleges and universities, especially large research universities, have such scant coherence of purpose that the president of the University of California observed that one of the few points of cooperation among departments within a modern university was to share a central heating system (Kerr, 1963). Today, either ambition or pursuit of fresh revenue streams means that many universities tend to add programs that seem to be timely and expedient. Incumbent programs are dropped sporadically, although not always as the result of thoughtful deliberation about institutional mission or educational purpose.

Solution: Rely on Distance Learning Technology

This would seem to be an appealing area in which over time technology could drive down instructional costs, an advantageous situation that then could be passed on to students as consumers in the form of lower price. Such a sequence is uncertain, probably unlikely. A more informed estimate is that as colleges and universities—including traditional, residential campuses with a full-time student body—add the option of distance learning courses on the Internet, the result will be to lower institutional expenses without lower tuition charges. In other words, distance learning and other forms of broadcast education have great appeal as a "cash cow" that, after initial startup costs are absorbed, have the potential to enroll increasing numbers of students at relatively little additional expense.

Some analysts have extolled innovations by such technology leaders as Stanford University and Massachusetts Institute of Technology (MIT) to share at no charge to students Internet broadcasts of lectures and courses in what is hailed as the University of Where Ever (Keller, 2011). Although such generous innovations are encouraging, they usually face crucial limits. The information and images may be free to students, but credentials are not. Most likely, one will have to pay if one wishes to receive academic credit or a degree for having participated in the courses.

Distance education follows no single model of price and cost. Indeed, there are selected programs in which distance learning commands the prestige to charge higher tuition rates than those for a full-time residential undergraduate program. An executive master's of business administration (MBA) program from a prestigious university such as Duke or MIT would be potential examples.

Solution: Rely on Private Fundraising

This makes good sense as a means for a college or university to supplement—and thus reduce reliance on—either increased tuition charges or state appropriations. In fact, since about 1980, virtually every institution, ranging from established private colleges and universities to all categories of public institutions, including community colleges, have established sophisticated, highly professional development offices. Success in this realm has been ironic and incomplete. For example, in 1994, a development officer at the University of Pennsylvania noted that although his university had just completed a successful $1 billion fundraising campaign, this was hardly sufficient as a panacea for all budget problems (Shepard, 1994). By 2011, several universities had campaigns for more than $2 billion.

The risk of emhasizing private philanthropy is that its success and appeal may have caused its effectiveness to be saturated. Numerous new private foundations have shifted their funding priorities from gifts to individual campuses in favor of support for thematic issues or causes such as serving modest income students or finding a cure for a particular disease—initiatives that cut across the higher education landscape. Colleges and universities also must share the fundraising stage with a growing number of organized, energetic nonprofit organizations. One consequence will be that for many educational institutions, fundraising will show a diminishing return.

Conclusion: Equity and Excellence in American Higher Education

Most analyses by economists and public policy researchers indicate that since 1985, colleges and universities in the United

States have shown little inclination or ability to reduce costs. The dominant approach over the past quarter century has been to seek new revenue sources, often with the hope that these will sponsor new initiatives that in turn will enroll more students, attract more research grants, draw more paying sports customers, or even persuade shoppers to buy products with college and university logos and other forms of "branding." The staples of annual income—student tuition payments, student financial aid from the federal government, and state subsidies for students—tend to be the magnetic attraction when colleges and universities seek an area in which to reduce spending and then transfer residuals to other projects and initiatives. On balance, one sees that the "buying the best" approach that was pioneered by a handful of academically prestigious and financially well-endowed institutions has been a source of emulation and aspiration that has diffused in varying degrees throughout virtually all of higher education in the United States (Clotfelter, 1996). An apt characterization of this pervasive institutional drive to increase one's reputation and resources is "Wannabe U" (Tuchman, 2009). In the small but powerful circle of research universities, the particular manifestation of Wannabe U is seen in the goal of "tapping the riches of sciences" in which universities are indelibly linked to the promise of economic growth (Geiger and Sa, 2008).

What is surprising is that these institutional strategies have worked as well as they have for several decades. What is sobering is that most likely they will not work indefinitely (McPherson, Schapiro, and Winston, 1993; Vedder, 2004). To the credit of colleges and universities, higher education underwent a "managerial revolution" starting in the mid-1970s that brought new accountability and energy to admissions, enrollments, fundraising, budget review and overall organizational planning (Keller, 1983). In retrospect, it has been no accident that the dire predictions about college closings were not fulfilled. One explanation is that the numerous books about "surviving the 1980s" were the source of administrative and planning lessons that colleges heeded. However, the sustained national economic downturn since 2007 combined with colleges and universities' investment portfolios having been especially hard hit by with stock market declines indicate that the emphasis on "ratcheting up" and leveraging existing monies into new projects with the university as an "economic engine" will not suffice indefinitely in the 21st century.

One insight from these changes and challenges offered by Arthur Levine in 1997 was the realization that higher education in the United States had become a mature industry. A downside of this maturation is that higher education no longer elicits the fresh enthusiasm it enjoyed with legislatures and taxpayers in, for example, 1960. It also is increasingly difficult for colleges and universities to persuade donors and legislators that academic institutions are struggling, emergent ventures. Finally, not only are parents and students concerned about rising college costs, in 2011, an increasing number of articles, reports, and studies argued that despite increases in tuition charges, public institutions may be relatively cheap to students—but not to taxpayers, who "are also bearing significant hidden costs" (Schneider and de Alva, 2011).

Students—that is, prospective students, enrolled students, and former students as alumni—fit into the complex picture as a constituency that is under increasing duress. For years, even during relatively prosperous periods for higher education and the national economy, such economists and policy analysts as Sandy Baum, Edward St. John, Michael McPherson, and James Hearn have been publishing systematic research based on thorough data that persistently has warned of cleavages in affordability and access, with modest income students being marginalized in realistic college choices. This tilt toward the advantaged students gaining leverage for yet more advantages in higher education brings this chapter full circle to a reminder of how such noncollege activities as summer camp with SAT preparation sessions tend to have increased rather than closed the gap of access and opportunity in American higher education over the past half century. It is a theme that permeates the patterns of institutional and student sorting and positioning.

One of the few benefits of the national economic recession since 2007 is that more students are "sharing the pain" in a direct, rather than vicarious, way. This is so because in each subsequent year since the severe downturn of 2007, a significant proportion of college students has shifted from the ranks of applicants with no financial need to newcomers in the ranks of those who cannot go to college—or at least the college of their choice as projected by them and their parents in prosperous times a few years earlier—without substantial aid from a combination of college as well as state and federal government. To exacerbate these financial pressures, the rising dependency on loans as a form of student aid has made college indebtedness an unwelcomed gift that keeps on giving well into the prime years of starting a career and/or pursuing advanced professional and graduate degrees.

To extend the interdependence scenario, by 2010 and 2011, reports on hiring in the learned professions of law and medicine indicated that even many graduates of the most prestigious law and medical schools faced bleak prospects for salaries and entry-level positions. The deferred gratification of an advanced professional degree that in the past made added student loans a reasonable investment has increasingly turned into a decision that is both expensive and risky. The net result is that at the end of the first decade of the 21st century, the traditional American commitment to excellence and equity is mired in a gridlock that no longer is confined to underserved low and modest income students; it now has extended upward in the pyramid of education, advantage, and aspiration of the middle and upper middle income realms of American society. The simultaneous reckoning for academic institutions is that this now is an era in which—according to an analyst writing for the *New York Review of Books*—colleges and universities are "in trouble" (Delbanco, 2009). One ray of hope is that out of the adversity of high tuition and growing student indebtedness, the pervasiveness of the problem associated with the rise of both college costs and college prices is now less likely to be ignored by stakeholders in serious policy deliberations.

Where and how will these renegotiations take root? A good chance for renegotiations will be that educational leaders, legislators, and other constituents will both heed and make use of the new generation of readily available databases and analytic tools. New research on the financing of higher education worldwide may prompt decision makers to pay more attention to how colleges and universities in the United States fare in comparison to their international counterparts (Johnstone and Marcucci, 2010). For prospective students and their parents, the new website launched by the U.S. Department of Education in June 2011 as part of the Higher Education Opportunity Act of 2008 provides free access to comprehensive and comparable data on net prices and costs of colleges nationwide (Lewin, June 30, 2011). This promise of clear consumer information, however, were not without problems. According to a *New York Times* editorial (February 26, 2012) about comparison shopping for college tuition, a study by the Institute for College Access and Success found wide variation in quality and clarity in the information colleges are providing to prospective students via their websites. A possible antidote—probably best seen as a partial solution—was the Department of Education's feature on its College Navigator site that allows students to sort colleges by average net price.

One of the most promising developments in the quest for both equity and excellence is the appearance of data conduits such as the Boston-based ConnectEDU, an organization that aims to increase the knowledge and options of underserved students, including those in geographically remote areas, so that decisions about college choice and student financial aid shift increasingly to the students as consumers, whereas before these resources tended to be more in the province of the admissions offices, especially at academically prestigious, selective colleges and universities (Carey, 2011). For state and national policy deliberations, the open forum and interactive capacities of the Delta Cost Project bring enhanced transparency to the getting and spending that characterizes the enterprise of American higher education (Desrochers and Wellman, 2010). After about a quarter century of pressures promulgated both by institutions and individuals, the "new deal" for American higher education has the motive, timing, and tools to confront—and perhaps solve—the problem of increased inequities and high prices of a college education.

References

Almanac of Higher Education for 2011–2012 (Washington, DC: Chronicle of Higher Education, 2012).

Anderson, Jenny. "For a Standout College Essay, Applicants Fill Their Summers." *New York Times* (August 5, 2011), A1.

Anderson, Jenny. "With Admission Rates Tougher than Harvard's, Schools Reconsider Policies." *New York Times* (September 6, 2011), A22.

Anonymous. "Comparison Shopping for College Tuition." *New York Times* (February 26, 2012), SR 10.

Archibald, Robert B. *Redesigning the Financial Aid System: Why Colleges and Universities Should Switch Roles with the Federal Government.* Baltimore and London: Johns Hopkins University Press, 2002.

Archibald, Robert, and Feldman, David. *Why Does College Cost So Much?* New York: Oxford University Press, 2010.

Archibald, Robert B. and Feldman, David H. "Explaining Increases in Higher Education Costs." Williamsburg, Virginia: College of William & Mary Department of Economics Working Paper No. 41 (September 2006).

Baldwin, Roger G., and Chronister, Jay L. *Teaching without Tenure: Policies and Practice for a New Era.* Baltimore: Johns Hopkins University Press, 2001.

Bartlett, Thomas. "Phoenix Risen: How a History Professor Became the Pioneer of the For-Profit Revolution." *Chronicle of Higher Education* (July 10, 2009) A1, A10–A13.

Bauerlein, Mark. "Ignorance by Degrees: Colleges Serve the People Who Work There More Than the Students Who Desperately Need to Learn Something." *Wall Street Journal* (August 2, 2010) http://online.wsj.com/article/SB1000 1424052748703720504575377140202306852.html.

Baum, Sandy. "College Education: Who Can Afford It?" In Michael B. Paulsen and John C. Smart, eds. *The Finance of Higher Education: Theory Research, Policy and Practice*. New York: Agathon Press, 2001, 39–52.

Baumol, William J., and Bowen, William G. *Performing Arts: The Economic Dilemma*. Washington, DC: Twentieth Century Fund, 1966.

Baumol, William J., and Blackman, Sue Anne. "How to Think about Rising College Costs." *Planning for Higher Education* 23(Summer 1995), 1–7.

Berg, Ivar. *The Great Training Robbery: Education and Jobs*. New York: Basic Books, 1972.

Berrett, Dan. "Wrong Kind of Accountability?" *Inside Higher Ed* (May 10, 2011) http://www.insidehighered.com/news/ 2011/05/10/texas_faculty_and_president_criticize_regents _measurement_of_professors.

Bok, Derek. "The Federal Government and the University." *Public Interest* (Winter 1980), 80–101.

Bowen, Howard R. *Investment in Learning: The Individual and Social Value of American Higher Education*. San Francisco, Washington, D.C., and London: Jossey-Bass for the Sloan Foundation and the Carnegie Council on Policy Studies in Higher Education, 1978.

Bowen, Howard R. *The Costs of Higher Education: How Much Do Colleges and Universities Spend per Student and How Much Should They Spend?* San Francisco: Jossey-Bass for the

Carnegie Council on Policy Studies in Higher Education, 1986.

Bowen, Howard R., and Schuster, Jack. H. *American Professors: A National Resource Imperiled.* New York and Oxford: Oxford University Press, 1980.

Bowen, William, and Levin, Sarah. *Reclaiming the Game: College Sports and Educational Values.* Princeton, NJ and Oxford: Princeton University Press, 2003.

Bowen, William G., Chingos, Matthew, and McPherson, Michael. *Crossing the Finish Line: Completing College at America's Universities.* Princeton, NJ: Princeton University Press, 2009.

Callan, Patrick M., and Finney, Joni E., eds. *Public and Private Financing of Higher Education: Shaping Public Policy for the Future.* Phoenix, AZ: American Council on Education and the Oryx Press, 1997.

Carey, Kevin. "The End of College Admissions as We Know It." *Washington Monthly* (August–September 2011) http://www.washingtonmonthly.com/magazine/septemberoctober_2011/features/the_end_of_college_admissions031636.php.

Carnegie Foundation for the Advancement of Teaching. *The Control of the Campus: A Report on the Governance of Higher Education.* Princeton, NJ: Carnegie Foundation for the Advancement of Teaching, 1982.

Cheit, Earl F. *The New Depression in Higher Education: A Study of the Financial Conditions at 41 Colleges and Universities* (New York: McGraw-Hill for the Carnegie Council, 1971).

Clotfelter, Charles. *Buying the Best: Cost Escalation and Elite Higher Education.* Princeton, NJ: Princeton University Press for the National Board of Economic Research, 1996.

Cuban, Larry. *How Scholars Trumped Teachers: Change without Reform in the University Curriculum, Teaching, and Research, 1890–1990.* New York: Columbia University Teachers College Press, 1999.

"College: Is It Worth the Cost?" *New York Times* Sunday Review (August 28, 2011), SR 12.

Davies, Gordon K. "The Importance of Being General: Philosophy, Politics, and Institutional Mission Statements." In John C. Smart, *Higher Education: Handbook of Theory and Research.* New York: Agathon Press, 1986, 85–102.

Davis, Kenneth L. "Urban Teaching Hospitals Disproportionately Targeted for Medicare Cuts." *New York Times* (September 27, 2011), A19.

Delbanco, Andrew. "The Universities in Trouble." *New York Review of Books* 56(May 14, 2009). http://www.nybooks .com/articles/archives/2009/may/14/the-universities-in -trouble/?pagination=false.

Desrochers, Donna M., and Wellman, Jane V. *Trends in College Spending, 1999–2009: Where Does the Money Come From? Where Does It Go? What Does It Buy?* Washington, DC: Delta Cost Project, 2010.

Draper, Joe, and Thomas, Katie. "As Colleges Compete, Major Money Flows to Minor Sports." *New York Times* (September 2, 2010), A1, A20.

Ehrenberg, Ronald. *Tuition Rising: Why College Costs So Much.* Cambridge, MA and London: Harvard University Press, 2000.

Ehrenberg, Ronald, ed. *What's Happening to Public Higher Education?: The Shifting Financial Burden.* Baltimore: Johns Hopkins University Press, 2006.

Fain, Paul. "Faculty Pay Is Not Part of Academe's Cost Crisis, Expert Tells Trustees' Conference." *Chronicle of Higher Education* (April 4, 2006), A1.

Fain, Paul. "New Web Tool Helps Both Experts and Public Grasp Colleges' Costs," *Chronicle of Higher Education* (July 9, 2010) http://chronicle.com/article/New-Web-Tool-Helps -Experts-and/66222/.

Finn, Chester E., Jr. *Scholars, Dollars and Bureaucrats.* Washington, DC: Brookings Institution, 1978.

Frederick M. Breneman, David W., Leslie, Larry L., and Anderson, Richard E., eds. *ASHE Reader on Finance in Higher Education.* Needham Heights, MA: Simon and Schuster for the Association for the Study of Higher Education, 1996.

Gabriel, Trip. "Learning in Dorm, Because Class Is on the Web." *New York Times* (November 4, 2010), A1.

Gardner, John W. *Excellence: Can We Be Equal and Excellent Too?* New York: Norton, 1961.

Geiger, Roger L. *Knowledge and Money: Research Universities and the Paradox of the Marketplace.* Stanford, CA: Stanford University Press, 2004.

Geiger, Roger L., and Sa, Creso M. *Tapping the Riches of Science: Universities and the Promise of Economic Growth.* Cambridge, MA: Harvard University Press, 2008.

Ginsberg, Benjamin. "Administrators Ate My Tuition: Want to Get College Costs in Line? Start by Cutting the Overgrown Management Ranks." *Washington Monthly* (September/October 2011) http://www.washingtonmonthly.com/magazine/septemberoctober_2011/features/administrators_ate_my_tuition031641.php.

Ginsberg, Benjamin. *The Fall of the Faculty: The Rise of the All Administrative University and Why It Matters.* London and New York: Oxford University Press, 2011.

Glazer, Nathan. "Regulating Business and the Universities." *Public Interest* (Summer 1979), 42–65.

Hacker, Andrew. "They'd Much Rather Be Rich." *New York Review of Books* (October 11, 2007), 31–34.

Harris, Gardiner. "Calling More Nurses 'Doctor,' A Title Physicians Begrudge." *New York Times* (October 2, 2011), 1, 18.

Healy, Michelle. "Ivy League Settles Price-Fixing Suit on Aid." *USA Today* (May 23, 1991), 1A.

Hearn, James C. "The Paradox of Growth in Federal Aid for College Students, 1965–1990." In Michael B. Paulsen and John C. Smart, eds., *The Finance of Higher Education: Theory Research, Policy and Practice*. New York: Agathon Press, 2001, 267–320.

Heller, Donald E., ed. *The States and Public Higher Education Policy: Affordability, Access, and Accountability*. Baltimore and London: Johns Hopkins University Press, 2001.

Hermanowicz, Joseph C., ed. *The American Academic Profession: Transformation in Contemporary Higher Education*. Baltimore: Johns Hopkins University Press, 2011.

Hess, Frederick M., ed. *Footing the Tuition Bill: The New Student Loan Sector*. Washington, DC: American Enterprise Institute, 2007.

Hess, Frederick M., Schneider, Mark, Carey, Kevin, and Kelly, Andrew. *Diplomas and Dropouts: Which Colleges Actually Graduate Their Students (And Which Don't)*. Washington, DC: American Enterprise Institute, 2009.

Jencks, Christopher, and Riesman, David. *The Academic Revolution*. Garden City, NY: Doubleday Anchor, 1968.

Johnstone, D. Bruce, and Marcucci, Pamela N. *Financing Higher Education Worldwide: Who Pays? Who Should Pay?* Baltimore: Johns Hopkins University Press, 2010.

Keller, Bill. "The University of Wherever." *New York Times* (October 3, 2011), A21.

Keller, George. *Academic Strategy: The Management Revolution in American Higher Education* (Baltimore and London: Johns Hopkins University Press, 1983).

Kennedy, Donald. *Academic Duty*. Cambridge, MA and London: Harvard University Press, 1997.

Kerr, Clark. *The Uses of the University* (Cambridge, MA: Harvard University Press, 1963).

Khalaf, Rhoula. "Customized Accounting," *Forbes* (May 25, 1992), 50.

Knight Commission on Intercollegiate Athletics, "First of Its Kind Survey Reveals Dilemma of

Reform." Miami, FL: Knight Foundation press release of October 26, 2009.

Knight Commission on Intercollegiate Athletics. *Restoring the Balance: Dollars, Values, and the Future of College Sports.* Miami, FL: Knight Foundation, June 17, 2010.

Koblik, Steven, and Graubard, Stephen R., eds. *Distinctively American: The Residential Liberal Arts Colleges.* New Brunswick, NJ: Transaction Publishers, 2000.

Kramer, Martin. "The Unsmart Choices of Smart Students." *Change Magazine* (March/April 2000), 50.

Levine, Arthur. "Higher Education's New Status as a Mature Industry." *Chronicle of Higher Education* (January 31, 1997), A48.

Lewin, Tamar. "What's the Most Expensive College? The Least? Education Department Puts It All Online." *New York Times* (June 30, 2011), A13.

Lewin, Tamar. "Universities Seeking Out Students of Means." *New York Times* (September 21, 2011), A18.

McPherson, Michael. Schapiro, Morton Owen, and Winston, Gordon C. *Paying the Piper: Productivity, Incentives, and Financing in U.S. Higher Education.* Ann Arbor: University of Michigan Press, 1993.

Middaugh, Michael F. *Understanding Faculty Productivity: Standards and Benchmarks for Colleges and Universities.* San Francisco: Jossey-Bass, 2001.

Miller, Claire Cain, "In Silicon Valley, the Night Is Still Young: Despite Investor Fears, Start-Up Money Flows," *New York Times* (August 21, 2011), BU 1, 4.

O'Keefe, Michael. "Where Does the Money Really Go?: Case Studies of Six Institutions." *Change* (November/ December 1987), 12–34.

O'Donnell, Richard F. *Higher Education's Faculty Productivity Gap: The Cost to Students, Parents and Taxpayers* (Austin: Report for University of Texas System, 2011).

O'Donnell, Rick. "Why Productivity Data Matter." *Inside Higher Ed* (July 20, 2011) http://www.insidehighered.com/views/ 2011/07/20/o_donnell_on_faculty_productivity_data.

Paulsen, Michael B., and Smart, John C., eds. *The Finance of Higher Education: Theory, Research, Policy & Practice.* New York: Agathon Press, 2001.

Rosenzweig, Robert M. *The Research Universities and Their Patrons.* Berkeley, Los Angeles, and London: University of California Press, 1982.

Rosenzweig, Robert M. *The Political University: Policy, Politics, and Presidential Leadership in the American University.* Baltimore and London: Johns Hopkins University Press, 1998.

Rosovsky, Henry. *The University: An Owner's Manual.* New York and London: W. W. Norton, 1990.

Ruch, Richard. *Higher Ed, Inc.: The Rise of the For-Profit University.* Baltimore: Johns Hopkins University Press, 2001.

Sanoff, Alvin P. "Serving Students Well: Independent Colleges Today." In *Meeting the Challenge: America's Independent Colleges and Universities since 1956.* Washington, DC: Council of Independent Colleges, 2006, 37–62.

Schneider, Mark, and de Alva, Jorge Klor. *Cheap for Whom? How Much Higher Education Costs Taxpayers.* Washington, DC: American Enterprise Institute, 2011.

Shepard, Robert S. "How Can a University That Raises a Billion Have a Tight Budget?" *Chronicle of Higher Education* (January 12, 1994), A48.

Singer, Natasha. "When S'Mores Aren't Enough: The New Economics of Summer Camp." *New York Times* (July 9, 2011), A1.

St. John, Edward, and Parsons, Michael D., eds. *Public Funding of Higher Education: Changing Contexts and New Rationales,* Baltimore and London: Johns Hopkins University Press, 2004.

Sperber, Murray. *College Sports, Inc.: The Athletic Department vs. The University.* New York: Henry Holt, 1990.

Suggs, Welch. "How Gears Turn at a Sports Factory: Running Ohio State University's $79 Million Program Is a Major Endeavor, with Huge Payoffs and Costs." *Chronicle of Higher Education* (November 29, 2002), A1, A32–A37.

Trow, Martin. "Reflections on the Transition from Elite to Mass to Universal Higher Education." *Daedalus* 99 (Winter 1970), 1–42.

Tuchman, Gaye. *Wannabe U: Inside the Corporate University.* Chicago and London: University of Chicago Press, 2009.

Veblen, Thorstein. *Theory of the Leisure Class: An Economic Study in the Evolution of Institutions.* New York: Macmillan, 1899.

Vedder, Richard. *Going Broke by Degree: Why College Costs Too Much.* Washington, DC: American Enterprise Institute, 2004.

Vladek, Bruce. "Buildings and Budgets: The Over-Investment Crisis." *Change* (December 1978–January 1979), 39.

Wallace, Thomas. "The Age of the Dinosaur Persists." *Change* 25 (July–August 1992), 56–63.

Wilson, James Q. *Bureaucracy: What Government Agencies Do and Why They Do It.* New York: Basic Books, 1989.

Introduction to the Forum on Policy Perspectives

The rising costs of higher education has been an attractive, often volatile, topic among policy analysts and advocates. This chapter presents an anthology of 10 original essays written by several prominent influential participants in this discussion whose leadership and research involve policy planning at the institutional, state, national, and international levels. They provide a forum of timely information and lively discussion that suggests the complexities and varieties of concerns associated with the topic of college costs. The forum opens with Jane V. Wellman's broad contextual commentary on trends within the United States, based on the highly regarded Delta Cost Project. The forum concludes with a worldwide perspective on the costs of higher education, provided by D. Bruce Johnstone's analysis that draws from the International Comparative Higher Education Finance and Accessibility Project. Between these endpoints, readers will find a succession of informed diverse viewpoints and emphases on the topic of higher education costs.

The College Cost Problem: The View from the Delta Cost Project

Jane V. Wellman, Founding Director, Delta Project on Post-secondary Education Costs

---

(Baona/iStockphoto.com)

Defining the College "Cost Problem"

One of the challenges in getting a handle on the college "cost problem" lies in the fractured conversation about college costs, and the inconsistent and sometimes even oppositional views about the nature of the college cost problem as that is viewed by the general public, policy makers, and within higher education. Opinion research by John Immewahr for Public Advocates documents this "fractured conversation," as briefly summarized below and as presented in Table 3.1.

A second problem relates to the diversity of types of institutions in the United States, and the very different way that the "cost problem" manifests itself between different types of institutions. Some institutions are spending a lot more money than they did twenty years ago, and are charging more in tuition to pay for it. Many institutions are spending more money because of the changing types of students they are serving, and the rising demand for student services and for student aid. For many

Table 3.1   Outside/Inside: Perceptions of college costs by different stake-holder groups

Group	Definition of the problem	Solution
Public	Caught between the growing importance of college and declining access and rising costs	Protect college access! Stop raising tuitions!
State finance officers and legislators	Need more college graduates	Increase productivity through retention and increases in graduates
College faculty	Deteriorating quality of students and declining standards	Raise standards, improve K-12, and stop talking about productivity!
Public college presidents	Caught in the "iron triangle" between costs/quality/access	Reinvest public resources in higher education
Private college presidents	Caught in a spending "arms race"	Find ways to reduce competition, beginning with reductions in tuition discounting

Source: John Immewahr, 2009.

institutions, the "cost problem" is caused by shifting subsidies, as actual spending is going down despite increases in tuitions. The fact that there is no consistent framing of the college cost issue is a frustration to policy makers and analysts alike, as the complexity of the topic frustrates the search for solutions to it.

To help frame the discussion about college costs, this paper very briefly summarizes some of the major conclusions from research by the Delta Cost Project into basic patterns of finance in higher education: where the money comes from, where the money goes, the reasons for continued high rates of tuition increases, and what the data say about where attention should go to reduce pressure on tuition increases. Although the paper stops short of recommendations, the hope is that greater clarity about the nature of the problem will help pave the path to eventual solutions for it.

Because of the focus on spending, as well as revenues, there is a time lag in the Delta data, as spending data take longer to post than revenues. The patterns described herein rely on data through the 2009 academic year—the first year of the "Great Recession." It is clear that the revenue situation has continued to deteriorate since then, particularly in the public sector, but the broad patterns behind these numbers—the dynamics between revenues and spending, and the role of the market in cost structures—are pretty consistent, reasonable indicators of the main cost dynamics facing institutions and students in 2012. The primary themes from this research show five patterns: 1) growing economic stratification; 2) a growing price/cost gap; 3) slight declines in the instructional share of spending; 4) large increases in spending for employee compensation; and 5) modest but palpable increases in instructional productivity overall, through higher rates of degree production against enrollments, and declines in SCH per completion.

Growing Economic Stratification between Institutions

The "cost problem" is very different as it affects different types of institutions, with dramatically different patterns in revenues and spending between public and non-profit private institutions, as well as between research universities, liberal arts colleges, and community colleges. Looking at spending patterns across the major types of institutions over the last ten years, one of the first pictures that emerges is of growing economic stratification between institutions—with revenues and spending continuing to go up in a relatively small number of institutions—against spending cutbacks and very constrained resources among the public and non-profit access institutions serving the majority of students in our country. For this and other measures of spending, the Delta Project uses a metric called "education and related" spending per student. The measure is an aggregate of average operating spending per student. It combines spending for instruction, student services, and the educational share of overhead (academic and institutional support and the physical plant). Sponsored research, auxiliary enterprises (hospitals and clinics and dormitories) are excluded, as is capital outlay. See "Trends in College Spending, 1999–2009," for more details, available at http://www.deltacost project.org.

The frequent media focus on the wealthiest and most selective institutions tends to skew public perceptions about higher education finance. It is true that the US has some of the very richest institutions in the world—but the large majority of students are being served in institutions with no more money per student than we have in our K-12 schools. Spending patterns for the core educational functions vary dramatically across the major sectors of postsecondary education—ranging in 2009 from around $35,000 annually per student among private research universities, who collectively enroll around 1 million students, and compared to less than a third of that among public community colleges, where nearly 7 million students were enrolled.

One of the more dramatic changes that occurred during the decade between 1999 and 2009 was the growth in economic stratification within higher education, leading to a real and growing gap in resources between public and non-profit private institutions (See Table 3.2). During that decade, private research

Table 3.2   Sector differences in average spending per student, against nationwide enrollments within that sector, AY 2009

Sector	Average education and related spending per student	Total # HC students enrolled, nationwide
Private research universities	$35,596	1,135,649
Private bachelor's institutions	$21,392	834,891
Private master's institutions	$16,810	1,313,669
Public research universities	$15,919	4,124,090
Public master's institutions	$12,363	2,553,889
Public community colleges	$10,242	6,654,006

institutions added on average an additional $7,000 in CPI adjusted new spending for education and related expenses per student—an increase of nearly 20% in just a decade. In contrast, public community college spending per student remained virtually flat.

A Growing Price/Cost Gap

The second theme is that tuitions are continuing to rise—but much faster than spending or costs in the majority of institutions. For the majority of institutions, increases in tuition do not translate into comparable increases in spending. The reason is because of cost-shifting—tuitions are going up in large part to replace revenues from state/local appropriations or because of declines in gifts or endowment earnings.

Cost shifting is most dramatic in the public sector, where revenues per student from state and local appropriations have been declining, but it is also evident among the majority of private institutions that are very tuition dependent, and don't have large endowments and rely on private gifts. In times of recession, such as 2009, institutions are both raising tuitions and cutting spending. The price/cost gap—the amount being charged to students versus what institutions are spending on them—has been a problem for years, and something that is probably unsustainable going forward. In 2009, among public institutions, tuition increases attempted to compensate for lost revenues from state and local

Table 3.3   2008–2009: One-year change in revenues per student from tuition/
state appropriations compared to changes in spending

Sector	One-year change in net tuition revenue per student	One-year change in state and local appropriations per student	One-year change in education and related spending per student
Public research	+$369	–$751	+$92
Public masters'	+$225	–$590	+$26
Public community colleges	+$113	–$488	–$254
Private research	+$293	NA	+$907
Private masters'	+$536	NA	+$352
Private bachelors'	+$381	NA	+$298

budget reductions, but new revenues from tuition increases covered less than half of the reduction in state and local appropriations. (See Table 3.3.)

Between 2008 and 2009, looking at public research institutions, for example, average net tuition revenue increased by $369 per student between 2008 and 2009, but the loss in state and local appropriations per student was $751, slightly more than twice the amount generated in increased tuition revenues. (Net tuition revenue means that this measure looks only at tuition revenue after deducting for tuition discounts, which are also going up.) Despite that, institutions were able to maintain education and related spending at roughly the same level as in prior years. To keep spending flat in the face of revenue losses, public institutions were clearly taking measures to reduce spending, as well as pulling from reserves or other revenue sources. The spending reductions will undoubtedly be larger in 2010 and 2011 when reserves are depleted and the federal stimulus funding from the "ARRA"—American Recovery and Reinvestment Act of 2009—money runs out.

Among public community colleges, revenues from state and local appropriations declined an average of $488 per student between 2008 and 2009, whereas tuition increases generated

Table 3.4 Ten-year change in revenues per student from tuition/state appropriations compared to changes in spending

Sector	Net tuition revenue per student	State and local approps revenue per student	Education and related spending per student
Public research	+$2,650	–$1,502	+$1,566
Public masters'	+$1,848	–$955	+$1,058
Public community colleges	+$811	–$346	+$38
Private research	+$3,538	NA	+$7,575
Private masters'	+$2,969	NA	+$1,962

new net tuition revenues of only $113 per student. Spending declined overall by –$254/student—an absolute decline of around 2% overall.

The tuition/spending story is somewhat different in the private sector, particularly within the private research sector where some of the institutions with the biggest endowments are lodged. Education and related spending in private research universities increased considerably more than increases in tuition revenue ($907 in spending per student compared to $293 in tuition revenue per student), suggesting that they still had plenty of new revenue in endowments despite suffering heavy paper losses in that year. This was not the case, however, for students in private master's or bachelor's institutions, where tuition revenues were larger than spending increases.

If one examines these figures over a ten-year period, the evidence of the price/spending disconnect is even starker, with tuition increases more than replacing state/local revenues, allowing for fairly modest spending increases in the research and masters institutions ($100 and $150/student/year, or around 1% per year despite losses in state/local appropriations). Among private institutions, the research sector is again the one area where prices are going up more slowly than spending. In this sector, spending increases over the decade were around $700 per student per year, or around 2%. (See table 3.4.)

A Slight Decline in the Instructional Share of Spending

Looking just at average spending for education and related expenses, the data show modest but important differences in spending patterns across the decade. The data reported below show average spending per student within the E&R category by sector, and how these spending levels have changed over the decade. These data distinguish between spending for the direct cost of instruction—primarily faculty salaries—and expenses going either for student services or for shared overhead between institutional and academic support and maintenance.

As the data show, the instructional share of E&R spending is highest among the research institutions, largely because of higher faculty salaries in those institutions. The data further show that there has been a slight reduction in the share of spending going to pay for the direct cost of instruction among all types of institutions over the 1999–2009 period, with those reductions being most evident among public community colleges, which showed an average decline in instructional spending of around 2% per FTE [Full Time Equivalent] enrollments over the ten year period. The changes are not dramatic, nonetheless, they do belie the commonly held view that the primary inflationary factor on college costs is the rising cost of faculty.

Employee Benefits Increasing—Particularly in Public Institutions

The single biggest factor contributing to spending increases in higher education are employee benefits—a particular problem among public institutions (See Table 3.5). Spending for employee salaries has been growing less than 1% a year on average—in part because institutions have been cutting costs by turning to part-time faculty. But even as salary costs are being managed, benefit costs have been growing in the public sector by an average of 5% per year. This effectively means that pretty much all of the new money coming in from tuition increases were going out the door to pay for the growing cost of health care.

Table 3.5   Changes in salary/benefit cost per employee: 2002–2009

Public institutions	Salary outlay per employee	Benefit cost per full-time employee
Research	0.9%	5.2%
Master's	−0.6%	4.6%
Community colleges	0.7%	5.2%
Private institutions		
Research	−0.3%	1.6%
Master's	−0.8%	2.4%
Bachelor's	−0.5%	1.3%

Modest but Promising Increases in Productivity

The absence of good measures of quality, and the general inability to tease apart value-added measures separating inputs from outputs, make measures of productivity in higher education very problematic. Recognizing that, the Delta Project endeavors to get some notion of gross measures of outcomes, by looking at the relationship between enrollments and degrees or credentials produced over time, and in student credit hours per degree produced. Looking at these measures, the ten-year trends between 1999 and 2009 show some promising signs of increases in instructional productivity in public institutions—meaning a slight uptick in the production of degrees relative to student enrollments (See Table 3.6). Aggregate degree productivity is measured by comparing overall production of degrees against enrollments. It is not a measure of student cohort graduation rates, but a gross measure showing how enrollments are converted into degrees or certificates. All types of institutions saw increases in degree and certificate productivity between 1999 and 2009, with the greatest gains in public and private masters' institutions. Community colleges also saw gains in completions, in this case, primarily in a great increase in certificates rather than in more degrees.

Public institutions also increased instructional productivity through reductions in credit hours per completion. Data on credit hour production are newly available beginning in 2002, so this measure captures activity for only the 2002–2009

Table 3.6   Degrees and certificate awards per 100 FTE students enrolled

		Total degrees per 100 FTE students	Total certificates and awards per 100 FTE students
Public research	1999	23.6	0.3
	2009	24.4	0.5
Public masters'	1999	22.3	0.3
	2009	23.3	0.6
Community colleges	1999	14.7	8.0
	2009	15.0	10.6
Private research	1999	30.5	0.4
	2009	31.5	0.9
Private masters'	1999	29.7	0.8
	2009	31.7	1.3
Private bachelors'	1999	22.1	0.6
	2009	22.9	0.4

period. During this period, undergraduate credit hours per degree/credential went down between eight and ten credit hours—translating into a "savings" of nearly a half a semester's worth of credits (See Table 3.7). Instructional productivity also increased at the graduate level for both public and private institutions. While the trends suggest credits are being used more efficiently, this metric does not necessarily mean that the average number of credits per graduate is also declining. From these data, we do not know if the gains are occurring because of declines in attrition, or reductions in "excess" credits beyond those required for the degree. Either way, it portends good news for policy makers interested in increasing productivity in higher education.

Conclusions

The long term fiscal trends facing American postsecondary education are not good: demand for higher education is increasing, even as public subsidies for it are declining. State governments are increasingly unable to maintain support for higher education at levels comparable to those provided in prior generations.

Table 3.7   Undergraduate and graduate credit hours/completion, 2002–2009

	Undergraduate			Graduate		
	2002	2009	2002–2009 Change	2002	2009	2002–2009 Change
Public research	164	153	−10	77	70	−8
Public masters'	169	160	−9	66	59	−7
Public community colleges	173	164	−9	—	—	—
Private research	141	140	−1	71	65	−6
Private masters'	134	132	−2	62	58	−3
Private bachelors'	148	152	4	—	—	—

Note: Graduate data excludes first professional; data were winsorized to adjust for outliers.
Source: Delta Cost Project IPEDS Database, 1987–2009; 11-year matched set.

Prospects for shifting funding to the federal government, either through student aid or in direct support to institutions, are similarly bad. Public rebellion over continued cost shifting and rising college tuitions is high, and institutional leaders and policy makers alike are feeling the heat. Attention to cost cutting—and to productivity—will continue to grow. As that occurs, it will be important for policy makers and institutional leaders to be clear about the problem they are trying to solve—whether on the revenue side, the spending side, or in the performance of the institutions. Greater consistency in language, and better information about where the money comes from, where it goes and what it buys, will be essential to the success of those efforts.

References

Delta Cost Project (2009). Trends in College Spending, 2009: Where does the money come from? Where does it go? What does it buy? Washington, DC: Delta Cost Project, available at http://www.deltacostproject.org.

John Immewahr. "The Fractured Conversation," Presentation to the Texas Higher Education Coordinating Board, January 2010, available from http://www.thecb.state.tx.us.

Perspective on the Rising Costs of Higher Education

Ronald G. Ehrenberg, Cornell University

Introduction

This essay focuses on the rising costs of undergraduate education at America's public and private nonprofit educational institutions. At the onset, it is important to distinguish between three interrelated concepts—posted levels of tuition and fees, academic institutions' expenditures per student, and the net (after institutional, governmental and other forms of grant aid and tax credits for tuition) tuition levels that students and their parents pay—which are often confused by the public.

The growth of posted undergraduate tuition and fees is what is reported in the popular press and what draws the most public attention. So, for example, during the last three decades tuition increases at private four-year colleges, public four-year colleges, and averaged 3.5%, 5.1%, and 3.5% a year more than the rate of inflation (as measured by the Consumer Price Index), respectively (Baum and Ma, 2011).

As was originally pointed out by Gordon Winston (1999), the expenditures per undergraduate student that institutions make each year is typically substantially higher than the tuition and fee levels students pay because of subsidies that students receive in the form of annual giving received by institutions from alumni, other individuals, foundations and corporations, from earnings from the institutions' endowments, from (primarily in public institutions) state appropriations, and from the implicit value of the services provided to students from buildings on campus that were paid for by private gifts or government appropriations in earlier years. Ignoring the implicit value of the services, over the last three decades, tuition increases in private higher education have been associated with increases in real expenditures per student. In contrast, as I detail below, tuition increases in public higher education have been largely efforts to compensate for reductions in states support (Desrochers, Lenihan, and Wellman 2010).

Finally, the net tuition levels (after grant aid and tax credits) that, on average, undergraduate students pay have gone up in recent years by less than the growth in posted tuition and fee levels, because of the growth in institutional and governmental grant aid and tax credits. For example, the College Board reports that during the 1990–91 to 2011–12 period, posted tuition rates at private nonprofit and public four year institutions grew at average annual rates of 5.3 and 7.0% respectively, but during the same period the net tuition levels paid by students and families grew at lower rates of 3.4 and 4.1 percent, respectively. Average tuition increases at public 2-year colleges were 5.6 percent a year during the period, but net tuition actually declined at these colleges during the period due primarily to the growth in the federal Pell Grant program, according to unpublished data from the College Board provided to me by Sandy Baum.

Why Tuition Kept Rising

The forces that have caused private academic institutions' undergraduate tuition levels to continually increase at rates that exceed the increase in the CPI have been extensively discussed by others and me elsewhere and I only briefly summarize them here (Ehrenberg, 2002, 2006, 2007, 2010; Archibald and Feldman, 2011). These include:

1. The aspirations of academic institutions, similar to other non-profit institutions, to be the very best that they can in every dimension of their activities, which calls for ever- increasing resources. Like the Sesame Street character Cookie Monster, who is on a continual quest for cookies which he (or she) then devours, academic institutions continually are searching for more resources to attract the best students, to hire and retain the best faculty, to have the best academic and nonacademic facilities, and to have the best support services. Put simply, the quest for excellence leads to continual efforts to enhance revenues from all sources, including undergraduate tuition.

The perceptions by students and parents that in a world of increasing inequality in earnings, even among college graduates, that where students go to college is almost as important as whether they go to college, and their perceptions that high priced selective private institutions confer unique educational and economic advantages on their students, which leads to ever increasing numbers of applicants applying to these institutions and only limited market forces to limit their tuition increases. Most studies, including Brewer, Eide, and Ehrenberg (1999) and Eide, Brewer, and Ehrenberg (1998) support the belief that selective private academic institutions confer unique advantages on their students; the only studies that disagree are Dale and Krueger (2002, 2011).

2. As the selective privates increase their tuition, this provides a "cover" for the less selective private institutions to raise their tuition levels.

3. The belief, at least at private liberal arts colleges, that the essence of a liberal arts education is small class sizes and substantial interaction between faculty and undergraduate students; this makes it difficult to achieve productivity gains and cost reduction.

4. Published rankings, such as those of *U.S. News & World Reports*, which are based partially on institutionally expenditures per students. This leads rate of spending, as any institution that unilaterally held its expenditures down, or whose expenditures grew at slower rates than its competitors, would fall in the rankings. Research by Monks and Ehrenberg (1999) confirm the importance of the USNWR rankings to institutions' admissions outcomes.

5. The growing use of technology, which often comes at high costs and leads to improvements in the quality of the higher education experience (but not necessarily the amount that students learn). Examples are online electronic reserves, class web pages, email, and tiered classrooms with internet connections. Unlike the CPI, where adjustments are made

for changes in product quality (e.g., automobiles) in the computation of the rate of inflation, no adjustments for changes in product quality are made when tuition increases are reported.

Of course all of these factors hold for public higher education as well, but the public institutions also face the added pressure that cutbacks in state support have put on tuition. In public higher education, tuition increases have been largely efforts to offset a long-run decline in per full-time equivalent (FTE) student state appropriations. State appropriations per FTE averaged $6,454 in fiscal year 2010; at its peak, in fiscal year 1987 the comparable number (in constant dollars) was $7,993; a decline of 19 percent (State Higher Education Executive Officers, 2011, figure 3). Even if one leaves out the effects of the "Great Recession," real state appropriations per FTE students were still lower in fiscal year 2008 than they were 20 years earlier. The financial problems of state governments make it likely that continual cutbacks in state support for public higher education institutions are likely in the future and this will put added pressure on public sector tuition increases.

Will Tuition Keep Rising?

Will private and public tuition increases continue at rates far exceeding the rate of inflation in the future? We may be rapidly approaching a turning point in private higher education. The *tuition discount rate*—the share of each tuition dollar that institutions return to their undergraduate students in the form of need-based or merit grant aid—has dramatically increased at private 4-year institutions. In the fall of 1990, the average tuition discount rate for first-time full-time first year students was 26.7 percent; by the fall of 2008 this tuition discount rate reached 42 percent (National Association of College and University Business Officers, 2009, 2010). Much of the increases in tuition revenues at private colleges and universities has been plowed back into undergraduate aid; at all but a handful of the very wealthiest privates, the vast majority of undergraduate financial aid dollars come largely from tuition revenue.

The wealthiest privates, which have no problem achieving desired enrollment levels, dramatically increased the generosity of their financial aid policies during the period 2008 to 2012 for a number of reasons. First, concerned that they remain accessible to students from all socioeconomic backgrounds, they responded to evidence that relatively small fractions of their students were coming from lower- and lower-middle income families, as measured by the share of their students that were Pell Grant recipients (Supiano and Fuller, 2011). Second, the rapid growth rates of their endowments during much of the period, when coupled with their relatively low endowment spending rates, led to pressure from the U.S. Senate Finance Committee for them to increase endowment spending on undergraduate financial aid; they voluntarily did so to avoid possible legislation that would specify minimum endowment spending rates for them. Finally, the dramatic increase in the financial need of their applicants because of the decline in family income levels and housing and financial asset levels after the financial collapse in 2008 put added pressure on their financial aid budgets.

Other private institutions, which use both need-based and merit aid to craft their classes and achieve desired enrollment levels, found that market forces do matter. Competition from lower price public institutions, along with stagnating real family income levels during much of the period, and then the decline in family incomes and assets after the financial collapse, dramatically increased their need to increase grant aid and offer larger tuition discounts both to fill all their seats and to achieve desired class composition.

"Net price calculators," which each academic institution is now required to have on its web page, offer the promise of providing more transparency about the true costs of college to potential students and their families. They also offer the possibility that some pressure will be taken off of private academic institutions to limit tuition increases, if the public becomes aware of how large typical tuition discounts are at private institutions. However, these "calculators" typically can provide accurate information only in the small number of cases in which institutions have "mechanical" needs-based or merit-based financial aid policies, so public pressure to reduce private higher education tuition increases probably will continue. The privates will have to increasingly make the arguments to potential students and their families about the advantages they may provide students relative to their public sector counterparts. A few privates have announced their intent to cap tuition increases at lower rates than they have in the past, or have announced plans to cut their posted tuition levels and to shift their focus from merit to need-based aid policies. Whether either strategy will benefit an institution in the short or long run is an open question.

Public higher education institutions, where most American college students are educated, face enormous pressures to increase enrollments, and persistence and graduation rates, at the same time that their state support per student is being continually reduced. They also face pressures to use faculty resources more efficiently and to serve as engines to enhance employment and tax revenues in their states. Concern that tuition increases will limit access and persistence may limit their ability to increase tuition for resident undergraduate institutions in some states. Other states have allowed their public institutions to charge differential tuition levels for majors that offer high income earning possibilities and/or whose curriculum is more expensive to offer (Ehrenberg, 2012, table 5). Many flagship public institutions have sought to respond to economic pressures by raising their undergraduate tuition for nonresident students and increasing the share of students that they enroll from out of state; state policy makers are less concerned about keeping out of state tuition levels low, although they are sometimes resistant to having a greater share of the seats at their flagship institutions filled by out of state students.

Finally, lurking beneath the surface is the elephant in the room: why historically didn't academic institutions take steps to improve the efficiency of their academic and nonacademic operations and reduce costs rather than increasing tuition. Some attribute this to shared governance, others (including Ginsberg, 2011) to a growing bureaucracy and the decline in faculty governance. I think a simpler explanation is that historically they did not face the pressures to do so. However, things have changed. The public institutions have faced financial pressures for years and have been forced to reduce their costs. And, as I have detailed elsewhere, in effort to reduce instructional costs the nature of the faculty has changed and expensive full-time tenured and tenure track faculty are now a declining species (Ehrenberg, 2011, 2012).

After experiencing the collapse of financial markets and the great recession, a number of major private and public universities hired external consultants to advise them on how to reduce their administrative costs and are taking serious steps to do so. Cornell, for example, is well on its way to reducing the administrative costs on its Ithaca campus by $75 to $85 million a year; this represents 5 to 6 percent of its base annual operating budget (excluding external research funding) (http://dpb.cornell.edu).

The 64–academic institution SUNY system, where I am currently a trustee, is taking steps to reduce administrative costs by centralizing activities where possible (purchasing, library acquisitions, information systems) to take advantage of economies of scale and by pushing campuses to achieve efficiencies by sharing back office functions such as registrar, human resources, and finance across campuses. All of these efforts are being made to devote increasingly scarce state resources to the core educational and student service missions. Moreover, campuses do not have to be public or even part of the same system, to achieve economies of scale in purchasing or to share back office functions. Two notable examples are the Wisconsin Association of Independent Colleges and University Collaboration Project (www.waicu.org/collaboration) and the Coalition for College Cost Savings (www.thecoalition.us).

Finally, the core academic mission of colleges and universities is an area that is ripe for changes to improve student learning and to reduce the costs of delivering education. Both synchronous and asynchronous technology can be used to share academic resources across institution. The growing for-profit higher education sector, which now enrolls almost 10 percent of all students, has been among the leaders in restructuring methods of delivering education through the use of technology to improve learning and reduce costs (Ehrenberg, 2011, 2012). Notable efforts from the nonprofit sector to restructure methods of delivering education include the work of the National Center for Academic Transformation (http://www.thenatcat.org) and the Open Learning Initiative at Carnegie Mellon University (http://oli.web.cmu.edu/open learning/initiatives). These latter two efforts have taught us that it is possible to use information technology to simultaneously improve learning outcomes and reduce costs in a variety of academic institutions and a variety of different types of introductory and remedial classes (Ehrenberg, 2011, 2012). The speed with which these approaches are more widely adopted may have a significant effect on the future rate of tuition increases at America's public and private nonprofit higher education institutions.

References

Archibald, Robert B., and David H. Feldman. 2011. *Why Does College Cost So Much?* New York: Oxford University Press.

Baum, Sandy, and Jennifer Ma. 2010. *Trends in College Pricing 2010*. New York: The College Board.

Brewer Dominic J., Eric E. Edie, and Ronald G. Ehrenberg. 1999. "Does It Pay to Attend an Elite Private College? Cross-Cohort Evidence of the Effects of College Type on Earnings." *Journal of Human Resources* 34(1): 104–123.

Dale, Stacy, and Alan B. Krueger. 2002. "Estimating the Payoff to Attending a More Selective College: An Application of

Selection on Observables and Unobservables." *Quarterly Journal of Economics* 117(4): 1491–1527.

Dale, Stacy, and Alan B. Krueger. 2011. "Estimating the Returns to College Selectivity over the Career Using Administrative Earnings Data." *National Bureau of Economic Research Working Paper* No. 17159. Cambridge MA: National Bureau of Economic Research.

Desrochers, Donna M. et al. 2010. *Trends in College Spending: 1998–2008.* Washington, DC: Delta Cost Project (http:// www.deltacostproject.org) (accessed on March 25, 2011).

Ehrenberg, Ronald G. 2002. *Tuition Rising: Why College Costs So Much.* Cambridge MA: Harvard University Press.

Ehrenberg, Ronald G. 2006. "The Perfect Storm and the Privatization of Public Higher Education." *Change* 38(1): 46–53.

Ehrenberg, Ronald G. Ed. 2007. *What's Happening to Public Higher Education? The Shifting Financial Burden.* Baltimore: Johns Hopkins University Press.

Ehrenberg, Ronald G. 2010. "The Economics of Tuition and Fees in American Higher Education." In Barry McGraw, Penelope Peterson, and Eva Baker, eds., *The International Encyclopedia of Education* (3rd ed., Vol. 2, 229–234). Oxford UK: Elsevier.

Ehrenberg, Ronald G. 2011. "Rethinking the Professoriate." In Ben Wildavsky, Andrew Kelly, and Kevin Carey, eds., *Reinventing Higher Education: The Promise of Innovation* (101–128). Cambridge, MA: Harvard Education Press.

Ehrenberg, Ronald G. 2012. "American Higher Education in Transition." *Journal of Economic Perspectives* 26(1): 1–26.

Eide, Eric, Dominic J. Brewer, and Ronald G. Ehrenberg. 2008. "Does It Pay to Attend an Elite Private College? Evidence on the Effects of Undergraduate College Quality on Graduate School Attendance." *Economics of Education Review* 17(October): 371–376.

Ginsberg, Benjamin. 2011. *The Fall of the Faculty: The Rise of the All-Administrative University and Why It Matters*. New York: Oxford University Press.

Monks, James, and Ronald G. Ehrenberg. 1999. "U.S. News & World Report's College Rankings: Why Do They Matter?" *Change* 31(6): 42–51.

National Association of College and University Business Officers. 2010. *2009 NACUBO Tuition Discounting Study of Independent Institutions*. Washington, DC: National Association of College and University Business Officers.

National Association of College and University Business Officers. 2009. "Newly Released NACUBO Tuition Discounting Study Survey Report Shows Rates Remain Stable." (http://www.nacubo.org) (accessed on March 25, 2011).

State Higher Education Executive Officers. 2011. *State Higher Education Finance: FY 2010*. Boulder: Author.

Supiano, Beckie, and Andrea Fuller. 2011. "Elite Colleges Fail to Gain More Students on Pell Grants." *Chronicle of Higher Education* 57(March 27) http://chronicle.com/article/Pell-Grant-Recipients-Are/126892/.

Winston, Gordon C. 1999. "Subsidies, Hierarchy and Peers: The Awkward Economics of Higher Education." *Journal of Economic Perspectives* 13(1): 12–36.

College Cost: Over Hyped and Misunderstood

Robert B. Archibald and David H. Feldman, Department of Economics

The College of William & Mary

After writing a book titled *Why Does College Cost So Much?*, we have gotten quite an earful from people who want to talk about our topic. Among the many reactions we have received, two stand out as common misconceptions. First, people systematically overestimate how much someone actually has to pay for a year of college education. Colleges and universities do themselves no favors here. Well-intentioned policies of colleges and universities have led to practices that obfuscate information flows and contribute to the sense that college is outrageously expensive. This is one reason that talk of crisis is over hyped. Second, people misdiagnose the reasons that college tuition is rising. Many people argue that wasteful practices are the driver of needless cost increases that then translate into tuition hikes. Colleges are not the most efficient organizations one can find, but growing inefficiencies are not the major cause of rising college tuition.

Poor Pricing Information

On August 17, 2010, *US News and World Report* ran a story titled, "Is a $50,000 College Tuition Worth It?" In the fall of 2011 a large number of magazines and newspapers reported on the growing number of colleges and universities with a total cost of attendance exceeding $50,000. Most people can do the math. If it takes $50,000 for one year of college, it will take more than $200,000 for four years (since tuition and fees will continue rising). This is indeed frightening. Any family that reads these numbers can easily conclude that they can never afford to send their kids to college.

The facts are quite different. The $50,000 price tag for a year of college is light years from what most students pay. Still, these stories about colleges with $50,000 price tags have a real impact on the way many people think about what a year in college actually will cost. Surveys consistently show that people dramatically overestimate the cost to them of attending college. For example, a report written by Stanley O. Ikenberry and Terry W. Hartle, *Too Little Knowledge Is a Dangerous Thing: What the Public Thinks and Knows about Paying for College*, (American Council on Education, 1998) shows that people overestimate tuition and fees at public institutions by a factor of 3.

Psychologists explain that people answer questions such as, "what is the tuition bill for a year at college?" by a process of anchoring and adjustment (e.g., Tversky and Kahneman, *Science*, 1974, 1124–1130). They have a number in mind, for example, the $50,000 that gets so much press. This is the anchor. They know that this number is too high, so they adjust. In many experiments people under adjust and make a guess about college tuition substantially higher than reality.

While the stories about $50,000 price tags may have an impact on the way randomly selected people answer a survey question, one would like to think that these stories do not determine the behavior of students and families as they consider applying to schools. Surely these people can replace the $50,000 anchor with better information. There is good information out there that families can use. The College Board's *Trends in College Pricing 2011* (CEEB, Figure 2, page 11) shows that the median student attending a public or private four-year institution is charged a tuition of $9,936, and only 2.5% of students attend a school with tuition and fees as high as $42,000. With a little search, students and their families should be able to find lots of anchors well below over-hyped numbers like $50,000.

Finding the list price that colleges charge is quite easy, but determining exactly how much an individual student will have to pay to attend any particular college is much more difficult. At many institutions, particularly those with high list price tuitions, the actual price most students are charged is well below the posted tuition. Again the College Board has good information. *Trends in Student Aid 2011* (Table 17B, page 27) shows that institutions accepting fewer than 35% of their applicants, and this constitutes the most desirable institutions, offer on average $13,400 in grant aid to their students. Some students get more than the average and others get less, and many students receive aid from sources other than the institution they attend. This means that the actual cost a student has to finance depends on his or her particular circumstances.

Since financial aid awards are individualized, people cannot easily determine how much a particular institution is going to cost them as they begin to evaluate their choices. The actual price they will face is one of the last pieces of information they receive in the admission process. Colleges now provide net price calculators to help students estimate what the net price of attendance actually will be. Unfortunately, these net price calculators are often very difficult to use. They can require almost as much information as a FAFSA. Also, they are not designed to estimate merit aid, which is very important to many students, especially in the middle and upper middle-income groups that receive little or no need-based assistance.

The lack of clear price information has consequences. Students who might find more selective schools affordable never begin the process of seriously exploring those alternatives. And some families, especially from the lowest income groups, may not think that a college education is even in the realm of the possible. If we are to achieve the goal of raising the percentage of the working-age population holding a college degree, we need to improve the information people have about their educational opportunities.

Misconceptions about the Factors Driving College Costs

Even if most people overestimate the true cost of attendance, a year in college can be quite expensive. And there is no doubt that the cost of attending a college or university has grown dramatically in recent years. The rate of increase of college tuition consistently exceeds the overall inflation rate. Many commentators conclude that there has to be something wrong with any industry whose "firms" consistently raise prices rises faster than the inflation rate.

Is it really unusual for an industry to experience price growth that consistently outpaces inflation? Table 2.4.4 in the National Income and Product Accounts gives price indexes for Personal Consumption Expenditures by Type of Product. There are 69 industries at the same level of aggregation as higher education. Over the period 1947–2010, the price index for higher education rose more rapidly than the overall price index in 52 of the 64 years. The higher education price index does indeed consistently rise more rapidly than inflation rate. But it turns out that higher education is not all that unusual. The price indexes for 9 of the 68 other products had counts above 52.

What are the other industries whose prices outpaced the overall price index even more consistently than higher education? They are things like dental services, life insurance, hospital services, and professional and other services. This latter category includes legal services and the services of accountants. These are all personal services provided by highly educated service providers. This finding is not a coincidence, and it should shape the public discussion of rapidly rising college costs. Common stories of rising college costs that focus on factors such as tenure, faculty sloth, administrative bloat, and country-club amenities cannot account for the similarity between all of these personal services. The similarity suggests that the same economic forces are driving costs in all of these industries. There is certainly some room for industry-specific factors, but the basic underlying story is the same for a group of industries that includes higher education.

Economists have known for a long time that the prices of services tend to rise more rapidly than the prices of goods because productivity improvement is very difficult in most services, especially personal services. Your barber probably uses the same basic technology barbers used fifty years ago. And a college professor does much the same thing Plato did at the Academy. Most manufactured goods and agricultural products are different. Technological progress has allowed us to produce these goods using fewer workers and less energy. Technological progress has held down the cost of production in these industries, but it has not had nearly the same effect on services.

The primary service provider in these industries are all highly educated, e.g., college professors, dentists, lawyers, and accountants. The wages of college graduates with advanced degrees have risen consistently more than the wages of college graduates since

1980. And the gap in wages with the less educated workers that predominate in manufacturing and agriculture has positively yawned wide. As a result, any industry whose workforce and wage bill reflects a predominance of educated labor has faced extra cost pressure since the early 1980s. Not coincidentally, this is the year that college costs, which had been flat to declining in the 1970s, began a sustained rise that continues to this day.

The final common thread that links these education-intensive personal services is the impact of new technology. These services have not been technologically stagnant. Quite to the contrary, they have experienced rapid change. But in these industries, new techniques and ways of using technology have raised costs more often than lowered them. In most industries firms will not embrace technologies that raise costs. Higher education and other personal services industries are different. They have to meet a standard of care. Physicians will face malpractice suits if they do not. Colleges won't be sued for malpractice, but the incentives are similar. If there is a new technology used by employers, colleges and universities must make their students aware of and competent with the new techniques. The parallel with malpractice is clear. Higher education institutions are early adopters of new technology because of the value to the faculty and students alike of being on the technological cutting edge. As a result, college costs tend to rise as new technologies are developed and work their way into the economy. This effect is most clear in STEM fields—i.e., science, technology, engineering, and mathematics—but it also affects the social sciences and humanities.

We think these three economic forces provide a convincing explanation of the main drivers of college costs. They are the same drivers that have put upward pressure on the prices of most other personal services provided by highly educated services providers. The technological forces that have reshaped the American economy over the last century have pushed up all service prices, and the prices of personal services that use highly educated labor most of all.

References

Ikenberry, Stanley O. and Hartle, Terry W. *Too Little Knowledge Is a Dangerous Thing: What the Public Thinks and Knows about Paying for College* (Washington, D.C.: American Council on Education, 1998).

The College Board, *Trends in Student Aid 2011* (New York: The College Board, 2011).

Tversky, Amos and Kahneman, Daniel. "Judgment Under Uncertainty, Heuristics and Biases," *Science* (1974) 1124–1130.

How Much Have College Prices Really Increased?

Terry W. Hartle, Senior Vice President, Government Relations and Public Affairs, American Council on Education

It's no secret that the posted price of a college education has increased faster than inflation over the last 30 years. Much faster. The most readily available information about the price of higher education is always the posted or list price published by individual institutions. And the changes in these prices in recent years are substantial enough to scare almost any family. Indeed, the rate of increase—particularly at public institutions—appears to have accelerated in the last decade. Table 3.8 shows the average inflation-adjusted percentage change in posted price at colleges and universities, along with changes in median family income for each of the last four decades.

Posted Price Has Increased Sharply in the Last Decade

The posted price of higher education has changed over the last decade compared to other items commonly purchased by families. According to the tuition and fee data reported by institutions to the U.S. Department of Education, the published price at public four-year colleges increased by 73 percent in real terms between 1999–2000 and 2010–11. At for-profit colleges,

Table 3.8   Posted Price of Higher Education

	Inflation-adjusted percentage change by decade			
	1970–1979	1980–1989	1990–1999	2000–2009
Public, 4-year	−17%	47%	39%	53%
Private, not-for-profit	−13%	54%	26%	20%
Public, 2-year	1%	28%	27%	38%
Median family income	5%	10%	10%	−5%

Source: *Digest of Education Statistics*, 2010; table 345.

the after-inflation change was 39 percent. For private, non-profit four-year institutions, the gain was 32 percent, while community colleges were at 26 percent. This brief analysis relies on percentage changes in posted price. Using percentage change can mask the actual dollar impact on students and families. For example, between 2000–2001 and 2009–2010 public, four-year tuition increased by 53 percent in real terms as opposed to the 20 percent gain at private, four-year institutions. However, the dollar impact of the change is actually greater at private colleges—$3,900 vs. $2,300.

The trend lines vary considerably across sectors. Prices at private, non-profit colleges increased at a relatively steady rate over the decade but for other parts of the postsecondary universe the trends are more complex. Real tuitions increased steadily at public, four-year colleges until 2008–09, when the economic downturn and state budget cuts led to significant tuition increases. Public community colleges show even more variation. In the early years of the last decade, steady state funding and modest tuition increases meant the real posted price at community colleges actually declined. Inflation-adjusted tuition began to rise in 2002–03 and grew slowly but steadily for four years. After declining slightly in the middle of the decade, prices jumped sharply in response to state and local budget problems.

It's difficult to determine precisely how tuition changed at private, for-profit colleges and universities because the way many of these institutions report tuition data varies. The available information, however, suggests the real price of a for-profit education increased steadily between 1999–2000 and 2005–06 when it dipped noticeably. The following year, however, it began to climb steadily. Not only is the inflation-adjusted posted price at postsecondary institutions increasing rapidly, it is increasing faster than many other goods and services that consumers buy. For example, during this time period, tuition at public four-year colleges increased faster than medical care, prescription drugs, a new car or housing. Indeed, only health insurance premiums increased faster. Public two-year colleges and private non-profit and for-profit institutions had a slightly better record, but they too increased far faster than the price of a new car or housing. Perhaps most problematic, posted prices increased far more rapidly than family income. Over the last decade real median family income actually declined by 5 percent (according to the U.S. Census Bureau). In short, for many families, college does appear to be increasingly out of reach.

It's a somewhat different pattern for the well-to-do. During this same time period, the income of families at the 90th percentile declined as well, albeit by just 2 percent. In short, while published tuition is likely to represent a larger share of family income for all families, the situation over the last decade is much worse for low- and middle-income families than the well-to-do. There are multiple reasons for the increase in posted price and there are offsetting considerations. As any higher education analyst knows, posted price is not the same thing as net price. Unfortunately, families are not higher education analysts and many find "net price" a confusing concept. Despite a new federal mandate that all institutions of higher education publish a "net price calculator" prominently on their websites, it can be difficult for a family to connect the concept of net price with what they must actually pay.

But the fact remains the dramatic increases in posted price have been considerably offset for many families by a sharp increase in need- and merit-based financial aid. Indeed, if anything, it appears the amount of student aid has increased faster than tuition over the last decade. According to the College Board's annual *Trends in Student Aid* report, between 1999–2000 and 2009–10, the total amount of student aid available to finance higher education went from $94 billion to $199 billion— an increase of 112 percent *after* inflation. Breaking this down further, federal grants and loans jumped 136 percent, state grants rose 66 percent, institutional aid grew 69 percent, and private and employee grants increased by 53 percent. (Preliminary College Board data for 2010–11 suggests that total aid now stands at $227 billion, which represents an inflation adjusted gain of 132 percent.)

Although posted college prices have continued to increase, the growth of student aid has resulted in a decrease in the net tuition of public two-year and private, not-for-profit four-year schools. Between 2006–07 and 2011–12, the actual tuition students paid after accounting for student aid increases fell by $780 at community colleges and $550 at private not-for-profit four-year institutions. Thanks to the sharp increases in posted price, public four-year colleges and universities saw a slight increase in net tuition of $170.

The net price data provides some welcome news in what otherwise represents a pretty dismal picture. Still, it's hard to feel comfortable when posted prices have increased so rapidly and the media and government officials all claim that higher education is increasingly "unaffordable." At least in the short run, total student aid funding has at least kept pace with tuition increases and net tuition shows very modest gains (or has actually fallen).

Given the widespread concern about the growing "unaffordability" of higher education, it's somewhat surprising to discover that college enrollments have boomed—almost 50 percent in the last decade alone. It's hard to imagine that higher education is unaffordable if enrollments are growing so rapidly. But college officials cannot take as much comfort as we might wish. Many families are digging deeper to pay for college. Some students are attending different institutions because of concerns about how much higher education will cost. And even if the best case scenario is true—posted price increases are offset by rapid growth in student aid—this is not a trend likely to continue.

Even more troubling, perhaps, is that a complex, nuanced explanation, even if completely accurate, may not matter very much. We do not live in a world that values careful, detailed assessments of complex issues. To the contrary, civic discourse is continually simplified and streamlined. In such an environment, perceptions can become reality, regardless of their accuracy. If policymakers and the public think higher education is "unaffordable" and readily available evidence seems to support that view, it can be exceptionally difficult to have a rational public policy discussion. That, like it or not, is the situation the higher education is facing today.

Why Cost Matters: The Taxpayer Burden of Higher Education

Jorge Klor de Alva, President, Nexus Research and Policy Center

Is the Price and Cost of a Degree Worth It to Taxpayers?

The current conversation on the rising costs of higher education has been focused primarily on the steeply increasing tuitions faced by parents and students. The continually mounting price of a college education is widely blamed for making it increasingly more difficult for students to obtain the college degree believed to be necessary to enter and remain in the middle class. Not surprisingly, college affordability has become a topic worthy of presidential politics (e.g., Lichtblau 2012; Obama 2012). However, because little attention is paid by the press and policymakers to the *cost* of making higher education possible, as opposed to the *price* paid for that education, the burden borne by taxpayers to educate postsecondary students has been mostly neglected.

To help address this neglect, in 2011 Mark Schneider, former commissioner of the U.S. Department of Education's National Center for Education Statistics, and I explored taxpayer costs in two related studies (Klor de Alva and Schneider 2011; Schneider and Klor de Alva 2011). Our aim was to widen the concern over spiraling tuition rates by including the benefits and costs to all of us, whether enrolled or not, to make higher education a reality. As part of our research we investigated whether taxpayers, as many claimed, were being left holding the bag due to both increasing default rates on government funded financial aid and the high dropout rates at most public colleges and universities. In what follows I summarize our findings as relevant to *The Rising Costs of Higher Education*.

Because escalating tuitions are leading some commentators to question the value of a college degree, we first worked on answering the question, *Do students who earn a bachelor's degree and participate in the labor force experience returns, such as higher wages, that justify the costs incurred by them in earning that degree?* Our answer, consistent with a large body of work by labor economists, was an unequivocal "yes." After taking into account the costs students incurred earning a bachelor's degree, over a lifetime the net present value of additional earnings derived from that degree ranged, on average, between $235,000, for a graduate from a non or less competitive not-for-profit college, to $552,000, for a graduate from a most competitive not-for-profit institution. If a bachelor's degree pays for the individual, what about the taxpayer? This led us to the second question we sought to answer: *Do taxpayers get a positive return on their investment in higher education?*

To get to answers others would find supported by the data, we used only publicly available sources such as those produced by the U.S. Department of Education, the U.S. Census, PayScale.com, the Board of Governors of the Federal Reserve System, the Tax Foundation, and the Internal Revenue Service (for sources and methodology see Klor de Alva and Schneider 2011, Appendix; Schneider and Klor de Alva 2011, Appendix). Furthermore, to make sure we were not comparing apples to oranges, in both studies we reported on eleven selected categories of institutions arrived at by cross-classifying information by control (whether they were public, not-for-profit, or for-profit) with levels of selectivity, ranging from open admissions to most selective using *Barron's Profiles of American Colleges* (2009). Although we recognize that taxpayers receive indirect benefits from their investment in higher education, such as the avoided costs of incarceration, social services, taxpayer-supported health care, and the like, our calculations focused strictly on direct, economically measurable costs and benefits.

The answers to our questions were based on calculating, from the perspective of a *bachelor's graduate*, the full cost of earning a degree subtracted from the benefits of increased earnings over the graduate's work life (in comparison to the earnings expected if the graduate had only completed high school). From the perspective of the *taxpayer*, we calculated the costs, which include direct appropriations and foregone taxes, subtracted from the benefits, which include taxes derived from the higher salaries and lifetime earnings of graduates.

We show that taxpayers benefit from the higher state and federal income taxes paid on the higher salaries earned by college graduates, varying from $60,000 in additional taxes paid over the work life of a graduate from a less selective public institution to almost $150,000 in additional income taxes paid over the work life of a graduate from the most selective not-for-profit schools. We then calculated the amount to which taxpayers subsidize the education that students receive in most colleges and universities. This was done by estimating the direct state appropriations for public universities and the complex set of tax exemptions enjoyed by not-for-profit ones.

These calculations (all adjusted to 2010 dollars) are summarized in Table 3.9, which shows that taxpayers subsidize bachelor's degrees in all not-for-profit institutions, except the most

Table 3.9 Taxpayers benefit from the higher income of college graduates

Sector	Lifetime addi-tional income taxes paid	Taxpayer benefit/cost per bache-lor's degree	Net benefit/cost to taxpayer
Non-/less competitive			
For-profit	$54,800	$6,100	$60,900
Public	$60,100	–$67,600	–$7,500
Not-for-profit	$52,100	–$8,000	$44,100
Competitive			
Public	$66,700	–$62,600	$4,100
Not-for-profit	$58,200	–$8,700	$49,500
Very competitive			
Public	$78,100	–$61,200	$16,900
Not-for-profit	$78,600	–$8,600	$70,000
Highly competitive			
Public	$97,100	–$74,300	$22,800
Not-for-profit	$93,600	–$8,800	$84,800
Most competitive	$98,700	–$108,000	–$9,300
Not-for-profit	$147,100	–$58,700	$88,400

Source: Authors' calculations (Klor de Alva and Schneider 2011, Tables 2, 3 and 6 summarized in Schneider and Klor de Alva, Table 2).

competitive, at around $8,000 to $9,000 per degree. In public institutions the taxpayer investment ranges from $61,000 to $74,000, except in the most competitive category, where the subsidy rises to approximately $108,000 per graduate. Further, because for-profit institutions do not receive state subsidies and pay taxes rather than receive tax exemptions, even after including the cost of government-funded financial aid and accompanying defaults, taxpayers benefit by around $6,000 per bachelor's degree.

In the same Table we also see that, even after netting out the subsidies they put into America's colleges and universities, in most cases, taxpayers make a "profit" by sharing in the added income graduates earn. Not surprisingly, but important from a public policy perspective, at every level of selectivity, taxpayers gain less from public institutions than from private ones, whether these are not-for-profit or for-profit. The two categories where schools are on average in the "red" from the taxpayers' perspective include only public institutions: non/less competitive schools, whose high drop out rates are very costly, and most selective public institutions (mostly flagship schools), where the cost of undergraduate education is exceedingly high due to the many expenses involved in being research institutions, including a costly faculty teaching few courses and the building and maintenance of research facilities.

Concerning the cost of dropouts, in the first of our previous studies (Klor de Alva and Schneider 2011, Appendix, Table 9) we calculated how much, on average, the cost per degree could be lowered if the number of dropouts were reduced by 50 percent. Among non/less competitive and competitive public institutions, the cost of the degree drops by more than $10,000 (from $67,000 to $53,000 and from $62,000 to $51,000, respectively). Not surprisingly, a recent study on the cost of dropouts reports that they cost the nation well over $1 billion each year in taxpayer dollars (Schneider 2010). As for the flagship campuses, we recognize that more is involved in evaluating them than simple profit/loss calculations given their importance in maintaining the competitiveness of the American economy. This benefit may balance out the higher taxpayer costs these institutions incur for producing bachelor's degree students, but this is a policy decision for governors, state legislators, and other stakeholders to make, informed by accurate considerations of costs.

Public Institutions Cost Taxpayers More Than Private Ones

When we compared the "sticker price" (the advertised tuition) and "net price" (what is actually paid after "discounts" and financial aid) of colleges across the eleven categories in our study perhaps the most surprising pattern was just how close the net price is for schools in different sectors at the lower levels of selectivity. For non/less-competitive schools and for schools in the competitive category (the selectivity category with the largest number of schools and students), the difference in what students actually pay is less than $3,000 (even though the sticker prices are separated by far larger amounts, ranging, on average, from $15,000 to $29,000). Schools in these lower levels of competition tend to lack a valuable brand name and the competition between them leads to a predictable result—true prices converge. When we turn to schools with name recognition, schools can charge a premium, and the most selective not-for-profit schools, schools that own marquee names, have the largest premium, with a net price more than twice as great as the most selective public institutions ($14,000 vs. $29,000).

But price does not equal cost.

The large amount of money taxpayers invest in institutions of higher education creates a divergence between what consumers pay for their education and what a college education actually costs. For public institutions, the money comes mostly in the form of direct appropriations from the state government, averaging about $10,000 per student per year. For not-for-profit colleges and universities, the major subsidy comes from their tax exempt status, which removes their endowment income from taxation and makes any gifts they receive from individuals or corporations also tax-free.

In our first study we documented the flow of money to and from campuses (Klor de Alva and Schneider 2011, Appendix Table 7). There we calculated the total cost to students and taxpayers of a bachelor's degree, accounting for the time to degree and the costs of educating students who drop out from college (about 40 percent of students who start a bachelor's degree do not complete it). In our calculations the net price for students in these schools averaged $8,077, lower than the average net price of $8,758 for students in for-profit institutions and even lower than the $10,510 estimated net price for students in not-for-profit schools in this category.

Keeping in mind that public colleges and universities were found to be "cheaper" than either not-for-profits or for-profit institutions in the same selectivity category, in Table 3.10 we

Table 3.10   Public institutions cost taxpayers more than private ones: examples of annual net cost or benefit per FTE student, 2010 dollars

	Non-/less competitive for-profits	Non-/less competitive publics	Non-/less competitive not-for-profits
Total amount received from government	$246,987,677	$4,504,066,609	$64,209,498
Total amount paid to government	$331,109,879	–$97,121,925	–$6,029,340
Total annual benefit (cost) to taxpayers	$84,122,203	–$4,601,188,534	–$70,238,838
Number of FTE students	$106,755	582,785	67,997
Annual taxpayer benefit (cost) per FTE student	$778	–$7,895	–$1,033

Source: Authors' calculations (Klor de Alva and Schneider 2011, Table 4).

summarize the calculations for schools in the non/less competitive categories. As Table 3.10 makes evident, taxpayers annually contribute around $8,000 per student for public institutions in this category of selectivity, but only around $1,000 per year for students in not-for-profit institutions. Even more striking, taxpayers actually *earn* nearly $800 per year per student in taxpaying, for-profit institutions. Clearly, while the *price* of public schools is low for the student, the *cost* of these schools for the taxpayer is much higher than either not-for-profit or for-profit institutions.

Percent of Total Annual Cost to Taxpayers per Student Earning a Bachelor's Degree

In Table 3.11, where we combine the information about the student net cost and the taxpayer cost (Klor de Alva and Schneider 2011, Table 3 and Appendix Table 7 respectively), we see that the overall annual taxpayer *cost* of educating a student differs substantially across the eleven categories as does the student contribution to the total cost.

While many have argued that for-profit institutions are costly, when we combine the net price that students pay with the fact that these institutions on average generate a net profit to the taxpayer,

Table 3.11   Annual cost of bachelor's degree per student with estimated amounts paid for by the student and the taxpayer

	Net price to student	Annual benefit (cost) to taxpayer	Combined cost	Percent of total cost paid for by taxpayer
Non/less competitive				
For profit	$8,752	$788	$7,964	0%
Public	$8,077	−$7,895	$15,972	49%
Not for profit	$10,510	−$1,033	$11,543	9%
Competitive				
Public	$9,075	−$8,729	$17,804	49%
Not for profit	$11,897	−$1,405	$13,302	11%
Very competitive				
Public	$10,926	−$10,534	$21,460	49%
Not for profit	$15,004	−$1,536	$16,540	9%
Highly competitive				
Public	$13,270	−$14,370	$27,640	52%
Not for profit	$22,196	−$1,869	$24,065	8%
Most competitive				
Public	$14,222	−$23,617	$37,839	62%
Not for profit	$29,565	−$13,216	$42,781	31%

Source: Authors' calculations (Klor de Alva and Schneider 2011, Table 3, Appendix Table 7).

the combined cost is far lower than schools in other categories and the taxpayer ends up *gaining* rather than contributing to the annual combined per student cost. When we look at not-for-profit campuses, we find that the total annual cost of attendance in every category, but the most selective one, is lower than in public institutions. In effect, while the *price* of public institutions is indeed lower than the price of most not-for-profit schools, the *costs* to the taxpayer are not.

Furthermore, in Table 3.11 we see that taxpayer support increases with greater selectivity among public institutions. The rate of increase of taxpayer support for not-for-profits is much more gradual, until we turn to the *most selective* not-for-

Table 3.12 More selective institutions enroll fewer students with Pell Grants
         and Receive more government subsidies

Barron's rating	Percentage of students with Pell Grants	Average annual government subsidy per student*
Non/less competitive	45.3	$6,056
Competitive	32.3	$7,189
Very competitive	22.4	$8,288
Highly competitive	15.4	$10,625
Most competitive	11.2	$15,102

Source: Authors' calculations (Klor de Alva and Schneider 2011, Table 5).
The average annual government subsidy per student is derived by adding the total annual benefit (cost) to taxpayers of each of the Barron's ratings and dividing this sum by the total number of full-time equivalent (FTE) students in that rating. (See Klor de Alva and Schneider 2011, Appendix Table 8.)

profit colleges and universities, where the taxpayer subsidy increases by almost a factor of 10.

Conclusion

In Table 3.12 we display the concentration of Pell Grant students in schools in Barron's selectivity levels. In our two previous reports we documented substantial taxpayer subsidies to students in most colleges and universities—either through direct appropriations to public institutions or tax subsidies to not-for profit schools. The federal government also supports students directly through the Pell Grant program, which is targeted at students with financial need. But Pell Grants pale in comparison to the size of these other subsidies.

When the percentages of Pell Grant enrollments by selectivity are combined with levels of taxpayer subsidies, we can see that low income and minority students—the fastest growing segment of the population—are concentrated in colleges and universities that get the lowest levels of taxpayer support.

There may be legitimate reasons supporting the various patterns of taxpayer subsidies noted above and across the institutions we studied. However, we believe that in this time of fiscal shortages debate about the rising costs of higher education must be informed by the data we have presented, which show that while taxpayers benefit from nearly all college graduates, taxpayers do not benefit equally from all higher education sectors.

References

Barron's Profiles of American Colleges. Hauppauge, N.Y.: Barron's Educational Series, Inc., 2009.

Klor de Alva, Jorge and Schneider, Mark. *Who Wins? Who Pays? The Economic Returns and Costs of a Bachelor's Degree.* San Francisco: Nexus Research and Policy Center and Washington, D.C.: American Institutes for Research, 2011. (Retrieved January 25, 2012, from http://www.nexu sresearch.org.)

Lichtblau, Eric. "Romney Offers Praise for a Donor's Business." *New York Times*, January 15, 2012, p.1. (Retrieved January 25, 2012, from http://www.nytimes.com/2012/01/ 15/us/politics/mitt-romney-offers-praise-for-a-donors -business.html?_r=1&ref=ericlichtblau.)

Obama, Barack. "2012 State of the Union Address." *New York Times*. (Retrieved January 25, 2012, from http://www .nytimes.com/2012/01/25/us/politics/state-of-the-union -2012-transcript.html?ref=stateoftheunionmessageus.)

Schneider, Mark. *Finishing the First Lap: The Cost of First-Year Student Attrition in America's Four-Year Colleges and Universities.* Washington, D.C: American Institutes for Research, 2011. (Retrieved January 25, 2012, from http:// www.air.org/files/AIR_Schneider_Finishing_the_First _Lap_Oct101.pdf.)

Schneider, Mark and Klor de Alva, Jorge. *Cheap for Whom? How Much Higher Education Costs Taxpayers.* American Enterprise Institute for Public Research, Education Outlook, No. 8, October 2011. (Retrieved January 25, 2012, from

http://www.aei.org/files/2011/10/05/08-EduO-Schneider
-Oct-2011-gnew.pdf.)

Too High a Price? The Impact of College Prices on Underserved Students

Brian A. Sponsler, Associate Director for Research, Institute for Higher Education Policy
Alisa F. Cunningham, Vice President for Research, Institute for Higher Education Policy

Discussion of rising college prices has become unavoidable. Once the province of academic literature and wonky think tank–inspired dialogues, college prices have become a mainstay of news reporting, political leaders' talking points, and the kitchen table discussions of millions of American families struggling to support college-going.

The heightened attention paid to college prices is a result of the convergence of factors. Steady increases in tuition have outpaced inflation nearly three-fold over the past few decades. Stagnated wages for most American workers over a similar time period have made paying for college all the more difficult. And the ensuing reliance on student loans has resulted in increased indebtedness of college students and graduates, who often leave school with tens of thousands of dollars in student loan debt, whether they ever earn a degree or not. As a result, both the perception and the reality of an affordable college education have diminished in the eyes of many and the topic has become a source of widespread discussion.

There are a number of explanations for increasing prices. Among the most notable are declining state appropriations per student at public colleges and universities; rising costs of technology, energy, and healthcare; expansion of services offered to students; and increasing use of merit aid scholarships. In addition many students, aided by the availability of student loans and expanding financial aid from institutions, continue to be willing to pay high fees. Yet beyond these root causes, the *effects* higher prices have on students have not been uniform. The reality is that rising prices over the past few decades have had a disproportionate impact on traditionally underserved student groups, including individuals who are the first in their family to go to college, come from less-affluent backgrounds, are racial/ethnic minorities, returning adult students or military veterans. These student groups face many hurdles in gaining access to college and successfully earning a degree, but financing their education is often of paramount concern. For those fortunate enough to possess higher levels of financial resources and social capital, increasing prices have made college going more difficult, but not impossible. But for a larger and growing number of students, high college costs threaten to become an insurmountable barrier to college attendance and degree completion, potentially eroding decades of efforts to expand access and increase educational attainment.

As public policies and institutional practices are amended to make college going more affordable and accessible, it is imperative that postsecondary decision makers be aware of the responses of underserved student groups to high college prices, and understand the implications these responses have for students' chances of earning degrees. Herein we highlight some of the ways traditionally underserved students have responded to high college prices, noting the issues of non-enrollment, institutional selection, and educational financing.

Underserved Student Responses to High College Prices

Research confirms what common sense unearthed, namely that the price of college has a critical impact on a student's likelihood of pursuing a degree. Students are intensely focused on the price of college (or their perception of that price) before making decisions about whether, when, and where to enroll. In response to high prices, low-income and other underserved student groups often behaved in logical ways given their personal context and college knowledge. These responses, however, may not ultimately benefit their chances of successfully earning a degree. Three "truths" of high college prices are especially critical be aware of as they wrestle with solutions to the college cost quandary.

Truth Number One: The "sticker shock" of college prices causes many students to abandon college before they even begin

The price of going to college is a critical piece of the access equation. Despite progress over the past few decades in increasing access to college, rising college prices contribute to disturbing enrollment gaps between more and less affluent individuals; recent data indicates that barely half of low-income students enroll in college immediately after graduating from high school compared to 84 percent of their more affluent peers (U.S. Department of Education, National Center for Education Statistics, 2011).

Although academic and social factors play a role in inhibiting access for underserved students, price sensitivity contributes mightily to a non-enrollment choice. As the nation seeks to build human capital through education, those groups that would most benefit from college-going face a pricing structure that dissuades enrollment. More disturbing, even among low-income students who are academically qualified to pursue a college degree, non-enrollment is pervasive. High prices are putting pressure on all students—but they are threatening to push an entire generation of traditionally underserved students out of the educational pipeline altogether.

Truth Number Two: High prices impact students' institutional choice, leading to clustering of underserved student groups in institutions least able to support educational success

Underserved students may also react to high prices by choosing to enroll in certain types of postsecondary institutions—even when other institutions might be more suitable to their needs or more beneficial to their chances of earning a degree. This institutional under-matching may come in the form of choosing relatively low-priced institutions, or those located closest to home, purely as cost-cutting strategy—even when a student is academically qualified to attend an institution where their chances of graduating are higher (Bowen, Chingos & McPherson, 2009). Low-income students are disproportionately likely to enroll in community colleges, which tend to have significantly lower prices than in other sectors, but also carry lower completion rates; low-income students financially dependent on their parents are more than twice as likely to enroll at community colleges as students from families with incomes of $100,000 or more. Conversely, fewer than one in five low-income college students are enrolled in a public or private four-year institution.

The impact of enrollment choices is clearly driven by more than just price. But when the majority of low-income students end up clustered in institutions that are least able to support them to graduation, it's clear that high prices are having a significant effect on enrollment patterns.

Truth Number Three: To pay high college prices, enrolled students often make choices that delay or hinder their completion

The majority of low-income and other underserved students receive grant aid of some sort to support college going and offset, in part, high college prices. Expenditures on federal Pell Grants, which target low-income students, have increased considerably in recent years (Baum and Payea, 2011). However, over the last three decades the maximum Pell Grant has consistently covered less than half of the average total price at public four-year institutions; in some years merely a third of tuition costs have been covered by these grants. Even when taking into account grant aid from federal, state, and institutional sources, low-income and other disadvantaged student groups are challenged to cover the high price of college attendance.

As a result, to finance their education underserved students are likely to make decisions that hinder their chances of leaving college with a degree. Students have a number of options to cover college costs, including working significant hours while taking classes, living at home with parents or other family members, enrolling on a part-time or reduced basis, or taking out student loans. These funding strategies are not mutually exclusive, and students commonly employ several of them at any one time.

Yet research illustrates that each of these strategies carry its own risks. Working full-time, enrolling on a part-time basis, or living with a parent has been shown to reduce the likelihood of earning a degree (Cunningham and Santiago, 2008). Additionally, although student loans have been an essential tool in helping low-income students gain access to college, the excessive use of student loans by some students at some institutions carries significant short- and long-term costs, particularly for students who drop out without a degree.

High college prices have largely erased the impact of need-based grant aid programs, leaving low-income students with difficult choices—support college-going with financing strategies that harm their chances of completion, become indebted through excessive use of student loans, or forgo enrolling at all.

Addressing Student Perceptions of High Prices

College prices impact all students. Yet high prices are particularly consequential for traditionally underserved student groups. The responses to high college prices by low-income and other underserved students have striking and negative consequences on their likelihood of earning a degree. A first step toward reducing the impact of high prices is to make sure students and families are taking full advantage of existing programs that can make earning a degree less costly in both the short and long run.

Given the responses to prices discussed above, federal and state governments, community-based organizations, and institutions themselves have implemented a number of programs to assist students in building knowledge of how to cover college costs. Unfortunately, many low-income and other underserved students are not taking advantage of these existing initiatives.

Despite the availability of need-based grant aid, for example, many students who are eligible for Pell Grants never apply for financial aid (Kantrowitz, 2009; see also King, 2006). Similarly, although extensive financial literacy programs exist that aim to help students avoid financial pitfalls, far too many students remain either unaware or unengaged by these programs to make them as effective as they could be. Finally, for students who struggle to repay their student loans, a number of federal options exist, including income-based repayment plans, loan deferments, and forbearance programs. Yet many borrowers do not use those tools and end up unnecessarily going into default, with dramatic personal consequences (Cunningham and Kienzl. March 2011). To assist underserved student groups in dealing with the consequences of high college prices, it is necessary to increase knowledge of these programs and others, as well as ensure they are used to their full effect.

Learning from Student Reactions to High Price

In the end, the inescapable truth of high college prices is clear: high prices make it difficult for historically underserved students to access college and complete a degree. Underserved students face a maddening higher education landscape. On one hand they are inundated with messaging that the only reliable means of improving their financial prospects is through obtainment of a college degree. Yet at the same time colleges continue to raise costs of attendance at a pace that outstrips federal and state aid, and those institutions most likely to enroll underserved students are the least able to support successful educational outcomes.

As constituents of higher education wrestle with containing costs and designing financial aid policies to offset costs for those in need, it is essential that a focus is kept on low-income and other disenfranchised student groups. Reducing costs for existing college students and recent graduates is a necessary endeavor. But if the nation is truly committed to increasing educational attainment it must find ways to provide underserved students with accessible choices that don't come with the high price of reducing their chances of finding educational success.

References

Baum, Sandy and Kathleen Payea. 2011. *Trends in Student Aid: 2011*. (New York: The College Board, 2012).

Bowen, William G., Matthew M. Chingos and Michael S. McPherson. 2009. *Crossing the Finish Line: Completing College at America's Public Universities*. Princeton University Press.

Cunningham, Alisa F. and Gregory S. Kienzl. 2011. *Delinquency: The Untold Story of Student Loan Borrowing*. Washington, DC: Institute for Higher Education Policy.

Cunningham, Alisa F. and Deborah Santiago. 2008. *Student Aversion to Borrowing: Who Borrows and Who Doesn't*. Washington, DC: Institute for Higher Education Policy.

Kantrowitz, Mark. 2009. *Analysis of Why Some Students Do Not Apply for Financial Aid*. Available at FinAid.org.

King, Jacqueline E. 2006. *Missed Opportunities Revisited: New Information on Students Who Do Not Apply for Financial Aid*. ACE Center for Policy Analysis.

U.S. Department of Education, National Center for Education Statistics. 2011. *Condition of Education: 2011*. Washington, DC: Author.

Just Say No to "Sticker Price"

Andrew P. Kelly, American Enterprise Institute

Public anxiety about the cost of college has reached critical mass. A 2011 poll found that 57 percent of Americans thought that a college education was not worth the investment (Pew

Research Center, 2011). From the state house to the White House, policymakers have told colleges and universities that current trends are unsustainable. President Obama famously put colleges "on notice," warning that a failure to contain costs will result in fewer federal aid dollars.

While this national conversation about cost containment is worthwhile, these discussions must define "college costs" precisely and in a way that is helpful for various audiences. Unfortunately, the conventional narrative focuses exclusively on "sticker prices" as the preferred measure of cost. While sticker prices are easy to come by, they are less useful to two audiences—families and taxpayers—than more accurate measures of cost. From the perspective of prospective students and their families, the most useful measure of cost is the "net price" after subtracting grant aid. Sticker prices may cause families more trouble than they are worth.

From the taxpayer perspective, a focus on the sticker price actually understates the actual cost of higher education to society, particularly at public institutions. As I argue below, once we expand the lens to include public subsidies, foregone tax revenue, and degree productivity, however, our notion of what qualifies as "low cost" looks dramatically different.

Families Need Net Prices

Colleges engage in what economists call "price discrimination": they set a sticker price and then tailor aid packages to discount the actual cost of attendance based on student characteristics like family background, academic qualifications, and other accomplishments. Price discrimination is an important recruiting tool for colleges and universities, who use aid packages to attract the desired mix of students.

An example shows that the gap between sticker price and net price after aid can be substantial, particularly for lower-income students. According to the National Center for Education Statistics (NCES) College Navigator, Stanford's total cost of attendance (tuition, living expenses, and books and supplies) was more than $55,000 per year in 2011, while California State University at Long Beach was considerably less expensive at about $21,000. But the average net price for a low-income student (families making less than $30,000 a year) in 2009–2010 was about $4,500 at Stanford, and $3,600 at Cal State Long Beach. This is a stylized example, but more systematic data suggest that such discounting is fairly common. This is especially true for low- and middle-income families, where the difference between net and sticker price are likely to be the largest.

The problem is, the net price of college generally remains hidden until far too late in the process. In general, students will not know what they'll actually pay in terms of net price until after they have applied to the college, filled out the Free Application for Federal Student Aid (FAFSA), gotten accepted by the college, and received a formal offer of financial aid. This lack of transparency leaves consumers at a severe disadvantage in the higher education market. Without accurate information about prices, prospective students will fail to consider the most selective colleges because of huge sticker prices, while others—particularly first generation college hopefuls—may give up on college altogether.

The federal government has done its part to make sure that net price information is available. Under the latest installment of the Higher Education Act, colleges are required to develop "net price calculators" that will provide prospective students with a reasonable estimate of what they will have to pay, given their family income and other characteristics.

Making these data available is an important step. But if parents do not recognize the distinction between sticker and net prices, how can we expect them to seek out the net price calculators? My own research on parental information suggests that while a majority recognize the distinction between sticker price and net price when primed to think about a lower-income student, lower-income parents were the least likely to recognize this distinction (Kelly, 2011).

In a survey of 1,000 parents from California, Florida, Illinois, New York, and Texas, I asked parents to estimate the cost of attendance at three colleges in their state: two publics and one private. I then asked parents to estimate the cost, after financial aid, for a student from a family of four with an annual income of $60,000. Finally, the survey asked them to estimate what they would have to pay for their own child.

Overall, somewhere between 65 and 75 percent of parents adjusted their estimate of costs downward between the first and second question, recognizing that students from modest means pay discounted tuition. The results suggest that parents may (rightly) perceive that top private colleges are the most likely to discount their tuition with financial aid for less-advantaged students.

Beneath these encouraging patterns, parents from families making less than $30,000 were significantly less likely than their high-income peers to ratchet their cost estimate downward from question one to question two; just over half of the parents from the lowest income group did so when asked about the public colleges (compared to about ¾ of parents in the highest income group). Parents from the lowest income groups were also the most likely to overestimate what they would have to pay for their own child to attend. Fully 60 percent of low-income parents overestimated the price at the public flagship.

These survey results suggest that most parents will recognize the distinction between net price and sticker price *when they are primed to think in those terms*. From a public policy perspective, these patterns reveal why it is critical to actively frame discussions of college costs in terms of net price, particularly when it comes to informing low-income families. As such, policymakers, educators, and nongovernmental organizations should take pains to introduce consumers to the net price *concept* if they want them to use the net price *calculators*. In short, a college cost debate that harps on sticker prices will do little to help consumers make more informed choices.

Broadening Definitions of Cost

A reliance on sticker prices can also distort policy debates. Because of state subsidies, endowments, and other sources of revenue, prices typically bear little relation to costs in higher education. Tour guides cite this fact with pride as they walk across campus: it actually costs the college double or triple the amount of money they charge in tuition to educate their students. Translation: sticker price is a decidedly poor proxy for what postsecondary education costs to deliver.

Despite this disconnect between cost and price, debates about higher education often define "low-cost" programs on the basis of sticker prices rather than a more accurate measure total costs per student or per degree produced. In an era of tight public budgets and growing human capital needs, measures of total cost and return on investment are arguably more important than posted tuition and fees. Policymakers aiming to make strategic investments in the most productive institutions need information about the number of positive outcomes per dollar spent. Colleges with low sticker prices, high public subsidies, and low completion rates may not be such a great public investment after all. They are cheap for individual consumers, but quite expensive from the perspective of taxpayers.

Two recent studies show that when we take a more global view of the cost to taxpayers, our notion of low cost institutions changes considerably. In the first, Klor de Alva and Schneider (2010) looked at college costs through the eyes of the taxpayer, counting direct public support (state appropriations and grants to students), foregone tax revenue, and taxes paid by for-profit colleges to calculate the total cost per degree produced. They found that private colleges—both for-profit and non-profit—cost taxpayers less per degree than public colleges. Their analysis shows that for-profit colleges actually boast a positive benefit/cost ratio because they pay taxes on their earnings and receive little by way of direct subsidies. In contrast, selective public colleges cost taxpayers between $60,000 and 75,000 per bachelor's degree.

In the second study, Schneider and Yin (2011) calculated the cost of community college attrition. Policymakers often hold up community colleges as a low-cost pathway because of their low tuition. But community colleges also have low retention and graduation rates, which raises their cost per degree. Schneider and Yin estimate that over the five years between 2004 and 2009, the state and federal governments spent almost $4 billion on community college students that did not return for a second year.

On some level, it is not surprising that public institutions are costly for taxpayers. These institutions soak up taxpayer dollars via public subsidies in part because they provide positive externalities for the communities where they are located. The point is not to argue that policymakers should spend less on public institutions. Rather, policymakers should insist on a definition of cost that actually reflects the full extent of public investment and institutional productivity. Steering the conversation about college costs away from sticker price to more accurate measures is an important first step.

Summing Up

One can only hope that the brewing debate about college costs will drive us toward better measures of cost that are useful to the various stakeholders in the higher education community. Part of the challenge is that data are not always immediately available. Generating good estimates of net price, for instance, requires analyzing the student aid records of current students. More precise measures of education and related expenses per degree are difficult to come by because colleges often fail to categorize expenses in such neat boxes.

But these logistical hurdles should not deter the push for more accurate information on costs. Increasing higher education productivity and improving consumer choice will prove difficult without it.

References

Kelly, Andrew P. (2011). "Nothing But Net: Helping Families Learn the Real Price of College." *Education Outlook*, No. 10. (Washington, DC: American Enterprise Institute.)

Klor de Alva, Jorge and Mark Schneider. (2010). *Who Wins? Who Pays? The Economic Returns and Costs of a Bachelor's Degree*. (Washington, DC: American Institutes for Research.)

Pew Research Center. (2011). *Is College Worth It? College Presidents, Public Assess Value, Quality, and Mission of Higher Education*. (Washington, DC: Pew Research Center.)

Schneider, Mark and Michelle Yin. (2010). *The Hidden Costs of Community Colleges*. (Washington, DC: American Institutes for Research.)

Forecasting Our Risks

Kristine E. Dillon, President, Consortium on Financing Higher Education (COFHE)

In the 1970s and early 1980s, despite widespread hardships of the so-called New Depression in higher education, flagship state universities appeared to be reasonably positioned to weather most coming storms (Cheit, 1973, p. 150). From that vantage, the most at-risk institutions were the independent colleges that were relatively small in size, not the most selective academically, and with relatively low endowments. Yet contrary to dire predictions by higher education scholars like Lewis Mayhew, the Carnegie Council and others, the mortality rate of these smaller independent colleges has been amazingly low. In fact, the resilience of the independent colleges across the "status pyramid" of American higher education's much valued diversity of institutional types has been remarkable—and likely represents an under-appreciated success story. Furthermore, whereas in the 1970s, while at least a few nonprofit, independent universities did go into receivership and became public (e.g., University of Pittsburgh and University of Louisville), such transformations in 2012 would be very unlikely. Indeed, today's state universities are at risk financially and, arguably, floundering in mission, finding themselves buffeted by the pressures to compete for national "rankings" as well as to serve the needs of the states that created them. What explains the inaccuracy of this forecast?

Charles Clotfelder's 1996 book, *Buying the Best*, signaled that by about 1985 all higher education (and, the national economy) had emerged from a terrible decade—and that a handful of independent colleges and universities not only survived the 1980s but in fact, flourished. While such "elite" schools should not be confused as representative of the median for their sector, even the less well-endowed colleges that were challenged by stiff competition from low-cost state colleges and universities largely survived the difficult preceding period by adhering to a similar financing model: raising their tuition prices and increasing substantially their offers of financial aid. A lower cost structure— offsetting lack of endowment—allowed this approach. As we examine the 30-year period that has passed since the mid-80s, we can see that the majority of small independent colleges may not be flourishing but still they survive, and their pricing and cost structures have largely continued to follow the model of high price combined with high aid, along with costs per student as high as their resources allow.

The picture for state supported higher education is less rosy. Even before the Great Recession began precipitously eroding sources of state funding across a wide spectrum of services and public institutions, publically financed higher education showed many signs of stress in matching its aspirations with its sources of revenues. Flagship universities began seriously to experiment with the model previously implemented within the independent sector: higher pricing strategies, aggressive admissions recruitment, extensive fundraising programs and increased budgets for financial aid. Out of state recruitment and foreign recruitment at much higher tuition pricing, as well as increased in-state tuitions, became core to the model.

Continuing the tradition of studies like Cheit's (1973) and Howard Bowen's (1980), the Delta Cost Project developed metrics to compare changes from year to year in average spending per student, starting in 1999. This analysis has also examined revenues from tuition and states, and local and private sources. Delta discovered that, for the majority of institutions, increases in tuition do not translate into increases in spending. In fact, at most public institutions, tuition increases have attempted to offset lost revenues from state and local budget reductions. Further, such actual tuition increases have been less than half of the real reduction in state and local appropriations:

> [A]t public research institutions, for example, average tuition revenue increased by $369 per student between 2008 and 2009, but the loss in state and local appropriations per student was $751, slightly more than twice the amount generated in increased tuition revenues. Despite that, institutions were able to increase educational and related spending per student by $92. To realize greater spending in the face of revenue losses, public institutions were clearly taking measures to reduce spending as well as finding new revenue sources. (*Trends in College Spending, 1999–2009*)

The media soundtrack for higher education in the second decade of the millennium is punctuated by discordant sound bites, including those from President Obama who says, "We are putting colleges on notice—you can't assume that you'll just jack up tuition every single year. If you can't stop tuition from going up, then the funding you get from taxpayers each year will go down" (Jan. 27, 2012 University of Michigan speech). Other comments focus on frustration with the increased competition for entry into the nation's most selective schools, irrespective of price:

"Getting into Harvard is like winning the lottery twice," said Barmak Nassirian (American Association of Collegiate Registrars and Admission Officers). "You're getting into Harvard, and if you don't have the adequate resources, you're getting into an institution that has the financial resources to package you properly."

Harvard requires no contribution from families with annual incomes below $60,000 and no more than 10 percent of income from typical families who earn up to $180,000. Currently, 70 percent receive some aid, the school notes. (*Philadelphia Inquirer*, February 2, 2011, Susan Snyder)

What do these—quite different—public comments about higher education have in common? The cost of producing an education, especially at the schools most in demand, has grown even as the *net price* (tuition paid after financial aid) for these high-demand schools has dropped. But, we also see the price of attending a public institution has grown, even as its costs per student have been constrained. Is the president asking for reductions in the costs of education resulting from increasing expenditures on financial aid? Not likely. What about cost constraints on educational quality? Possibly, but presumably with reluctance. Is there likelihood that top private schools will cut the expenditures made on an undergraduate education that is sought by many more students than can possibly be admitted to the seats available? Probably not. As economist Howard Bowen famously said, "The incentives inherent in the goals of excellence, prestige, and influence are not counteracted within the higher education system by incentives leading to parsimony or efficiency" (1980, 20).

Very recently, Archibald and Feldman, two economists from The College of William and Mary, tackled a comprehensive analysis of higher education's apparently "dysfunctional" model to evaluate whether the cost of producing undergraduate education could (or should) be significantly overhauled. Their book,

Why Does College Cost So Much?, makes a reasoned case that there are underlying drivers that will continue to raise costs in the production of undergraduate education (2011). In particular, they explore the implications for higher education of "cost disease" in the personal services sector, contrasted with productivity gains in the manufacturing sector enabled by capital investment, innovation and skills—breakthroughs often contributed by those with college educations. Similar productivity gains have not been achieved within the services sector, meaning that so far, we have yet to implement viable ways to replace the high-cost production functions within higher education. These authors argue that the "standard of care" (or quality expectations) for a college graduate have implied continued investment by colleges and universities in the newest, best technologies and learning opportunities available in order to meet the expectations of students, employers and graduate schools. The differentials in earnings for those who are college educated versus those without college degrees have also grown, likely strengthening the argument that college graduates' contributions offer advantages to the economy. These authors state:

> The key consideration is the quality of the service. Productivity growth that would be accepted by service providers and customers alike will have to be productivity growth that maintains the quality of the service. (p. 41)

The schools with the strongest applicant pools and the best reputations have maintained and burnished a model of striving for excellence by using their resources to produce a better and more costly product, rather than focusing on cutting costs and prices for all their customers. But, while doing so, they *have* cut prices paid by lower and middle income students by offering generous institutional, need-based financial aid. As other types of colleges and universities, both public and private, have faced both external threats to funding (e.g., state and federal support) and competition for students (e.g., increased application activity, use of merit scholarships), the cost-price issues raised by the media and politicians have become increasingly difficult for most of us to sort out. And this confusion has consistently affected those who attempt to forecast the future for American higher education, as well.

Recall that the 1970s' forecasts for higher education saw a troubled future for independent colleges especially in comparison with the public universities. The "financing" model adopted by private colleges and universities has generally been successful in averting that future, and the commitment and capacity of states to play the role forecast for them in sustaining support for public institutions has eroded badly. While productivity gains in the service sector would certainly be welcomed—not only in higher education but also in health care—the contributions of the services sector to our economy and quality of life remain significant. Lawrence H. Summers, an economist and former Harvard president, made this forecast:

> A good rule of thumb for many things in life holds that things take longer to happen than you think they will, and then happen faster than you thought they could. . . . Here is a bet and a hope that the next quarter century will see more change in higher education than the last three combined. (*New York Times*, Jan. 22, 2012 "The 21st Century Education")

Concerns about how to produce high quality education for young people required in order to advance the country's economic goals are valid. But simplistic actions involving cuts to public resources for colleges and universities or price controls to cap tuition growth cannot address realities of service sector productivity models. At present, there are exciting experiments underway at many schools to test the potential for uses of educational technology that may yield improvements in educational productivity and cost reductions. But, until such productivity breakthroughs can be identified that will achieve quality educational outcomes on a broad scale, undermining the current model of American higher education can only be harmful to the economy's best interests.

References

Archibald, Robert B. and David H. Feldman. 2011. *Why Does College Cost So Much?* New York: Oxford University Press.

Bowen, Howard R. 1980. *The Costs of Higher Education.* San Francisco: Jossey-Bass.

Cheit, Earl F. 1973. *The New Depression in Higher Education.* New York: McGraw-Hill.

Obama, Barack. 2012. Speech at the University of Michigan. January 27, 2012.

Snyder, Susan. "Competition for Colleges Increasing as Applications Rise." *Philadelphia Inquirer*, February 2, 2011. http://articles.philly.com/2011-02-02/news/27095484_1 _financial-aid-applications-rise-eric-j-furda.

Summers, Lawrence H. "The 21st Century Education." *New York Times.* January 22, 2012. http://www.nytimes.com/ 2012/01/22/education/edlife/the-21st-century-education .html?pagewanted=al.

The Delta Cost Project. September 2011. *Trends in College Spending, 1999–2009.* <http://www.deltacostproject.org/ analyses/delta_reports.asp>

Commotion at the Gates: Higher Education's Evolving Role in U.S. Inequality

James C. Hearn, University of Georgia

For older observers, the fall of 2011 brought memories of the 1960s on campus. The nation's growing income and wealth inequality was at levels unmatched since the Roaring Twenties (Krueger, 2011), and was attracting angry attention. President

Obama (2011) assailed the trend as "mindboggling." Numerous colleges around the country forcibly removed demonstrators and their tents from campus-based "Occupy" sites, including such iconic locations as Harvard Yard and Berkeley's Sproul Hall (*Inside Higher Education*, November 14, 2011; Carmichael and Baker, 2011; Krupnick, 2011). Outside the national eye, but perhaps even more evocatively, protesters were evicted from their posts at the University of Georgia's historic Arch, an iconic gateway to campus that appears on the state's seal (*11Alive News*, 2011).

Not surprisingly, when the "99% movement" first stirred nationally, higher education seemed less on the mind of protesters than business practices, taxation, housing, healthcare, and labor markets. But campuses have long been home for dissent and argument about individual opportunities for advancement, and soon such issues as college costs and the weak job markets awaiting graduates became additional, even primary, targets (Domonell, 2012). Arguments that "my tuition is too high" predictably struck some observers as merely self-serving but, in fact, the rising costs of higher education do merit deeper attention, albeit at a less individualistic and more policy-oriented level. One observer of the 2011 Harvard protests crystallized the issue nicely by wryly posing a question: "Do you think it's a little ironic that the university that makes the 1 percent is protesting the 1 percent?" (Carmichael and Baker, 2011).

This perspective went largely undiscussed at the time, but its power comes from looking beyond Harvard, to encompass all of higher education. That is, is it a little ironic that college students pursuing coveted socioeconomic credentials are protesting that very process? Colleges and universities are in fact central players in inequality, serving a critical role as gatekeepers of advanced opportunities in the society. Thus, though the tents and placards are gone now on many campuses, the image of commotion at the gates is certainly apropos. The reality is that the myriad connections between higher education and the nation's extraordinary new level of socioeconomic stratification are well worth our attention, and our concern.

To whom is the college gateway to be opened, and to whom should its benefits in later life accrue? Higher education is absolutely integral, and indeed central, to socioeconomic inequality. College degree–holders enjoy far greater lifetime incomes than others, and most Americans are comfortable with that pattern (McMahon, 2009). But what is problematic is the extent to which college opportunities are being rationed more and more by factors other than desire and capability to benefit from attendance. Are parents' socioeconomic circumstances increasingly driving college enrollment patterns?

The evidence on this question is mixed, but tends to the affirmative. Lower-income students are entering higher education at rates greater than ever before, but increasingly do so attending part-time and via delayed enrollment after high school, and they increasingly are less successful than other students in earning their degrees, regardless of their institutional sector (Cabrera et al., 2005; Bailey and Dynarski, 2011). Lower-income students have fallen behind in the competition for the credentials that help ensure scholarships and other aids to college affordability (Bastedo and Jaquette, 2011). Lower-income students are disproportionately enrolling in the institutional sectors with the lowest post-graduation payoffs in earnings and other favorable outcomes (Grodsky and Jackson, 2009). And, importantly, institutional choices are apparently becoming more stratified, not less: "There is no question that students from low-income families are under-enrolling in the most expensive, most selective institutions, even after controlling for their college preparedness and other observable characteristics" (Bowen et al., 2005, p. 94), and the fact is that those institutions can provide the greatest chances for socioeconomic mobility for students from disadvantaged backgrounds (Thomas and Zhang, 2005).

Now, let's be clear. Lower-income and minority high-school students have extraordinarily troubling rates of high-school drop-out, and that is a searing national problem. But if we focus on those who have been fortunate and able enough to earn a secondary degree, it is undeniable that virtually any of them can find a way to enter the nation's postsecondary system: we oversimplify the discussion when we speak of blocked access for that population. As noted above, postsecondary enrollments have been rising for years among lower-SES students. The real contemporary problem of higher-education opportunity is not full-blown blocking of access but rather constrained opportunity to enroll in ways that fit students' aspirations and qualifications. The nation's postsecondary system is increasingly open, and ambitious high-school graduates who do not enroll, or enroll only after years of delay, do so because their options are not fully known, limited, and unattractive, not because they have no options at all.

Thus, at the crux of the opportunity crisis for high-school graduates is being unable to attend desired institutions for which one is qualified, at enrollment levels one wants, at the times one wants, and in the long run, to graduate. When we look beyond high-school drop-outs, the issues are institutional choice, persistence, and success, not basic access. Ultimately, those constraints hamper the workings of a free educational and labor marketplace.

To understand how this came to be, we need to review ongoing tension between two, contrasting visions of the roles of colleges and universities in society. On one hand, these institutions comprise the nation's major *instrument of social mobility*, and are at the heart of innumerable rising-from-poverty stories in American life. One institution alone, the City College of New York, was central to the later careers of an extraordinary number of nationally influential sons and daughters of impoverished European and Caribbean immigrants in the 20th century. But, conversely, colleges and universities have also long been portrayed as central agents in the *reproduction of inequality*, their spaces allocated largely on the basis of socioeconomic background and their curricula comfortably confirming the traditions and values of capitalism (Bourdieu and Passeron, 1977; Bowles and Gintis, 1976). As Bowen et al. (2005) put it, are elite institutions to be "engines of opportunity" or "bastions of privilege"?

Neither view is fully right nor wrong, obviously—both have elements of truth. But the respective power of each vision unquestionably ebbs and flows, and it is hard to deny that higher education's reproductive role is currently ascendant. "Maximally maintained inequality," a classic notion in the sociology of education (e.g., see Raftery and Hout, 1993), contends that, as access expands to higher levels of education, status differentiation within and above that level grows, ensuring that the wealthiest in the society maintain their grounds of advantage and inequality is not reduced. For example, over the course of the nation's history, college attendance has gone from largely being the province of the elite to an activity open to a majority of the population, and in concert we have moved from little attention being paid to which institution one attended (being a college graduate alone was a critical determinant and marker of status) to ranking institutions and assigning varying levels of prestige to them. As access and the supply of postsecondary institutions have grown, status differentials among them (and thus among graduates) have grown in concert.

Need-based student financial aid plays a major part in the battle between competing visions of higher education's place in stratification. In the U.S., an institution's prestige, status, and ultimate socioeconomic "payoffs" have tended to parallel its price (Dale and Krueger, 2002), and as tuition levels have risen and student-aid levels fallen in their coverage of costs, attendance at the highest-status institutions has increasingly been rationed to favor those from the wealthiest reaches of society (McPherson and Shapiro, 1998). As noted earlier, there is reasonably solid evidence that attendance at the highest-prestige institutions has real payoffs in post-graduation outcomes such as income and occupational status so, in recent years, lower-income students' movement into higher-income careers has been constrained in good part by the increasingly powerful mediating mechanism of status-differentiated entry into higher education. It is not solely in the elite institutions that we see this at work: students enroll in institutions, at certain times and at credit-load levels, in ways that are increasingly connected to their SES origins. The nation's postsecondary students appear increasingly diverse socioeconomically and in race/ethnicity and gender when we examine college enrollments at the most aggregated level, but as we move toward a focus on full-time students in highly regarded four-year institutions, the population grows decreasingly diverse. Put another way, as affordability of different postsecondary options declines, stratification and social reproduction rise.

In this sense, in the current context, our colleges and universities arguably have become increasingly complicit in the very social ills their students have been vociferously protesting. The wry Harvard student had it just right. Yet, it's important to remember that the institutions themselves are not at all in full control of their role in society, and are in fact only one of a sizable number of players in these processes. Governments for years invited acceptance of the notion of expanding educational opportunity as a public responsibility. Through the historic low and no-tuition policies of many public institutions and the remarkable expansion of student aid in the years following the U.S. Higher Education Act of 1965, higher-education leaders came to take for granted the continuing partnership of state and federal governments with institutions in financing attendance for lower- and middle-income students (Hearn, 2001; McPherson and Shapiro, 2001). As government's role in this partnership has eroded, blaming the institutions for the aftermath is simplistic. With their budgets for student aid highly constrained, and rising tuitions a necessity, institutions have few choices but to direct admissions and aid policies for students toward maintaining financial solvency, at the risk of further constraining educational opportunity. They need to craft a student body whose composition helps assure not only their academic vitality but also their financial health, and if that imposes growing limits on the socioeconomic diversity of the institution, then that can be a price worth paying for survival.

Where then, to turn for answers? If colleges and universities increasingly serve as preservers of origin statuses, rather than vehicles for mobility, and if both their leaders and policymakers feel constrained by inexorable limitations on their ability to direct resources to ameliorating the problems, then one could argue that hope lies mainly with greater efficiency and more effective targeting of private and government funding. And there, we've been before. Federal student aid programs are a central component of ensuring equality of higher educational opportunity in this country. Earlier (Hearn, 1993), I argued that the federal student-aid programs lacked *philosophical coherence, well-considered patterns of policy development, programmatic clarity and distinctiveness, access to managerially needed information, a strong and supportive interest-group coalition, a beneficent resource environment*, and a *robust client base*. Yet, over several decades, the programs had grown remarkably, and helped assure opportunity for millions. I termed this situation a paradox. Revisiting the same points about decade later (Hearn, 2001), I found limited change over these fronts. Now, almost two decades later, the paradox surely remains.

Perhaps addressing that enduring paradox presents a way forward. Much of my earlier focus was on inefficiency. The continuing inefficiencies have real costs. Is it possible to imagine a federal aid application that is easily understandable to its clients, and a need-analysis system that is straightforward in its calculations and clear-cut in its individual applications to different attendance scenarios? Could we further winnow the supply of federal aid programs, removing duplication and streamlining client and institutional decision-making? Might it be possible to re-evaluate federal programs that allocate funds based on formulas that favor, in result if not design, greater numbers of privileged students? The campus-based aid programs, for example, are currently targeted on institutions that tend to serve lower proportions of lower-income students (Smole, 2005). Can federal policymakers work with those at various other levels to more effectively employ available research to design, implement, and continually evaluate information and pre-college counseling programs for prospective students and their families, especially those for whom college enrollment remains a clouded dream? Can we better ensure that students are provided not only well designed services but also given powerful incentives to *access and use* informational material and to *actively engage* with counseling programs?

And, importantly, might it be possible to reinvigorate the notion of a partnership around the equality of opportunity agenda? Might federal, state, private, and institutional actors do what needs to be done to create collaboration and shared goal-setting and collaboration in this arena, rather than lobbing accusations toward each other, as has so often been the case recently? Realistically, we all know that we are in "the new normal," with all that entails. Tough times at all levels lead to shrunken student-aid packages and higher tuition levels which, in concert with the continuing economic stagnation, are leading to less college affordability, pointing in turn to changes in enrollment behaviors toward more part-time attendance, less expensive institutional choices, longer periods to graduation, and greater drop-out, especially among the economically vulnerable. Ultimately, the results are greater stratification and lowered socioeconomic mobility in the society. As a start, we need more dialogue among the parties, with the goal of resisting this unfolding debacle. Physically, the commotion at the gates may be quieting now. Metaphorically, however, we ignore its implications at great risk.

References

11Alive News. (2011). Police evict "occupy" protest group from UGa's Arch. Online story, October 20, 2011. Available at http://www.11alive.com/news/article/209753/40/

ATHENS- Police-evict-Occupy-protestgroup-from-UGAs -Arch.

Bailey, M. J. and Dynarski, S. M. (2011). Gains and gaps: Changing inequality in U.S. college entry and completion. In G. J. Duncan and R. J. Murnane (Eds.), *Whither Opportunity? Rising Inequality and the Uncertain Life Chances of Low-Income Children*. New York: Russell Sage Foundation.

Bastedo, M. N. and Jaquette, O. (2011). Low-income students and the dynamics of higher education stratification. *Educational Evaluation and Policy Analysis, 33*(3), 318–339.

Bourdieu, P. and Passeron, J-C. (1977). *Reproduction in Education, Society and Culture*. Thousand Oaks, CA: Sage.

Bowen, H. (1977). *Investment in Learning*. San Francisco: Jossey-Bass.

Bowen, W. G., Kurweil, M. A., and Tobin, E. M. (2005). *Equity and Excellence in American Higher Education*. Charlottesville: University of Virginia Press.

Bowles, S. and Gintis, H. (1976). *Schooling in Capitalist America: Educational Reform and the Contradictions of Economic Life*. New York: Basic Books.

Cabrera, A. F., Burkum, K. R., and La Nasa, S. (2011). Pathways to a four-year degree: Determinants and transfer and degree completion. In A. Seidman (Ed.), *College Student Retention: A Formula for Student Success* (pp. 155–214). Westport, CT: Praeger.

Carmichael, M. and Baker, B. (2011). Occupy Harvard left up to students. Boston.com, November 11, 2011. Available at http://articles.boston.com/2011-11/news/30387781_1 _harvard-yard-protesters-tents.

Dale, S. B. and Krueger, A. B. (2002). Estimating the payoff of attending a more selective college: An application of selection on observables and unobservables. *Quarterly Journal of Economics, 107*(4), 1491–1527.

Dominell, K. (2012). Occupy higher ed. *University Business*, January. http://www.universitybusiness.com/article/occupy -higher-ed

Hearn, J. C. (1993). The paradox of growth in federal aid for college students: 1965–1990. In J. C. Smart (Ed.), *Higher Education: Handbook of Theory and Research* (Volume IX, pp. 94–153). New York: Agathon.

Hearn, J. C. (2001). Epilogue to "The paradox of growth in federal aid for college students: 1965–1990." In M. B. Paulsen and J. C. Smart (Eds.), *The Finance of Higher Education: Theory, Research, Policy, and Practice* (pp. 316-320). New York: Agathon Press.

Inside Higher Education. (November 14, 2011). Tensions over Occupy protests on campus. Available at http://www .insidehighered.com/quicktakes/2011/11/14/tensions -over-occupy protests-campuses.

Kreuger, A. (2012). The rises and consequences of inequality in the United States. Address to the Center for American Progress, Washington, DC, by the Chairman, Council of Economic Advisors. Available at http://www.whitehouse .gov/sites/default/files/krueger_cap_speech_final_remarks .pdf.

Krupnick, M. (2011). UC Berkeley policy defend Occupy crackdown, say tents won't be tolerated. MercuryNews.com, November 10, 2011. Available at http://www.mercurynews .com/occupy-oakland/ci_19306598.

McMahon, Walter W. (2009). *Higher Learning, Greater Good: The Private and Social Benefits of Higher Education.* Baltimore: Johns Hopkins University Press.

McPherson, M. S. and Shapiro, M. O. (1998). *The Student Aid Game: Meeting Need and Rewarding Talent in American Higher Education.* Princeton, NJ: Princeton University Press.

McPherson, M. S. and Shapiro, M. O. (2001). The end of the student aid era?: Higher education finance in the United

States. In M. C. Johanek (Ed.), *A Faithful Mirror: Reflections on the College Board and Education in America* (pp. 335–376). New York: College Board.

Obama, B. (2011). Remarks by the president on the economy in Osawatomie, KS, December 6, 2011. Available at http://www.whitehouse.gov/the-press-office/2011/12/06/remarks-president economy-osawatomie-kansas.

Raftery, A. E. and Hout, M. (1993). Maximally maintained inequality: Expansion, reform and opportunity in Irish education, 1921–1975. *Sociology of Education, 66*, 41–62.

Smole, D. P. (2005). *The Campus-Based Financial Aid Programs: A Review and Analysis of the Allocation of Funds to Institutions and the Distribution of Aid to Students.* Congressional Research Service Report for Congress RL32775. Washington, DC: Congressional Research Service.

Thomas, S. L. and Zhang, L. (2005). Post-baccalaureate wage growth within four years of graduation: The effects of college quality and college major. *Research in Higher Education, 46*(4), 427–459.

International Perspectives on the Rising Cost of Higher Education

D. Bruce Johnstone, Distinguished Service Professor, State University of New York and Director of the International Comparative Higher Education Finance and Accessibility Project

The costs of higher education in most countries have been rising steeply, both for individual colleges and universities and for systems or countries. The cost drivers in all countries are mainly two. The first is the tendency of unit, or per-student, costs in higher education, as in virtually all labor-intensive, productivity resistant, enterprises, to mirror at least the annual increases in faculty and staff compensation. That is, unlike the goods-producing, extractive, and agricultural sectors of economies in which a continuous substitution of capital and technology for labor lowers costs and generates real economic growth, the addition of capital and technology to colleges and universities may make them more *productive*, in the sense of being able to produce more written products and even to teach more effectively (e.g., with ubiquitous computers, digital libraries, PowerPoint projection, and the like), but it almost never make them *less costly*. Thus, as long as there is wage and compensation growth in the larger economies (driven by the real productivity gains), and as long as the compensation of faculty and staff tends to track all other compensation gains, the unit costs in higher education will increase at rates in excess of costs generally—and thus at rates greater than the prevailing rates of inflation (Baumol and Bowen, 1966; Johnstone 2001).

The second cost driver, which impacts systems and countries more than institutions and which magnifies the underlying annual increases in per-student costs, are the even more rapidly increasing enrollments. Enrollments in tertiary education worldwide increased from some 15 million in 1980 to more than 139.4 million in 2006, to as much as 150 million by the time of the 2009 UNESCO World Conference on Higher Education (Teichler, 2009; Altbach 2009). These increasing enrollments, fuelled by the realization that higher education is a way to higher incomes, greater status, more life options, and simply a way to get out of one's village, have been the product of three main forces: (1) demographics, or the growth of the college-going age cohorts, which is especially high in most low- and middle-income countries (although low or even negative in Japan, Russia, and some other European countries); (2) the growth in secondary school completion rates, which are also increasing rapidly in the low- and middle-income countries and which magnify the underlying growth in country age cohorts (although secondary school completion rates may be near saturation in many of the advanced industrialized countries); and (3) increasing levels, or amounts, of education per initial matriculate, which tend to be increasing in all countries as persistence and completion rates edge upwards and as graduates, often facing high rates of first degree graduate unemployment, go on for second degrees to be more competitive in crowded job markets.

These enrollment drivers differ greatly among countries, but are especially forceful in countries that combine high birth rates and low initial participation rates—which combination is particularly striking in Asia (with the exception of high-middle and high income countries like Japan, Korea, Taiwan, and Singapore) and most of the countries in Latin America, and Africa. From 1980 through 2007, for example, higher educational enrollments in Indonesia grew by well over 400 percent, Vietnam well over 600 percent, Malaysia by a factor of 11, and China by a factor of well over 12 (Asian Development Bank, 2008).

Thus, it is not just that the worldwide costs and revenue needs of higher education are high—although they are. It is that these costs, and especially the consequent revenue needs, are annually increasing in most countries at rates far in excess of the prevailing rates of inflation—and most importantly and seriously, at rates in excess of the available increases in governmental revenues. As these costs and revenue needs surge upwards worldwide, they are far outpacing the trajectories of available governmental revenues in almost all countries—and especially in low- and middle income countries, where taxes are difficult and costly to collect as well as frequently regressive, and where the competition for these available governmental revenues is especially great from other claims on public budgets, such as elementary and secondary education, public health, sanitation, public infrastructure, safety nets for the poorest, environmental preservation and restoration, and other socially and politically compelling public needs.

A consequence of these diverging trajectories of higher education's surging costs and revenue needs, on the one hand, and the limited available public revenues on the other, is increasing institutional austerity. This austerity is manifested in low-income countries by overcrowded lecture theatres and laboratories and deteriorating equipment, libraries, and the like—but also (even in the most affluent countries) by stagnant faculty and staff compensation, declining faculty/student ratios, and increasing reliance on part-time and adjunct faculty. In some countries, especially in Latin America and much of East Asia, austerity in public universities has been at least lessened by capping public university enrollments and turning instead to growing *demand -absorbing* private sectors. India, Malaysia, Turkey, South Africa, and other countries have attempted to use computer and instructional technology— which, as stated above have not proven particularly useful in reducing overall per-student costs at most institutions—to establish entirely new Internet universities to deliver distance instruction, especially to remote areas, in order to save on the costs of student living, the costs of expensive university physical plants, and some of the costs of faculty and staff. And a few countries—most notably the so-called *transitional* countries of Russia and the other countries emerging from the former Soviet Union as well as countries in East and Central Europe and in much of East Africa—have capped the enrollments of *governmentally sponsored* (that is, low or no tuition fees) students and begun separate privately sponsored, fee-paying, tracks within their public universities.

Finally, in almost all countries, the diverging trajectories between higher education's surging costs and increasingly limited governmental revenues is leading to a search for other-than-governmental revenues. Although this search is leading many countries to encourage faculty and institutional entrepreneurship as well as to seek US-style philanthropy (with little success), the most common policy of supplementing the increasingly inadequate governmental revenue is through a shift of some costs to parents and students, commonly termed *cost-sharing*. Cost sharing is partly a statement of fact: that the high and rising costs of higher education are *shared* mainly among four parties, or bearers of these costs, namely: (1) governments via taxes and deficit financing; (2) parents via current contributions, savings, or borrowing; (3) students via term-time and vacation earnings and borrowing; and (4) philanthropy via endowments, foundations, and current giving. Cost-sharing is also a description of the important—and both politically and ideologically contested—shifting of these costs from predominate reliance in most countries on governments (or taxpayer), to being shared with parents and students (Johnstone 1986, 2004, 2006; Johnstone and Marcucci, 2010; Marcucci and Johnstone, 2007).

Cost-sharing takes many forms, including:

- policies to charging tuition fees where public higher education was formerly free—as in the UK and China in 1997, or many European countries in the first decade of the 21st century (albeit most on a relatively nominal basis, with the Nordic countries, Switzerland, France and most of the German Länder continuing to resist tuition fees);

- very steep increases in tuition fees (that is, in the parent/student share of rising costs) where they had already existed, as in the United States, Japan, and many provinces of Canada, particularly since the beginning of the 21st century);

- the addition of private fee-paying tracks in countries that maintain smaller, selective free or low tuition fee public universities, as in Russia and many other former Communist / socialist countries as well as in East Africa;

- full- or nearly full-cost fees for food and lodging that was formerly borne by governments (as in most former communist / socialist countries, including China, Vietnam, and Mongolia);

- freezing student grants or bursaries, especially in the face of continuing high inflation, or shifting student financial assistance from grants to loans;

- decreasing governmentally borne subsidies within student loan schemes via increasing interest rates or decreasing the extent of interest-free in-school or grace periods;

- limiting enrollments in public institution and/or the capping the numbers of public institutions, and turning to private tuition fee-dependent colleges and universities to absorb more of the surging demand for higher education.

The costs and finance of higher education remain enormously complex, rapidly changing, and politically and ideologically contested, especially in an international comparative context. Among the questions that will continue to be contested, both within and among countries and that effectively illustrate the most significant differences and current issues are the following:

1. Can tax revenues to higher education in most countries be significantly and permanently increased from current levels in order to accommodate the steeply rising costs of higher education without shifting more of the burden to parents and students?

2. If the answer to #1 is *no* or *unlikely*, can costs—both the per-student costs of instruction and the system-borne costs of enrolment increases—be driven down further? That is, are there efficiencies yet to be made, such as greatly increased use of technologically aided instruction or shortened degrees that will not significantly erode either quality or accessibility? Or must the increasing austerity in higher education continue to be solved largely on the revenue side, with increasing tuition and other fees?

3. To what degree should public revenues to higher education be divided among the public universities more-or-less equitably (the model of most of Continental Europe), or should countries invest more selectively to boost the prestige of a few universities (as in the United States, the United Kingdom, Canada, Japan, China, and most recently and tentatively [as of 2010] Germany)? Or similarly, should countries shift some resources from their costlier research universities to the (somewhat) less costly colleges and short-cycle tertiary institutions?

4. Should greater higher educational efficiency and cost reductions in public colleges and universities, largely through managerial flexibility and greater reallocatiblity of resources, be pursued through changing the status of public institutions in more countries from *governmental agencies* to *public corporatizations* (as, for example, in the United States, the United Kingdom, Japan [beginning in 2004], and most recently in France)?

5. As to tuition fees, which are increasing in some form throughout much of the world, but which continue to be resisted in the Nordic countries, some other European countries, much of Latin America, and most of Central and West Africa: should they be *up-front*, expected mainly from parents (to the degree to which they are financially able), or should they be *deferred*, and paid by students in the form of loans? Expected parental contributions and up-front tuition fees, at least for first-degree students, are the model in most countries, including the United States, Canada. Continental Europe (where tuition fees exist), China, Japan, and most other countries in the world with tuition fees. In France and Germany, although with no or very low tuition fees, parents are still expected to support their children's costs of student living. However, in Australia as in England, Wales and Northern Ireland, tuition fees, while relatively significant, are *deferred* (that is, expected of students rather than parents) and are repaid in the form of income contingent loans. Thus higher education in England (which is almost entirely public) is correctly said to be *free at the time of matriculation*, even though it has become, as of 2012, a very expensive public university system, and most students will owe a significant debt upon completion, in addition to whatever debts they may have accumulated for their living expenses. (In the Nordic countries, by contrast, governments pay the entire costs of instruction, but students, as financially emancipated young

adults, rather than their parents are expected to pay for their generally high living expenses through student loans.)

6. Finally, where tuition fees exist and are generally expected to be paid by parents, how should these fees vary? The *dual track* tuition fee policy, in which instruction is free or nearly so for the governmentally sponsored students, but quite high for all who are admitted to the private, or fee-paying, tracks, may benefit mainly the privileged and thus be opposed by mot scholars and policy analysts, is far more politically palatable than would be the introduction of meaningful tuition fees for all. In addition, tuition fees can and do also vary by program or academic major more in other countries than in the United States, where tuition fees at the undergraduate level are generally the same for all degree programs at the same institution. However, in most other countries, where there are few of what Americans term *general education* courses taken by all students regardless of program, tuition fees tend to be considerably higher for programs in the highest demand, such as management, computer science, medicine (which is a first degree at most universities outside the United States), and the English language.

References

Altbach, Phillip G., Liz Reisberg, and Laura E. Rumbley. (2009). *Trends in Global Higher Education: Tracking an Academic Revolution*. Paris: UNESCO. A report prepared for the World Conference on Higher Education.

Asian Development Bank. (2008). *Education and Skills: Strategies for Accelerated Development in Asia and the Pacific*, Downloaded February 5, 2012 http://www.adb.org/Documents/Studies/Education-Skills-Strategies-Development/.

Baumol, William J. and William G. Bowen,. (1966). *Performing Arts: The Economic Dilemma*. New York: Twentieth Century Fund.

Johnstone, D. Bruce. (2006). *Financing Higher Education: Cost-Sharing in International Perspective*. Boston: Boston College Center for International Higher Education; and Rotterdam: Sense Publishers.

Johnstone, D. Bruce. (2004). The Economics and Politics of Cost Sharing in Higher Education: Comparative Perspectives, *Economics of Education Review* 20:4, pp. 403–410.

Johnstone, D. Bruce. (2001). "Those 'Out of Control' Costs," in Philip G. Altbach, D. Bruce Johnstone, and Patricia J. Gumport, eds., *In Defense of the American Public University*. Baltimore: Johns Hopkins University Press.

Johnstone, D. Bruce. (1986). *Sharing the Costs of Higher Education: Student Financial Assistance in the United Kingdom, the Federal Republic of Germany, France, Sweden, and the United States*. New York: College Entrance Examination Board.

Johnstone, D. Bruce and Pamela Marcucci. (2010). *Financing Higher Education Worldwide: Who Pays? Who Should Pay?* Baltimore: Johns Hopkins University Press.

Marcucci, Pamela N. and D. Bruce Johnstone. (2007). Tuition Policies in a Comparative Perspective: Theoretical and Political Rationales. *Journal of Higher Education Policy and Management*, 29:1, pp. 25–40.

Teichler, Ulrich and Sandra Bürger. (2009). Student Enrollments and Graduation Trends in the OECD Area: What Can We Learn from International Statistics?, in OECD (Organization for Economic Cooperation and Development) *Higher Education to 2030, Volume 1: Demography*. Paris: Centre for Educational Research and Innovation, pp. 151–172.

4 Profiles

In higher education, as in baseball, one cannot tell the players without a program. This is especially useful advice for following the issues associated with rising costs of college. It is also true that in higher education, one cannot tell the programs without a program. To provide useful guides, this chapter sets forth a concise outline of the profiles, respectively, of key organizations and programs, persons, and publications integral to the economics and financing of colleges and universities in the United States—and with selected attention to international higher education.

Key Organizations and Programs

Higher education in the United States is distinctive, perhaps unique, worldwide in its reliance on a complex blend of federal and state agencies along with numerous private not-for-profit centers and institutes, along with commercial and lobbying groups, involved in shaping and providing services and analyses related to the finances of going to college. Many of these are housed in Washington, DC and, as such, are illustrative of the creative energy (and tension) as representatives of each continuously interact to review and discuss new and old policies and programs. The groups range in size, complexity, and purpose.

(Steve Shepard/iStockphoto.com)

Some are large, highly professional bureaucracies whose primary function is to administer programs. Others may be small, relatively new start-up think tanks, foundations, or nonprofit organizations.

Over the past half-century an increasing number of lobbying groups representing such commercial and for-profit entities as bankers and loan agencies have joined the ranks. In addition, a number of established higher education associations are located in and around the One DuPont Circle area of Washington, DC. Although there is a concentration of organizations in Washington, the network of key higher education groups extends to agencies and offices in state capitols, along with headquarters for several national groups in New York, Boston, Chicago, the San Francisco Bay area, and other metropolitan sites nationwide.

Whether in formal congressional hearings or informal work groups and conversations, the numerous, diverse groups listed and summarized here are fluid in their continual movement among roles of allies, advocates, analysts, and adversaries. This fluidity is a defining hallmark of the politics and policies of higher education at the state and federal levels.

American Council on Education (ACE): http://www.acenet.edu

ACE, founded in 1918, represents the chief officers (presidents and chancellors) of a range of U.S. accredited, degree-granting institutions. These include both for-profit and nonprofit institutions, from community colleges to four-year institutions. ACE member institutions serve approximately 80 percent of current college students. ACE also represents over 200 directors of organizations and associations related to higher education. Through advocacy, research, and programming initiatives, ACE informs higher education leaders on 21st-century higher education issues and works as the main coordinating entity for U.S. higher education. ACE's goal is to influence public policy to advocate for a greater nation and world.

American Education Society (AES)

Founded in 1815 as the American Education Society of Pious Youth for the Gospel Ministry, AES represented one of the first and best examples of large-scale student financial aid programs whose purpose was to attract impoverished yet talented, dedicated young men to college—as the first and required step for ordination as Protestant ministers who would then serve as missionaries in underrepresented locales. Its founding leaders included a former president of Harvard and influential Protestant clergy and professors in New England. Between 1816 and 1866, the AES attracted a large number of donors and awarded generous college scholarships—about 200 in 1826, peaking with 1,100 scholarships in 1836, for a cumulative total of 5,302 scholarships. The AES was significant because it demonstrated the tradition of private donors and voluntary associations for supporting higher education. Its insistence that recipients pursue formal studies as part of a bachelor's degree program at an established liberal arts colleges helped to shape the concept of a "learned profession" in the United States. Its approach to student financial aid included the condition that recipients agree to maintain good academic standing, complete a college degree, and then continue studies and service. This model later would be adapted by federal agencies to attract and retain talented students in such professional fields as medicine, allied health, social work, and teaching. Excerpts from the original charter for the AES, published in 1816, appears in Chapter 5.

American Educational Society (AES): http://www .aessuccess.org

AES is a branch of the Pennsylvania Higher Education Assistance Agency (PHEAA) that, in conjunction with PHEAA's other loan servicer, FedLoan Servicing, provides guarantees and services for loan products, including private and alternative loans as well as Federal Family Education Loan Programs (FFELP). AES serves millions of borrowers nationwide. The Pennsylvania General

Assembly created PHEAA in 1963. It has evolved into a leading student aid organization. PHEAA provides loan guarantees, servicing, and other programs related to student financial aid and administering Pennsylvania's state-funded student aid offerings.

American Enterprise Institute for Public Policy Research (AEI): http://www.aei.org/

AEI is dedicated to public policy research and defines itself as "a community of scholars and supporters committed to expanding liberty, increasing individual opportunity and strengthening free enterprise." AEI pursues these unchanging ideals through independent thinking, open debate, reasoned argument, facts, and the highest standards of research and exposition. AEI's education policy division has published numerous anthologies and research reports on topics such as the student loan industry, cost-effectiveness in community colleges, factors and trends in tuition policies, and other topics related to costs of higher education. Without regard for politics or prevailing fashion, AEI dedicates its work to a more prosperous, safer, and more democratic nation and world. The education policy studies department focuses on issues of accountability, innovation, and entrepreneurship in K-12 and postsecondary education. Three times a year, the education policy department hosts the Future of American Higher Education Working Group, a gathering of the nation's top higher education scholars, practitioners, and entrepreneurs that is designed to discuss pressing issues and generate intellectual discussion in higher education reform.

American Institutes for Research (AIR): http://www.air.org/about/

AIR is a not-for-profit, nonpartisan behavioral and social science research organization founded in 1946. One of the largest of these types of organizations in the world, AIR employs over 1,500 experts from various fields, seeking innovative ways to approach issues. AIR's work is conducted independently and objectively, as its primary aspiration is to utilize effective ideas and methods to enhance life in the United States and abroad. In 2012, AIR became host and home for the Delta Cost Project on revenues and spending in higher education.

Association of American Universities (AAU): http://www.aau.edu

The AAU, founded in 1900, is a nonprofit organization comprised of the 61 foremost research universities in North America. AAU was initially established to enhance the international reputation of U.S. research universities. AAU currently focuses on issues that are significant to research-intensive institutions. These include undergraduate and graduate education, research funding, and research policy. AAU's primary activities advance issues pertaining to member institutions, including federal government relations, policy studies, and public affairs. Member universities are considered cutting edge in terms of national interests (e.g., economics, security, and public welfare), scholarship, and innovation. AAU works to foster a constructive relationship between the federal government and research universities. Fifty-nine member institutions are U.S. universities, and three are Canadian. In the United States, AAU universities award over half of all doctoral degrees, 55 percent of which are in science and engineering.

Association for the Study of Higher Education (ASHE)

ASHE is a national organization for advanced research and scholarship on higher education issues, including access, equity, and costs of going to college. Its conferences and research symposia devote great attention to attrition, retention, graduation, and affordability in higher education. ASHE also sponsors a major publication on these topics, *The Review of Higher Education*, a scholarly peer-reviewed journal that is discussed in greater detail later in this chapter in the "Publications" section. Founded in 1974, ASHE has sponsored and recognized such scholars as economists Howard R. Bowen, Edward St. John, William G. Bowen and such research organizations as IHEP. Each year its annual conference features a public policy forum. Membership includes established scholars, professors, policy analysts, and graduate students.

Brookings Institution: http://www.brookings.edu

The Washington-based Brookings Institution is consistently referenced as the most influential, quoted, and trusted think tank. It utilizes independent research addressing public policy issues to promote visionary, practical solutions for policy issues. The Brookings Institution's efforts advance three primary goals: strengthening American democracy; promoting American economic and social welfare, security, and opportunities; and fostering a candid, secure, flourishing, and collective international system.

Carnegie Foundation for the Advancement of Teaching (CFAT): http://www.carnegiefoundation.org/about-us/about-carnegie

CFAT was founded by U.S. steel magnate Andrew Carnegie in 1905. Its historical focus is the improvement of teaching and learning. As an independent research and policy center, CFAT works to address practical problems of education by collaborating with educational scholars, practitioners, and other experts. Currently, CFAT's research approach is based on four principles: shared learning, improvement of successful techniques, continued creation of new knowledge, and dissemination of practical findings. In 1970, CFAT began collecting data on colleges and universities to classify institutions by various criteria. This framework has been updated over time to reflect the changing landscape of higher education. It is widely adopted by researchers as representative in terms of primary differences between institutions, to control for institutional variance, and to establish that sampled institutions, students, or faculty are representative of their populations. As of 2012, the Carnegie framework utilized six classifications. The framework includes a basic classification (which is the traditional format for the Carnegie classification system); undergraduate and graduate instructional program classification; enrollment profile and undergraduate profile classifications; and a size and setting classification.

Center for College Affordability and Productivity (CCAP)
http://centerforcollegeaffordability.org/

CCAP is a Washington-based, not-for profit, independent research organization, founded in 2006 by economist Richard Vedder, who serves also as the center's director. CCAP's research agenda addresses issues facing higher education institutions throughout the nation. Currently, its focus includes student financial aid policies, efficiency issues, faculty and staff productivity, for-profit higher education, and accreditation. Some of CCAP's publications include pieces on college athletics, endowments, governmental spending and regulations, as well as studies on institutions within certain states.

College Entrance Examination Board (CEEB):
www.collegeboard.org

In 1900, the CEEB was established to provide standardized entrance examinations to students interested in attending colleges and universities. The exams, known as College Boards, were intended to assist institutions in identifying suitable applicants for admission. Although the acronym CEEB is still used for some purposes, the organization primarily uses the shorter name College Board. By 1926, the College Board replaced the original exams with the Scholastic Aptitude Test (SAT). The board has continued to use versions of the SAT over the years. When criticism over the SAT's ability to test "aptitude" arose, the name was changed to Scholastic Assessment Test. Currently, the SAT is comprised of a reasoning test and individual subject tests. The board has dropped the long form of the test's name, and it is referred to strictly as SAT (reasoning test) and SAT Subject Tests.

In 1947, the College Board collaborated with the American Council on Education (ACE) and the Carnegie Foundation for the Advancement of Teaching (CFAT) to create the nonprofit Educational Testing Service to administer exams. In 1955, the board acquired administration of the Advance Placement (AP) Program, where high school students can engage in college-level courses and apply for college credit upon completion. In 2000, the College Board started CollegeEd to encourage early college preparation and readiness. In 2010, after years of working with state agencies to address college preparatory issues for underserved students, the College Board founded its Advocacy and Policy Center to conduct research and offer recommendations regarding college preparedness. The board concentrates on college readiness, college connection and success, and advocacy. Programs include Readiness (Advanced Placement (AP), SpringBoard, ReadiStep, CollegeEd, CLEP, PSAT/NMSQT, EXCELerator, College Connection and Success: SAT, SAT Subject Tests, and SAT Readiness Tools, Student Search Service, College Planning, College Search, CSS/Financial Aid PROFILE, Scholarship Search, and its Advocacy and Policy Center.

Congressional Hispanic Caucus Institute's Education Center (CHCI) http://www.chci.org/education_center

In 1987, CHCI created its education center, to assist Latino students in navigating the educational process. Its mission is to develop the next generation of Latino leaders through education and career and development opportunities. CHCI provides information to students, parents, and educators to assist Latino youth to complete high school, attend college, and develop rewarding careers.

ConnectEDU

ConnectEDU represents a new generation of innovative institutes and applied research organizations that provide students as consumers with increasing access to the data and decision-making information previously considered the exclusive domain of college and university admissions offices or to highly select, affluent constituencies. As such, it energizes the dynamics of college choice and affordability. Its founder, Craig Powell, an alumnus of Brown University, has brought to this organization an interest in and personal knowledge of the difficulties children from remote geographic areas and modest income families face in navigating the complex maze of educational planning, college choice, and professional preparation. Located in Boston, ConnectEDU is a technology company, founded and grounded in education, committed to transitioning 21st-century learners on their pathways from school to college to career, helping them realize their potential, achieve a secure financial future, and ultimately connect to life's possibilities. ConnectEDU is the world's largest educational network, with nearly 20 million registered learners; over 4,000 educational institutions; and 130,000 employers.

Consortium on Financing Higher Education (COFHE): http://web.mit.edu/cofhe

Formed in the mid-1970s, the Consortium on Financing Higher Education (COFHE) consists of 31 highly selective, independent liberal arts institutions. The consortium has two offices in Cambridge, Massachusetts, where space is provided by both the Massachusetts Institute of Technology (MIT) and Johns Hopkins University, as well as an office in Washington, DC.

COFHE membership is voluntary and supported by dues paid by member institutions. COFHE is a think tank that collects data from member institutions in addition to conducting research and policy analysis. The principal focus of COFHE's work is access, affordability, and assessment of undergraduate education, particularly concerning admissions, financial aid, and cost. COFHE has created several surveys to examine undergraduate experiences. The Washington office tracks legislative matters of financial aid, tax policy, and related college cost issues.

Cornell Higher Education Research Institute, Cornell University (CHERI): http://www.ilr.cornell.edu/cheri/

CHERI was founded in 1998 as higher education research organization. The founding director and principal researcher is Professor Ronald G. Ehrenberg, a contributing author to Chapter 3 in this reference book. Its principal funding has come from the Atlantic Philanthropies and the Andrew W. Mellon Foundation. Additional funding has come from the Alfred P. Sloan Foundation, Lumina Foundation, and TIAA-CREF. The institute has an interdisciplinary mission, and professionals involved with CHERI are based out of five different colleges within Cornell University, as well as institutions around the globe. CHERI has several research interests associated with higher education costs, academic status, access, and retention. Currently, CHERI focuses on implications of financial resource distribution among institutions, burgeoning costs and significance of university science programs, and financial challenges to public institutions. In addition, CHERI researchers address faculty governance issues, enhancement of humanities and social sciences PhD programs, and access and retention rates within science, technology, and mathematics (STEM) fields and higher education as a whole.

Council of Independent Colleges (CIC): http://www.cic.edu

Established in 1956, CIC is an association of nonprofit, private (independent) colleges and universities.

CIC offers support for institutional leaders, promotes institutional excellence, and works to increase public awareness of the benefits that private higher education affords to society. It is the sole national association with the purpose of providing direct services to private colleges and universities. CIC also offers seminars, conferences, and additional programs to enhance the quality of education, institutional organization, and institutional recognition. It also supports the development efforts of private colleges and universities. CIC is open to all small and mid-sized private academic institutions, including selective liberal arts colleges, mid-sized private universities, religious colleges, historically black colleges, and single-gender institutions. Two-year private colleges and nonprofits that support the goals of independent higher education are also eligible to join CIC. Several organizations are affiliated with CIC as affiliate and state fund members.

Delta Costs Project at American Research Institutes: http://www.deltacostproject.org/index.asp

The Delta Cost Project at American Research Institutes is an independent nonprofit policy research organization with the mission of improving public transparency about higher education finance, including comparative data on the ways that institutions spend their resources. Founded in 2006 and based in Washington, DC, it is the only national organization that organizes data on revenues and spending for both public and nonprofit higher education. In 2012, the Association of Institutes of Research (AIR) assumed responsibility for the Delta Cost Project. Delta Cost Project data are derived from federal sources, adjusted for changes over time, normalized to put spending into context by Full Time Enrollment (FTE), and adjusted for inflation. This research includes a commitment to creating analytic tools to document trends in college spending, understand where and why college costs are increasing, translate technical accounting information into benchmarks for institutional and policy audiences, identify and promote best practices that generate the greatest return on investment for access and success, and promote institutional and policy strategies for improved productivity.

Education Sector (ES): http://www.educationsector.org

Education Sector, an independent think tank founded in 2005, is a nonprofit, nonpartisan organization that works to enhance existing educational reform initiatives and develop solutions for the most critical educational issues in the United States. Education Sector conducts research and policy analyses, and it provides opinion and editorial pieces to national news publications. ES presents its findings related to legislative issues and communications with policy stakeholders. Education Sector's target audience consists of federal, state, and local policymakers, educators, and media. The group attempts to offer policymakers unbiased, clear policy reports to support educational reform. Education Sector's expertise is in areas related to both K-12 and higher education.

Education Trust http://www.edtrust.org

The Education Trust's goal is to promote academic achievement for all P-12 students, particularly those from low income or minority backgrounds. The Trust advances this goal by partnering with educational stakeholders, including policymakers as well as community and business leaders, to offer practical assistance that will provide strong service to all students at all levels of education. To advance its goals, the Education Trust analyzes data from local, state, and national levels. Based on its research, the Education Trust engages in policy debates at state and national levels in an effort to influence policies that will assist students and institutions reach high achievement levels.

Educational Testing Service (ETS): http://www.ets.org/

ETS is a nonprofit organization that was established by the College Entrance Examination Board (CEEB), the Carnegie

Foundation for the Advancement of Teaching (CFAT), and the American Council on Education (ACE) in 1947. Each group remitted some of its assets and testing functions to form the centralized testing agency ETS. CEEB furnished assessments such as the Scholastic Aptitude Test (SAT) and the law School Admissions Test (LSAT). The Carnegie Foundation for the Advancement of Teaching (CFAT) provided its Graduate Record Examination (GRE) and Pre-Engineering Inventory. Finally, the American Council on Education (ACE) gave ETS its National Teacher Exams and Cooperative Test Service. ETS's early clients included a large number of postsecondary institutions, the Association of American Medical Colleges (AAMC), the U.S. Atomic Energy Commission, the State Department, and corporations such as Pepsi Cola. Throughout the 1960s, the number of individuals taking ETS tests, as well as the number of assessments available, continued to grow. ETS had become the leading U.S. testing agency by the mid-1970s.

ETS has faced criticisms that its exams are biased toward upper middle class audiences, which has led it to adjust its materials. Moreover, the proliferation of test preparation services, such as those provided by Kaplan Educational Centers and Princeton Review, has resulted in concerns over the security of ETS's copyrighted materials. ETS has sought protection by altering and removing some of its questions, and requesting that employees of such companies refrain from repeatedly taking ETS tests. By the 1990s, ETS had expanded its offerings, including computer-based exams and courses for additional areas outside of higher education. It administered courses for elementary schools, as well as exams for professionals such as manicurists and retail managers. A large amount of its revenue, however, was derived from administration of College Board programs. ETS eventually established for-profit subsidiaries— for example, Capstar—to undertake its assessment activities for governmental agencies and industry. Additional for-profit subsidiaries include ETS Technologies (for online learning) and ETS K-12 Works (for state scholastic testing). In recent years, ETS has acquired some of its competitors in the testing world. Its main competitors include ACT and Pearson VUE. ETS administered the Graduate Management Admissions Test (GMAT) for approximately 50 years, but in 2003, the Graduate Management Admission Council awarded that contract to Pearson VUE. Today, ETS also serves international students and employers. ETS administers, and scores over 50 million tests per year. Its tests include the Test of English as a Foreign Language (TOEFL), TOEIC (English language tests for non-native speakers), GRE tests, and PRAXIS Series (teacher certification exams used in numerous states).

Hispanic Association of Colleges & Universities (HACU): www.hacu.net

Eighteen inaugural institutions founded HACU in 1986. Today, HACU represents hispanic-serving institutions (HSIs) in the United States (including Puerto Rico), Latin America, Spain, and Portugal. In the United States, HACU members total less than 10 percent of colleges and universities, yet they educate over two thirds of all Hispanic postsecondary students. In the 1990s, HACU lobbied Congress for formal recognition of campuses with high Hispanic enrollment as HSIs, leading to federal appropriations for those institutions. HACU's mission is to advance development of its member institutions, increase access to and quality of Hispanic postsecondary education, and share resources and information with businesses, government, and industry. Focused on the largest minority population in the United States, HACU's Office of Policy Analysis and Information examines issues affecting the success of Hispanic students and HSIs. HACU manages several services: internships, scholarships, and study-abroad programs.

Hispanic Scholarship Fund (HSF): http://www.hsf.net

The Hispanic Scholarship Fund (established in 1975) has granted over $335 million in scholarships. It supports a wide range of educational programs for parents and students, ranging from admissions counseling to postbaccalaureate employment. HSF offers general college scholarships, as well as scholarships specific to current college students, community college transfers, and graduating high school students. In addition, HSF partners with the Gates Millennium Scholars Program. HSF offers awards that are based on need and on merit. Many of its scholarships are cosponsored by companies, for example, Verizon, Procter & Gamble, and ExxonMobil. HSF also collaborates with universities through its University Alliance Program to increase recruitment, retention, and performance of Latino students. Its mission is to raise the number of Hispanic students who pursue bachelor degrees and graduate from colleges and universities.

Institute for College Access & Success: http://www.ticas.org

The Institute for College Access & Success is an independent, nonprofit organization that conducts nonpartisan research and advocates access and affordability for all individuals. The institute works to improve processes and public policies related to higher education. Its current projects include the Project on Student Debt, to increase public knowledge of the implications of rising student debt; Simplifying the FASFA, a streamlined process where application questions can be answered through existing government data; and College InSight, an open website consisting of data and research on issues related to higher education, particularly affordability, diversity, and student success.

Institute of Higher Education Policy (IHEP): http://www.ihep.org/

IHEP is a nonpartisan, nonprofit organization that is committed to improving college access and success in higher education for all students—with a special focus on underserved populations—by providing timely research to inform public policy decisions. Based in Washington, DC, IHEP develops innovative policy as well as practice-oriented research to guide policymakers and education leaders who develop high-impact policies to address our nation's most pressing educational challenges. IHEP offers an independent perspective through a staff that includes some of the most respected professionals in the fields of public policy and research. It is committed to equality of opportunity for all and helps low income, minority, and other historically underrepresented populations gain access to and achieve success in higher education.

International Comparative Higher Education Finance & Accessibility Project (ICHEFAP) http://gse.buffalo.edu/org/inthigheredfinance/

ICHEFAP addresses higher education costs, particularly the rising shift in costs from government to individuals. ICHEFAP is housed in the Graduate School of Education's Center for Comparative and Global Studies in Education at the State University of New York at Buffalo. Shifting costs, that is, "cost sharing" or "revenue diversification," is studied by ICHEFAP as an economic concept based on equity and efficiency, while taking into account concerns that public revenues in most countries cannot maintain increasing enrollment and per-student costs.

ICHEFAP examines areas such as tuition increases in public and private universities, rising student living costs, and mounting utilization of student loans. ICHEFAP's research comprises multiple global initiatives. Current interests include introduction of tuition in China and Europe, reliance on tuition-supported colleges in much of Asia and Latin America, as well as the emergence of private colleges and universities in Russia.

Latino College Dollars: http://www.latinocollegedollars.org

Latino College Dollars, begun in 2005, is an initiative of the Tomás Rivera Policy Institute (TRPI). TRPI is a nonprofit organization that conducts research on significant issues influencing Latino communities. The organization hopes that this research will leadi to informed policy decisions. TRPI is associated with the University of Southern California School of Policy, Planning, and Development, as well as the Institute for Social and Economic Research and Policy at Columbia University. Latino College Dollars arose out of TRPI's 2005 study commissioned by the Walt Disney Company, which concluded that there was an abundance of information about college scholarships posted online, yet much of the data needed updating, was not actively distributed, and often posted only in English. By 2006, additional funding from the Sallie Mae Fund, Walt Disney Company, and Southern California Edison resulted in an original printed scholarship directory, which listed regional organizations that offered grants and scholarships to Latino students in California. Concurrently, AT&T funded the initial online directory, which built upon the print version. The online directory was expanded in 2007, with further funding, to include national grant and scholarship opportunities for eligible Latino students.

Lumina Foundation: http://www.luminafoundation.org

The Lumina Foundation for Education, established in 2000, is an Indianapolis-based private, independent organization. It is currently the largest higher education–focused private foundation. Moreover, Lumina is ranked among the top 40 private foundations for funds awarded. Lumina has invested over $1 billion in research and public policy initiatives. Its primary goal is increasing access to and success in postsecondary education. Its Goal 2025 initiative seeks to increase, by 60 percent, the number of Americans with world-class degrees and credentials by 2025. Lumina's plan includes identification and advancement of effective practices, influence of constructive public policy, and promotion of a public will to change. Lumina has provided grants to several colleges and universities, foundations with similar foci, and additional organizations that continue to work toward enhanced student access and success. Lumina also publishes the educational quarterly *Focus*. In 2010, Lumina committed

$43.4 million toward nearly 100 grants, ranging from awards of a few thousand to millions of dollars.

National Collegiate Athletic Association (NCAA): http://www.ncaa.org/

The NCAA is the major regulatory and coordinating association for intercollegiate athletics nationwide. NCAA involvement with and influence on the costs and prices of undergraduate education comes from their role in setting standards for terms and amounts of athletic grants-in-aid. Related policies include limits on aid and conditions of retention and degree completion, matters about which presidents, provosts, athletic directors, deans of admission, and directors of financial aid are involved and concerned. The NCAA in its role as sponsor and promoter of numerous championship competitions, many of which include broadcast rights as well as ticket sales, is a major source of revenues, which are ultimately channeled from the NCAA to member institutions. The NCAA also is significant in the college costs forum because the expenses of maintaining varsity sports program influences overall campus budgeting, with great variation depending on institutional type and the kind of athletics program a campus opts to offer. The NCAA website provides detailed, comprehensive statistics on the revenues and expenditures of intercollegiate athletics programs, according to individual institutions as well as to collective associations such as conferences and institutional types.

National Association of Independent Colleges and Universities (NAICU): http://www.naicu.edu/

Established in 1976, NAICU represents nonprofit, private colleges and universities on major government issues. NAICU conducts and publishes research on trends within higher education, coordinates activities at the state level, and lobbies policymakers regarding legislation and regulation that affects its members.

In particular, NAICU focuses on student financial aid, taxation, and government regulation. NAICU public initiatives include the Student Aid Alliance and the National Campus Voter Registration Project. The association has over 1,000 members across the United States. Reflecting the diverse landscape of contemporary private higher education, member institutions include liberal arts colleges, research universities, faith-related institutions, and professional and two-year colleges. Moreover, special interests and complementary groups are also members of NAICU. Members of the National Association of Independent College and University State Executives (NAICUSE) and Secretariat also belong to NAICU. To better serve their members, the Foundation for Independent Higher Education (FIHE) and the Council for Independent Colleges (CIC) have agreed to partner with NAICU to increase cooperation and collaboration.

National Center for Education Statistics (NCES): http://nces.ed.gov/

Housed in the U.S. Department of Education and the Institute of Education in Washington, DC, NCES is the principal federal unit for collection and analyses of U.S. and global education data. NCES collects data in areas of early childhood education and development, elementary and secondary education, international education, libraries, and postsecondary education. It is responsible for the National Assessment of Educational Progress (NAEP), also known as the Nation's Report Card, the National Education Longitudinal Study (NELS), and the Education Finance Statistics Center (EDFIN). Perhaps the data most familiar to colleges and universities is IPEDS, the Integrated Postsecondary Education Data System, which is engineered around a number of complementary surveys that collect institution-level data. IPED's system includes all institutions whose main purpose is provision of postsecondary education. The data are related to enrollments, graduation rates, faculty and staff, academic libraries, and institutional finances.

National Center for Public Policy and Higher Education (NCPPHE) http://www.highereducation.org

The National Center was an independent, nonprofit, nonpartisan organization established in 1998. Its mission was to promote public policy, which advances access to and achievement of postsecondary education. The National Center researched issues facing two- and four-year, public and private, and for-profit and nonprofit institutions at the state and national level. The National Center independently researched policy issues related to opportunities for, and attainment of, higher education. The National Center shared its findings with public, civic, business, and higher education leaders. The National Center was sponsored by the nonprofit corporation the Higher Education Policy Institute in San Jose, California. The National Center closed on June 30, 2011; however, its reports are still available online and questions can be directed to the Higher Education Policy Institute.

National Student Clearinghouse: http://www .studentclearinghouse.org

The Clearinghouse, located in Herndon, Virginia, has over 3,300 college and university participants, representing approximately 96 percent of students enrolled in public and private institutions in the United States. The Clearinghouse provides reporting, verification, and research for its participant institutions to organizations such as high schools and postsecondary institutions, student lending agencies, the U.S. Department of Education, and employers.

Student enrollment and degree data are provided by institutions, totaling over 110 million student records. The majority of services to postsecondary institutions are provided for a low fee or no charge. The Clearinghouse offers Family Educational Rights and Privacy Act (FERPA) compliant access to student educational records. Additional Clearinghouse offerings include transcript and research services to assist institutions in addressing budget and staffing distribution to meet student needs.

National Study of Instructional Costs & Productivity (University of Delaware): http://www.udel.edu/IR/cost/index.html

The National Study of Instructional Costs & Productivity at the University of Delaware provides a database to participant institutions that allows them to benchmark areas such as teaching loads, instructional costs, and productivity by discipline. Its basic benchmarking function is based upon the Carnegie Foundation for the Advancements of Teaching (CFAT) institutional classifications, highest degree offered by institutions, and disciplines. Institutions may also define custom benchmarks for data comparison. The database allows personnel to examine questions concerning tenured faculty teaching loads, proportions of undergraduate teaching performed by regular faculty, cost of instruction per student credit hour, and research and service within academic departments, comparative to other institutions.

Nexus Research and Policy Center: http://www.nexusresearch.org/

Nexus Research and Policy Center is an independent, nonpartisan, nonprofit organization founded by former executives of the University of Phoenix. Through the dissemination of its research, the promotion of evidence-based policies, and the development of a robust database, Nexus seeks to improve mutual understanding and cooperation among all higher education sectors (public, private, and proprietary) with the aim of advancing the educational performance of institutions that serve nontraditional students. Nexus applies cognitive science methods and "big data" analytics to help understand and improve teaching and learning processes. It also prepares data-based analyses of pressing policy issues such as the costs and benefits of higher education; the efficacy of affordability, access, and degree completion policies; and the challenges involved with making sound policy based on current data gathering practices.

Organisation for Economic Co-Operation and Development (OECD): http://www.oecd.org/education/

The mission of the OECD is to promote policies that will improve the economic and social well-being of people around the world. With headquarters in Paris, France, the OECD provides a forum in which governments can work together to share experiences and seek solutions to common problems. It includes work with governments to understand what drives economic, social, and environmental change. Projects include measuring productivity and global flows of trade and investment—and analysis of data to predict future trends. The OECD set international standards in numerous areas, from agriculture and tax to the safety of chemicals. Expansion of access to higher education has been one of its prominent commitments.

Pullias Center for the Study of Higher Education at the University of Southern California: http://pullias.usc.edu/

The Pullias Center focuses on issues of social justice, equity, access, and affordability in higher education. Its publications include reports and resources pertinent to national policy issues as well as a strong component of studies and policy discussions dealing with postsecondary education in the state of California. The director is Professor William Tierney, who also is president-elect of the American Educational Research Association. With a generous bequest from the Pullias Family estate, the newly named Earl and Pauline Pullias Center for Higher Education at the University of Southern California (USC) Rossier School of Education has been established (the center was previously known as the Center for Higher Education Policy Analysis). The gift allows one of the world's leading research centers on higher education to continue its tradition of focusing on research, policy, and practice to improve the field. The center is named in honor of Dr. Earl V. Pullias, one of the founding faculty of USC's department of higher education in 1957. He was the author of more than 100 research articles, primarily focused on philosophical issues in higher education, and the author and coauthor of numerous books.

State Higher Education Executives Office (SHEEO): http://www.sheeo.org

SHEEO was created in 1954 by executive members of nine state higher education boards. SHEEO's members are chief executives of 28 governing and 29 coordinating statewide boards of higher education. SHEEO emphasizes the significance of strategic planning and statewide management. It represents members in both public and private media to promote state interests in financing and planning for higher education. SHEEO also exchanges data with federal agencies, postsecondary institutions, and other organizations to develop standards related to practices, research conduct, and development of higher education. SHEEO makes public policy recommendations to state and federal agencies as well as legislators. As the states' federal government liaison, SHEEO researches and reports on policy issues, while employing projects meant to enhance to enhance higher education.

Student Loan Marketing Association (SLM), or Sallie Mae

The Student Loan Marketing Association (SLM) was established in 1972 as a government-sponsored enterprise, and it began privatizing its operations in the late 1990s. SLM, commonly known as Sallie Mae, is the nation's largest federally insured student loan originator. In addition to education loans, Sallie Mae's products for individuals include college savings programs, tuition insurance, and scholarship search tools. Sallie Mae's specialized subsidiaries and divisions also offer debt management services and technical products to clients in fields ranging from business and education, to loan guarantors. Included among Sallie Mae's multiple subsidiaries are Academic Management Services Corporation, Southwest Student Services Corporation, Student Assistance Corporation, Student Loan Finance Association,

Student Loan Funding, and UPromise. The Sallie Mae Fund is SLM's charitable organization, which provides scholarship funding focused on minority, low income, and first generation college students. SLM has provided over $10 million in scholarships since 2001. Moreover, SLM's acquisition of the nonprofit, education financing company Nellie Mae in 1999 provided the endowment for what is now the Nellie Mae Education Foundation, which focuses on systematic change in education.

United Negro College Fund (UNCF): http://www.uncf.org

Famous for its motto "A mind is a terrible thing to waste," the UNCF was established in 1944. It is a philanthropic organization that provides financial assistance to students and to its member universities and colleges. UNCF assists over 60,000 students annually. Students from families with low to moderate incomes are awarded scholarships, fellowships, and internships to assist with tuition and related expenses such as room and board. UNCF emphasizes the significance of education for all Americans, particularly students of color, with its UNCF An Evening of Stars campaign, which consists of public service announcements and national media commentary. Some of UNCF's support programs for undergraduate and graduate students include the Gates Millennium Scholars Program, the UNCF/Merck Science Initiative, and the Corporate Scholars Program. UNCF provides operating funds to its 38 member colleges and universities. All are small, private institutions, primarily located in the southern United States, with lower tuition costs than comparable colleges and universities. UNCF provides institutional support through its Institute for Capacity Building, an initiative focused on faculty development and curricular improvement, student recruitment and retention, and fundraising. UNCF institutions have graduated notable public figures, including Martin Luther King, Jr.; Spike Lee; and Ralph Ellison. Named after its founding member and former Tuskegee

University president, UNCF's Frederick D. Patterson Research Institute advocates public policy initiatives that can improve local educational practices. The institute's research focuses on African American education from preschool through adulthood and examines educational attainment.

U.S. Department of Education (USDoED or ED): http:// www.ed.gov

The ED was established in 1980 by dividing the Department of Health, Education, and Welfare into the Department of Education and the Department of Health and Human Services. ED is administered by the US Secretary of Education. ED has approximately 4,400 employees and an operating budget of $68 billion. ED also originates over $120 billion in new loans each year. The Department of Education's mission is to prepare for global competitiveness by promoting student access, achievement, and educational excellence. Its staff focuses on federal financial aid policies by distributing and monitoring funds. ED collects, analyzes, and shares data on U.S. schools as a means to focus national attention on significant issues. ED also enforces federal laws concerning educational civil rights and privacy. ED operates in conjunction with agencies such as the Federal Interagency Committee on Education, the Office of Postsecondary Education, and the Institute of Education Sciences. ED has the smallest staff of the 15 Cabinet agencies, but the third largest budget (behind Defense and Health and Human Services).

Williams Project on the Economics of Higher Education (WPEHE): http://sites.williams.edu/wpehe

The Williams Project, housed at Williams College in Massachusetts, began in 1989 with a grant from the Andrew W. Mellon Foundation. Additional funding has been awarded by the U.S. Department of Education, the National Science

Foundation, and the Spencer Foundation. WPEHE conducts research pertinent to managers, policymakers, and scholars concerning the economics of colleges and universities. Its research frequently addresses the heterogeneous nature of institutions, noting that an economic analogy between higher education and for-profit industry can be helpful, but also misleading. Past projects include research on institutional responses to differences in external research and scholarship funding, reformation of institutional accounting practices, and the effects of merit aid on the quality and allocation of educational opportunity. Projects include institutional accounting strategies and the economic structure of postsecondary education. Researchers have presented their work to the Association of Governing Boards of Universities and Colleges, at Department of Education workshops, and at national commission hearings on postsecondary finance.

Key Persons

Individuals and ideas are the heart of higher education institutions. The massive national and state programs of student financial aid and the funding of higher education are the result of policy debates and discussions that have led to advocacy and analyses. The result is a concentration of diverse talent and perspectives from past and present that has elevated the topic of college costs into high visibility—and high regard—in the public forum of national issues.

Adelman, Clifford

Clif Adelman has been influential as a higher education policy analyst with innovative interpretations of qualitative and quantitative data. He is currently a senior associate with the Institute for Higher Education Policy in Washington, DC. For much of Adelman's career, he has studied areas such as degree completion rates, standardized testing, and transfer patterns. Adelman holds a bachelor's degree in English from

Brown University, as well as a master's and PhD in history of culture from the University of Chicago. Adelman served as a senior research analyst for the Education Department (ED) for almost 30 years. His work included contributions to 1983's *A Nation at Risk* report, as well as *Involvement in Learning*, which helped to generate the assessment movement in higher education. As a senior research analyst, he authored studies, which served as standards in educational research and informed policy agendas. Adelman has also served as an educator and administrator at City College of New York and Yale University. He has written extensively on higher education. His books and reports published by the U.S. Department of Education include *The Way We Are: The Community College as American Thermometer; Answers in the Toolbox: Academic Intensity, Attendance Patterns, and Bachelor's Degree Attainment;* and *The Toolbox Revisited: Paths to Degree Completion from High School through College.*

Archibald, Robert

Economist Robert B. Archibald has presented over the past 15 years original, often counterintuitive recommendations for policies and programs related to student financial aid and the financing of higher education. At a time when there was widespread dissatisfaction with student financial aid, Archibald's research concluded with the policy reform of shifting responsibility for student loans from federal agencies to colleges and universities. At the same time, he presented the case for having federal agencies and campuses switch roles, with governmental programs providing grants and colleges offering student aid in the form of loans. Most recently, in collaboration with economist David Feldman, he has reasoned that the high costs of college have been exaggerated because they fail to give adequate attention to factors that lower the net price charged to students and their families. His research on higher education finance during the past 12 years has included two books: *Redesigning the Financial Aid System: Why Colleges and Universities Should Switch Roles with the Federal Government* (2002, Johns Hopkins University Press) and, with David H. Feldman, *Why Does College Cost So Much?* (2011, Oxford University Press). He received his BA from the University of Arizona and his MS and PhD from Purdue University. He is Chancellor Professor of Economics at the College of William & Mary, where he has been on the faculty since 1976. He has served as chair of the Economics Department, director of the Thomas Jefferson Program in Public Policy, interim dean of the Faculty of Arts and Sciences, and president of the Faculty Assembly.

Baum, Sandy

Sandy Baum is an independent policy analyst for the College Board and Professor of Economics Emerita at Skidmore College. Baum earned her BA in sociology at Bryn Mawr College and her PhD in economics at Columbia University. She has written extensively on issues relating to college access, college pricing, student aid policy, student debt, affordability, and other aspects of higher education finance. Baum is the coauthor of the *Trends in Higher Education* series and *Education Pays: The Benefits of Higher Education for Individuals and Society*. Other recent work includes studies of setting benchmarks for manageable student debt levels and of tuition discounting in public and private colleges and universities. She cochaired the Rethinking Student Aid study group, which recently issued comprehensive proposals for reform of the federal student aid system.

Blumenstyk, Goldie

Goldie Blumenstyk is a senior writer and "Financial Affairs" columnist for the *Chronicle of Higher Education*. She earned a bachelor's degree in history from Colgate University and a master's degree in journalism from Columbia University. Blumenstyk's areas of expertise include institutional finance, for-profit higher education, and academic technology transfer and research commercialization. Her work on university-industry partnerships with corporations including BP, ExxonMobil, and Novartis has been cited extensively in mainstream and scholarly articles. Her "Financial Affairs" column in the *Chronicle* concentrates on the business aspects of higher education.

Blumenstyk is nationally renowned for her expertise in institutional finance, for-profit higher education, and university technology transfer. She was awarded a special citation from the National Education Writers Association in 2008 for her articles on university finance. She has also been a guest on public radio programs, including NPR's *Talk of the Town*, and Boston's *On Point with Tom Ashbrook*. Prior to her long tenure with the *Chronicle*, Blumenstyk reported on politics and government for the *Orlando Sentinel*.

Bowen, Howard R.

Howard R. Bowen (1908–1989) was an economic scholar, expert on the economics of higher education, and former president of the Claremont University Center (now the Claremont University Consortium; 1970–1974), Grinnell College (1955–1964), and the University of Iowa (1964–1969). He authored several books, including 1983's, *The State of the Nation and the Agenda for Higher Education*, which earned the Ness Book Award for the most significant contribution of the year to the study of liberal education. He received a second Ness Book Award for his collaboration with Jack Schuster, *American Professors: A National Resource Imperiled*.

Bowen served in business and government, as well as university teaching and administration. He was chief economist for the Joint Congressional Committee on Internal Revenue Taxation (1944–1945), a Wall Street economist (1945–1947), and chair of the Johnson administration's National Committee on Technology, Automation, and Economic Progress.

In addition to his role as president at Claremont, Bowen was also R. Stanton Avery Professor of Economics and Education at Claremont Graduate University, returning to the classroom after his administrative role in 1974. Bowen's many awards include the Distinguished Service to Education Award of the Council for Advancement and Support of Education (CASE) and the Association for the Study of Higher Education's (ASHE) Distinguished Research and Distinguished Career Awards.

Bowen, William G.

Bowen is president emeritus of Princeton University and the Andrew Mellon Foundation. Bowen's writings on the economics of higher education have included studies of undergraduate retention and attrition along with works coauthored with Baumol on the "disease theory" of rising costs of higher education.

Callan, Patrick M.

Patrick Callan, president of the Higher Education Policy Institute, has written extensively on education, access, public accountability, and higher education financing. He is coeditor of 1997's *Public and Private Financing of Higher Education: Shaping Public Policy for the Future* as well as *Designing State Higher Education Systems for a New Century* (2001). He has served as advisor to higher education boards and governmental groups, and he has been a member of several national and regional commissions. Callan was founding president of the National Center for Public Policy and Higher Education (1998–2011) and executive director of the California Higher Education Policy Center (1992–1997), both of which were sponsored by the Higher Education Policy Institute. He served as vice president of the Education Commission of the States as well as executive director of the California Postsecondary Education Commission, Washington State Council for Postsecondary Education, and Montana Commission on Postsecondary Education.

Carey, Kevin: www.kevincary.net

Kevin Carey is director of the education policy program for the New America Foundation. His expertise is issues of P-12 and higher education. A self-described "serial think tank person," he previously worked as policy director at Education Sector and the Education Trust, and he was Indiana's assistant state budget director. Carey teaches education policy courses at Johns Hopkins University, and he has written pieces in publications such as the *American Prospect, Washington Monthly*, and *Democracy*. He also has columns in the *Chronicle of Higher Education* and the *New Republic*. Carey earned an Education Writers Association Award for commentary in 2010. He earned a master's degree in public administration from The Ohio State University and a bachelor's degree in political science from the State University of New York (SUNY)–Binghamton. He researches areas such as higher education reform, degree attainment, and college rankings.

Chambers, M. M.

M. M. Chambers (1899–1985) was a pioneering analyst of college and university fiscal patterns. He was author of a 1936 study for the Carnegie Foundation for the Advancement of Teaching that presented a model of higher education financial accountability. Chambers's annual reports on institutional income and spending became the foundation for an enduring institute and website, Grapevine, based at Illinois State University. A member of the American Association for the Advancement of Science, he held positions at the American Council on Education and was a visiting professor of higher education at Indiana University and the University of Michigan. His series of reports on the campus and courts became a staple of systematic higher education and was notable for its fusion of the study of higher education law and financing.

Cheit, Earl

Earl F. Cheit is Professor of Business Emeritus, and Haas School of Business Dean Emeritus at the University of California–Berkeley (UC Berkeley). Cheit's research interests include Asia Pacific economic relations, financing higher education, and trade policy. His publications include *More Than Survival: Prospects for Higher Education in a Period of Uncertainty* (1975), *The Useful Arts and the Liberal Tradition* (1975), and *Foundations and Higher Education: Grant Making from the Golden Years through Steady State* (1979). Cheit has also served as a senior advisor for the Asia Foundation, associate director of the Carnegie Council on Higher Education, and program officer in charge, Higher Education and Research, for the Ford Foundation. He is also a member of the Board of Control at the University of California Press, a trustee of Mills College, and trustee emeritus of the UC, Berkeley Foundation. A wing of the Haas School of Business, as well as the Earl F. Cheit Award for Excellence in Teaching at Berkeley, is named in his honor.

Cheit earned a bachelor's degree and a PhD in economics and law, all from the University of Minnesota. He joined UC Berkeley in 1957 and in addition to his faculty role has held positions that include executive vice chancellor (1965–1969), dean of the Haas School of Business (1976–1982), and interim athletic director (1993–1994).

Cunningham, Alisa Federico

Alisa Federico Cunningham is vice president of Research at the Institute for Higher Education Policy (IHEP), a nonpartisan, nonprofit organization located in Washington, DC that focuses on access to and success in postsecondary education. She oversees all of the organization's research studies as well as conducts her own research. Since joining IHEP in 1997, Cunningham's work has addressed topics such as higher education financing, financial aid, minority-serving institutions, and student persistence and attainment. In addition to presentations at numerous conferences and articles published in various journals and magazines, Cunningham is the author or coauthor of many of the institute's publications. She was awarded the 2010 Robert P. Huff Golden Quill Award for her contributions to financial aid literature, served on the Department of Education's Committee on Measures of Student Success in 2011, and currently is a member of the National Postsecondary Education Cooperative. Cunningham's original essay, coauthored with Brian Sponsler, is published in Chapter 3.

Dillon, Kristine E.

Dillon is president of the Consortium on Financing Higher Education (COFHE), a membership organization of 31 private colleges and universities (www.cofhe.org). COFHE examines financial aid policy; the factors affecting admissions, student enrollment, and retention; and university costs. Beginning with her graduate work with Howard R. Bowen on his seminal study for *The Costs of Higher Education*, she has engaged economic, evaluative, planning, management, and student services issues. Dillon held a number of research and administrative positions at the University of Southern California before joining Tufts University as dean of academic services and student affairs. She is a contributor to six books and has published and presented many papers about higher education. Her baccalaureate is from Whittier College and her PhD is from the Claremont Graduate University. Dillon's original essay is published in Chapter 3 and deals with the policy forum on rising costs of higher education.

Dingell, John D.

John D. Dingell (D-MI), known as America's Watchdog, has served 29 terms representing Michigan's 15th District in the U.S. House of Representatives. His role in public policies associated with rising costs of higher education was especially pronounced between 1990 and 1993 when he was chair of the subcommittee on oversights and investigation. He critically scrutinized university spending of federally sponsored research and development grants. Dingell was especially critical of universities that were charging between 60 and 75 percent on indirect costs, including reimbursements for expenditures Dingell did not consider pertinent to the scope of the funded research projects.

Ehrenberg, Ronald G.: http://faculty.cit.cornell.edu/rge2

Ronald G. Ehrenberg is the Irving M. Ives Professor of Industrial and Labor Relations and Economics at Cornell University, where he also is a Stephen H. Weiss Presidential Fellow, and Director of the Cornell Higher Education Research Institute (CHERI). He previously served as a vice president and trustee of Cornell, and is currently a trustee of the State University of New York (SUNY). A prolific labor economist and higher education researcher, his major publications include *Tuition Rising: Why College Costs So Much* (2002, Harvard University Press) and *What's Happening to Public Higher Education?* (2007, Johns Hopkins University Press). His honors include the Jacob Mincer Award for lifetime achievement from the Society of Labor Economists and honorary doctorate degrees from the State University of New York and Penn State University. His original essay appears in Chapter 3.

Feldman, David

David Feldman's current research explores the economics of higher education. Together with Robert B. Archibald, he is the author of *Why Does College Cost so Much?* (2011, Oxford University Press). The book explores economic forces that drive college cost and tuition setting, and how these affect access to higher education. Other recent articles in the *Journal of Higher Education* and in *Research in Higher Education* explore topics such as college graduation rates and accountability, the determinants of state higher education spending, and the testing of competing theories about the causes of rising college cost. In addition to his professional writing, he has also written commentaries for the *Chronicle of Higher Education, Inside Higher Ed,* the *New York Times,* and the *Washington Post.* He teaches in the economics department and serves as department chair at the College of William & Mary. His original essay, coauthored with Robert Archibald, is presented in Chapter 3.

Finn, Chester E., Jr.

Finn is a policy analyst whose 1978 work for the Brookings Institution—*Scholars, Dollars and Bureaucrats*—endures as a seminal guide to and analysis of the federal government's involvement in higher education, especially by means of student financial aid programs and agencies' respective sponsored research grant funding. Finn, president of the Fordham Foundation, served as assistant secretary of education during the administration of President Ronald Reagan. He also was a professor at Vanderbilt University.

George, Richard

Richard George gained national recognition for his role as executive with the Great Lakes Higher Education Corporation, a national leader in the student loan industry that provides services to borrowers, lenders, schools, and guaranty agencies. He served previously as a director of the National Council of Higher Education Loan Programs, as a director and chair of the Finance and Audit Committee of the Board of Directors of the National Student Clearinghouse, and as a designee of the U.S. comptroller general and the U.S. secretary of education to the study group for the Study of the Feasibility of Alternative Financial Instruments for Determining Lender Yields. He also has been a consultant on postsecondary education finance for the World Bank's International Finance Corporation subsidiary. He is a member of the American Enterprise Institute's working group on the future of higher education.

Grassley, Charles

Charles ("Chuck") Grassley has served as U.S. Senator from Iowa since 1980. Prior to his tenure in the Senate, Grassley served in the Iowa state legislature and the U.S. House of Representatives. He earned a bachelor's and master's degree in political science from Iowa State Teachers College (now the University of Northern Iowa) in the 1950s. Grassley also completed work toward a PhD in political science at the University of Iowa. He currently serves as Ranking Member of the Senate Committee on the Judiciary, working toward antitrust enforcement, updating the patent system, and immigration reform. In addition, he is a senior member of the Senate Committee on the Budget and a member of the Senate Committee on Agriculture. Grassley previously served as chair of the Committee on Finance. Senator Grassley supports tax incentives to increase the accessibility and affordability of higher education. He is also an advocate for cost-effective and efficient college savings instruments as well as tax breaks for colleges and universities as part of the federal tax code. He recently chaired a congressional oversight hearing to review tax provisions to assist with costs of higher education. Grassley has voiced concerns over institutions increasing tuition, particularly tax-exempt elite colleges with large endowments. Grassley's agenda is to improve American quality of life and enhance economic opportunities for individuals, families, and society.

Green, Edith Starrett

Edith Starrett Green (1910–1987) was a 10-term congressional representative from Oregon (1955–1974). She influenced nearly every education bill enacted during her tenure. Green was a graduate of the University of Oregon. She spent 11 years teaching and was the Oregon Congress of Parents and Teachers' legislative chairperson for three years prior to her work in Congress. During her first term, Green was recognized as an expert in educational policy and appointed to the Committee on Education and Labor. Her legislative efforts were so focused on education that she earned the nicknames Mrs. Education and the Mother of Education. Based on her personal experiences, Green was determined to introduce and endorse legislation that provided educational access to students of all economic backgrounds. She was involved in the passage of the 1958 National Defense Education Act, which established loans for low income students and provided graduate fellowships for prospective faculty. Green also drafted the Higher Education Facilities Act (1963) and the Higher Education Act (1965), and amended the Vocational Rehabilitation Act. Moreover, as chair of the Subcommittee on Higher Education of the Education and Labor Committee, Green presided over hearings that led to the passage of Title IX of the 1972 Higher Education Act, which kept federal funding from colleges and universities that discriminated against women. She spent much of her career working to remove social and legal obstacles that precluded women from attaining equality.

Hartle, Terry

Hartle is vice president for government relations at the American Council of Education (ACE), based in Washington, DC. For almost 20 years, Hartle has directed ACE's comprehensive effort to engage federal policymakers on a broad range of issues, including student aid, scientific research, governmental regulation, and tax policy. This work not only involves representation before the U.S. Congress, administrative agencies, and the federal courts, but it increasingly includes work on state and local issues of national impact. Given ACE's historic role in coordinating the government relations efforts of some 60 associations in the Washington-based higher education community, Hartle is widely considered American higher education's most visible lobbyist. He also oversees Higher Education for Development (HED), which supports the global development goals of the United States Agency for International Development (USAID), primarily by coordinating the engagement of the higher education community to address development challenges. Prior to joining the council in

1993, Hartle served for six years as education staff director for the Senate Committee on Labor and Human Resources, then chaired by Senator Edward M. Kennedy. Prior to 1987, Hartle was director of social policy studies and resident fellow at the American Enterprise Institute, and a research scientist at the Educational Testing Service. Hartle is quoted widely in both the national and international media on higher education issues; has authored or coauthored numerous articles, books, and national studies; and contributes regular book reviews to the *Christian Science Monitor*. Hartle received a doctorate in public policy from George Washington University in 1982, a master's in public administration from the Maxwell School at Syracuse University in 1974, and a bachelor's degree in history (summa cum laude) from Hiram College in 1973. He was awarded an honorary doctor of laws degree by Northeastern University in 1994. He is a member of Phi Beta Kappa, the Garfield Society at Hiram College, and the Hiram College Athletic Hall of Fame.

Hearn, James

Hearn is professor of higher education and associate director at the Institute of Higher Education at the University of Georgia. He holds a PhD in the sociology of education and an MA in sociology from Stanford University, and an AB from Duke University. His research and teaching focus on postsecondary education organization and policy. In recent work, he has examined the emergence and impacts of state policies in higher education, states' leveraging of university research in the pursuit of economic development, the development of new models for higher education organization and governance, faculty workforce issues in colleges and universities, and trends toward marketization and performance accountability in postsecondary systems and institutions.

Hess, Frederick M.

Hess is director of education policy studies at the American Enterprise Institute (AEI) and executive editor of *Education*

Next. His books include *Educational Entrepreneurship* (2006) and *Common Sense School Reform* (2004). His articles have been published in *Urban Affairs Review, Social Science Quarterly, American Politics Quarterly, Teachers College Record, Education Week*, and *Educational Leadership*. Prior to joining AEI, he was a professor of education and government at the University of Virginia.

Hodgkinson, Virginia Fadil

In the 1970s, Hodgkinson was founding research director for the National Institute of Independent Colleges and Universities (NICU), based in Washington, DC. She pioneered the compilation and analysis of systematic data on student enrollments and college costs in presentations for and deliberations with congressional staff. Her work was instrumental in bringing independent colleges and universities to the table in federal higher education and student financial aid legislation in part because her systematic data provided a compelling counter to casual stereotypes of independent colleges as being primarily institutions that enrolled relatively affluent students who tended to have little financial need. Hodgkinson also developed with colleagues effective studies on the "tuition gap" and affordability variations within American higher education. After leaving NIICU, she became a founding member of Nonprofit Sector. The Council for the Advancement and Support of Education (CASE) has named its annual research award in her honor.

Johnstone, D. Bruce

D. Bruce Johnstone is Distinguished Service Professor of Higher and Comparative Education Emeritus at the State University of New York at Buffalo and director of the International Comparative Higher Education Finance and Accessibility Project (CHEFAP). His principal scholarship is in international comparative higher education finance, governance, and policy formation.

He is the author of many books, monographs, articles, and chapters on these topics, the most recent being *Financing Higher Education Worldwide: Who Pays? Who Should Pay?* (with Pamela Marcucci; 2010, Johns Hopkins University Press). He has held posts as vice president for administration at the University of Pennsylvania, president of the State University College of Buffalo, and chancellor of the State University of New York system. He holds bachelor's and master's degrees from Harvard University and a PhD from the University of Minnesota. His original essay on trends in international financing of higher education is published in Chapter 3.

Kelly, Andrew P.

Kelly is research fellow in education policy studies at the American Enterprise Institute and a doctoral candidate in political science at the University of California–Berkeley. His research focuses on higher education policy, information and consumer choice in education, and public opinion. His recent influential studies include "Nothing But Net: Helping Families Learn the Real Price of College," which was published in *Education Outlook*. As a graduate student, Kelly was a National Science Foundation interdisciplinary training fellow. His research has appeared in *Teachers College Record, Educational Policy, Policy Studies Journal, Education Next, Education Week*, and popular outlets such as *Forbes*, the *Atlantic*, and the *Huffington Post*. He is coeditor of *Reinventing Higher Education: The Promise of Innovation* (2011, Harvard Education Press) and *Getting to Graduation: The Completion Agenda in American Higher Education* (forthcoming, Johns Hopkins University Press). His original essay about college and "sticker price" appears in Chapter 3.

Kennedy, Edward Moore "Ted"

Kennedy (1932–2009) (D, MA), served in the U.S. Senate from 1962 until his death in 2009. Kennedy was a graduate of

Harvard College, with a bachelor's degree in history and government (1956), the International Law School (the Hague, Netherlands, 1958), and the University of Virginia Law School (1959 where he earned the JD degree). Kennedy influenced virtually every significant federal student-aid program, ranging from Pell Grants (1972) to Academic Competitiveness and Smart Grants (2006). Kennedy worked toward several budget amendments that increased the maximum amount for Pell Grants. Early in his career, Kennedy contributed to the Higher Education Act of 1965, through the creation of the National Teachers Corp (which closed in the 1980s) that provided aid to student teachers who spent two years teaching in low income communities. He also cosponsored the 1972 Title IX Education Amendments, which ban gender discrimination at institutions that receive federal aid. In the 1990s, Kennedy served as chair of the education committee and was instrumental in the development of the federal direct-loan program, through which government aid is lent directly to students through their institutions. Kennedy's concerns over conflicts of interest in student lending led to legislative restrictions on lender compensation to colleges, which was the source of changes to the 2008 reauthorization of the Higher Education Act. He also supported the interests of Massachusetts colleges and universities. To protect the interests of some of the prestigious, well-established institutions in his state, he opposed attempts to revise the formula used to issue campus-based aid. Moreover, Kennedy supplemented the 1992 reauthorization of the Higher Education Act, permitting the Overlap Group (with eight institutions in Massachusetts) to continue sharing information concerning their financial aid packages.

Kerr, Clark

Kerr (1911–2003), considered to be the most influential figure in higher education in the second half of the 20th century, helped to design the policies and programs that made mass higher education accessible and affordable. He was emeritus professor of business administration, emeritus chancellor, and emeritus president of the University of California–Berkeley. Kerr was an expert in economics and industrial relations and, based on his administrative academic experience, devoted a large part of his research and writing to higher education. Kerr earned a bachelor's degree from Swarthmore (1932), master's degree from Stanford (1939), and a doctorate from UC–Berkeley—all in economics. He was a founder of the Industrial Relations Research Association and key contributor to both the California School or neoclassical revisionist approach and industrialism and industrial man movements in the study of industrial relations.

After six years as UC–Berkeley's first chancellor, he was named president of the University of California system in 1958. Kerr developed the California Master Plan for Higher Education, which accommodated growth throughout the three public portions of California's higher education system and incorporated private-sector planning for the approaching increase in students. He also decentralized the UC system and delegated daily decision making to individual campuses. Under Kerr's leadership, UC opened three campuses—Santa Cruz, San Diego, and Irvine—and began conducting graduate and research work at Davis, Santa Barbara, and Riverside. Moreover, he instituted parallel operational structures at each campus so that the UC system did not have a traditional flagship campus.

After leaving the presidency in 1967, Kerr became chair and research director of the Carnegie Commission on Higher Education, which later became the Carnegie Council on Policy Studies in Higher Education. During his tenure, over 140 volumes of research and analysis on higher education were produced. Kerr's writings include *The Uses of the University*, based upon his 1963 Godkin Lectures at Harvard, where he characterized the modern research university by the term *multiversity*, which is now widely used, and *The Gold and the Blue: A Personal Memoir of the University of California, 1949–1967; Volume I: Academic Triumphs* (2001); *Volume II: Political*

Turmoil (2003). In addition to his service at UC and for Carnegie, Kerr was involved in several committees such as President Eisenhower's Commission on National Goals, the Carnegie Foundation for the Advancement of Teaching, and the American Council on Education.

Klor de Alva, Jorge

Following his tenure as president of University of Phoenix, Jorge Klor de Alva became president of Nexus Research and Policy Center. He was founder, chair, and chief executive officer (CEO) of Apollo International, Inc., an education company with over 170,000 students in Europe, India, and Latin America. Previously he was Class of 1940 Professor at University of California–Berkeley; professor at Princeton University; a Fulbright scholar; John Simon Guggenheim fellow; a Harry Frank Guggenheim, NEH, and NSF grantee; and a Getty scholar, Getty Research Institute. He has published over 90 scholarly articles; coauthored nine social studies textbooks; and authored, coauthored, or edited another 15 books in the social sciences. He has been past consultant for Lumina's degree productivity initiative, and for the Educational Testing Service (ETS), the Graduate Record Examination (GRE), the College Board, the New York State Department of Education, and the Smithsonian Institution. His earned academic degrees include a B.A. and J.D. from the University of California, Berkeley and the Ph.D. from the University of California–Santa Cruz.

Lederman, Douglas

Douglas Lederman is one of the cofounders and editors of for *Inside Higher Ed (IHE)*, an influential daily electronic newspaper covering higher education. Prior to founding *IHE* in 2004, Lederman was a highly regarded writer for the *Chronicle of Higher Education* for 17 years. He started as athletics reporter and editor and then became special projects editor, which included expanding a provocative survey of college and university presidential compensation. He then focused on covering government and politics, and served as editor, assistant managing editor, and managing editor. In May 2003, he left the *Chronicle* with colleagues Scott Jaschik and Kathlene Collins to found *Inside Higher Ed*. A 1984 alumnus of Princeton University, he concentrated in sociology, served as co–sports editor, and served as sports and news reporter for the *Daily Princetonian*.

Lederman has this to say about his distinctive approach to higher education writing:

> Most journalism about higher education provides a flawed (or at least overly narrow) perspective. In most cases it is written from a consumer perspective (where will my kids get in to college?), and the leading national publications (NYT, WSJ) focus on a small subset of institutions where the reporters and editors either went themselves or want their kids to go. Because those publications are so visible, their coverage skews the national conversation about many higher education issues, especially pricing, by implying that the country's most expensive colleges are the norm for students, when in fact it isn't. At *Inside Higher Ed*, we aim to apply the best journalistic conventions—rigorous analysis, a watchdog orientation, strong storytelling—to a higher education industry facing enormous financial and technological pressure to change, and to explore how those pressures are changing how institutions behave. The resulting coverage both holds a mirror up to the professionals who work in higher education, and gives the public a window into an enterprise that, for many of them, can be a black box.

McPherson, Michael S.

McPherson is nationally renowned economist with special expertise in the relationship between economics and education. He is the fifth president of the Spencer Foundation. Prior to joining the Spencer Foundation in 2003, McPherson was president of Macalester College in St. Paul, Minnesota. Before his seven years as president of Macalester, McPherson was a professor (and chair) of economics, as well as dean of faculty at Williams College. He earned his bachelor's degree in mathematics as well as his master's degree and PhD in economics from the University of Chicago. McPherson has coauthored and edited several volumes, including *College Access: Opportunity or Privilege?*, *Keeping College Affordable*, and *Economic Analysis*.

McPherson has served as a trustee of the College Board, the American Council on Education, and the Minneapolis Institute of Arts. He has also been a fellow of the Institute for Advanced Study and a senior sellow at the Brookings Institution.

Middaugh, Michael F.

Middaugh shaped higher education policy during his 26-year tenure at University of Delaware when he ran the National Study of Instructional Costs and Productivity. He is an authority on strategic planning, assessment, and accreditation. Prior to being at the University of Delaware, Middaugh was chief institutional research officer for two State University of New York campuses. Middaugh's publications include *Planning and Assessment in Higher Education: Demonstrating Institutional Effectiveness* (2009) and *Understanding Faculty Productivity: Standards and Benchmarks for Colleges and Universities* (2001). He earned his bachelor's degree in biology at Fordham University, master's degree in liberal studies from SUNY–Stony Brook, and EdD from SUNY–Albany. He is a past president of the Society for College and University Planning (SCUP), the Association for Institutional Research (AIR), and the North East Association for Institutional Research (NEAIR). He has served as commissioner and chair of the Middle States Commission on Higher Education, is executive editor of the journal *Planning for Higher Education*, and has earned Distinguished Service Awards from AIR and NEAIR.

Morrill, Justin Smith

Morrill (1810–1898) was a Senator from Vermont who was champion of federal funding of state programs in agriculture, mechanical arts, mining, military and liberal education. This included the land grant act of 1862; and, in 1890, a second land grant act extended to states in the South, with funding for state choice in either public racial coeducation or creation of separate, distinct historically black public colleges and universities. Morrill and his acts were indelibly associated with the acronym of *A&M* as an affordable, expansive provision of state public higher education nationwide.

Odell, Morgan Sayre

Odell (1920–2010) served as founding president of the Association of Independent California Colleges and Universities from 1968 to 1985. He was effective in developing programs and legislation for California's state scholarship program, later renamed the Cal Grant Program. A leader among state higher education association executives in collaboration with such Washington, DC groups as the National Association of Independent Colleges (NAICU), he was central to deliberations on federal student financial aid programs. Odell was especially respected for his effectiveness in promoting the inclusion of independent colleges and their students as constituencies and recipients. An alumnus of Occidental College who received his doctorate in public administration from the University of California, he served as assistant to the chancellor of the California State University and Colleges System.

Pell, Claiborne

Pell (1918–2009) was a U.S. Senator (D, RI) who first took office in 1965 and was re-elected five times. Starting in 1968, his primary commitment was to creating and defining a large and well-funded program of student financial aid that emphasized student grants that were portable to an accredited college of the student's choice. The original grant program, approved as part of the 1972 reauthorization of the Higher Education Act, was known as the Student Educational Opportunity Grant program. Shortly thereafter, the program was renamed as Pell Grants in honor of the senator's leadership on this initiative. An alumnus of Princeton University who served in World War II, Pell also was a leader in the Senate in creating the National Endowment for the Arts and the National Endowment for the Humanities.

Perkins, Carl D.

Perkins (1912–1984) was elected to Congress in 1948. He served for several years as the ranking Democrat on the House Education and Labor Committee, as well as chair of the General Subcommittee on Education. Perkins was committed to social welfare programs, including federal scholarships, work-study, and student loans. He had served as a rural educator in Kentucky prior to graduating from Jefferson School of Law (now the University of Louisville Law School) in 1935, which influenced his position concerning educational assistance. The Carl D. Perkins Act, named in his honor, was passed in 1984 and reauthorized in 1990 (Perkins II) and 1998 (Perkins III). In 2006, the 1998 act was reauthorized as the Federal Carl D. Perkins Career and Technical Education Improvement Act (Perkins IV/CTEA). Perkins IV provides aid to postsecondary institutions that enroll students, particularly special populations, in career and technical education (CTE) programs. Funding can be allocated to areas including instruction, tutoring, and equipment. States and their institutions must submit assessment data annually to demonstrate federal compliance of their funded programs.

Rhoades, Gary

Gary Rhoades served as the general secretary of the American Association of University Professors (AAUP) in Washington, DC.

His work at AAUP included systematic analysis on problems of rising costs due to "administrative bloat" and other diversions from an institution's central educational mission. He has been a faculty member at the Center for the Study of Higher Education at the University of Arizona since 1986. Rhoades was professor and director of the Center from 1997 to 2009. His scholarly interests focus on comparative postsecondary education, science and technology policy, and restructuring of institutions and professions in the academy. Rhoades has written extensively in these areas, including his current volume, *Managing to Be Different: From Strategic Imitation to Strategic Imagination* (working title; forthcoming), *Academic Capitalism and the New Economy* (with Shelia Slaughter; 2004), and *Managed Professionals* (1998). Prior to joining the University of Arizona, Rhoades spent five years as a postdoctoral research scholar for the Comparative Higher Education Group at University of California–Los Angeles (UCLA). He earned a bachelor's degree, master's degree, and PhD, all in sociology, from UCLA.

Schneider, Mark

Schneider is vice president for new education initiatives at the American Institutes for Research (AIR) and a visiting scholar at the American Enterprise Institute (AEI) in Washington DC. Schneider served as U.S. deputy commissioner of education statistics and, subsequently, commissioner (2004–2008). He is Distinguished Professor Emeritus of Political Science at SUNY–Stony Brook. Schneider is a former president and vice president, public policy section, of the American Political Science Association (APSA). Prior to his faculty work at SUNY–Stony Brook, he was a member of the University of Michigan political science faculty. Schneider is one of the developers of www.collegemeasures.org, which offers the public data on college productivity. As a result, he serves as president of College Measures, LLC (a partnership of AIR and the Matrix

Knowledge Group). Schneider has written and edited several education policy works, including *Choosing Schools* (2000), *Higher Education Accountability* (2010), and *Getting to Graduation: The Completion Agenda in Higher Education* (forthcoming). His 2000 book *Choosing Schools* earned the Aaron Wildavsky Best Book Award from the Policy Study Organization. Schneider earned his bachelor's degree from Brooklyn College, City University of New York (CUNY) and PhD from the University of North Carolina–Chapel Hill.

Jeffrey Selingo: http://www.jeffselingo.com/about/

Selingo is vice president and editorial director of the *Chronicle of Higher Education*, in charge of long-term editorial strategy. He has spent the past 14 years in higher education reporting and editing, serving as editor of the *Chronicle* from 2007 to 2011. Illustrative of his writing on rising costs of higher education are articles published in the *Chronicle* such as "College Costs: Do Frills Have a Future?" (February 27, 2009) and "How Much Is Too Much?" (October 21, 2005). He has been a featured speaker before dozens of national higher education groups and appears regularly on regional and national radio and television programs, including for NPR, PBS, ABC, MSNBC, and CBS. His writing has also appeared in the *New York Times* and the *Washington Post*. He writes a regular blog and column for the *Chronicle* and the *Huffington Post*, where he explores innovation in higher education. Selingo's awards for outstanding reporting come from the Education Writers Association, Society of Professional Journalists, and the Associated Press. He was a finalist for the Livingston Award for Young Journalists. He received a bachelor's degree in journalism from Ithaca College and a master's degree in government from Johns Hopkins University.

Shapiro, Morton O.

Morton O. Schapiro is an authority on the economics of higher education, including college financing, affordability, and trends in educational costs and student aid. He is president of Northwestern University and also professor of economics in the Judd A. and Marjorie Weinberg College of Arts and Sciences. He holds appointments at Northwestern's Kellogg School of Management and School of Education and Social Policy. Prior to coming to Northwestern, Schapiro was president of Williams College (2000–2009). He was also a faculty member and assistant provost at Williams College (1980–1991). He was chair of economics at the University of Southern California and later dean of the College of Letters, Arts, and Sciences, and vice president for Planning (1991–2000). His scholarly works include *Keeping College Affordable: Government and Educational Opportunity* (with Michael McPherson; 1991), *Paying the Piper: Productivity, Incentives and Financing in Higher Education* (with Michael McPherson and Gordon Winston; 1993), and *The Student Aid Game: Meeting Need and Rewarding Talent in American Higher Education* (with Michael McPherson; 1998). He has also edited the volumes *College Access: Opportunity or Privilege?* (2006) and *College Success: What It Means and How to Make It Happen* (2008). Schapiro earned a bachelor's degree in economics from Hofstra University and a PhD from the University of Pennsylvania.

Sponsler, Brian A.

Vice president of research and policy at NASPA, the Student Affairs Administrators in Higher Education, appointed in May 2012. In this role, he leads and conducts research projects on and about college students and the institutions they attend, and he guides the association's strategic policy efforts. The unifying thread of his applied policy research is his work to assist practitioners, institutions, policymakers, and most critically students in advancing educational success. Prior to joining NASPA, he was associate director of research for the Institute for Higher Education Policy (IHEP). He is a scholar in the field of postsecondary education access, success, and public policy.

His research interests include the politics of higher education policymaking, undocumented student tuition policies, antecedents of state policy adoption, college access for disenfranchised populations, and the influence of governance and geography on student access. Prior to joining IHEP, Sponsler held professional positions in academic advising, college athletic administration and coaching, and nonprofit management. He holds a doctorate in higher education from George Washington University, an MA from Seattle University, and a BA from the University of Puget Sound.

Vedder, Richard

Richard Vedder is director of the Center for College Affordability and Productivity in Washington, DC and also adjunct scholar at the American Enterprise Institute (AEI), a think tank known for mostly libertarian and conservative perspectives. He has served as an economist with Congress's Joint Economic Committee. In his role with the AEI, he testified before the committee. Born in 1940, Vedder earned his BA in economics at Northwestern University in 1962 and his PhD in economics at the University of Illinois in 1965. He has since studied U.S. economic history, particularly as it relates to public policy. Some of his research has involved American immigration, economic issues in American education, and the interrelationship between labor and capital markets. Vedder's scholarly writings have appeared in journals such as *Explorations in Economic History*, the *Journal of Economic History*, and *Agricultural History*. He has written over 200 scholarly articles. Vedder's popular interest writings have appeared in the *Wall Street Journal, USA Today, Investor's Business Daily*, and the *Christian Science Monitor*. He has published the books *The American Economy in Historical Perspective: Unemployment and Government in Twentieth-Century America* (with Lowell Gallaway), *Can Teachers Own Their Own Schools?*, *Going Broke by Degree: Why College Costs Too Much*, and *The Wal-Mart*

Revolution: How Big-Box Stores Benefit Consumers, Workers, and the Economy (with Wendell Cox).

Wellman, Jane V.

Jane Wellman is a longtime leader in systematic policy research about revenues and expenditures in higher education in the United States. She was the founding director of the Delta Project on Postsecondary Education Costs, based in Washington, DC. In December 2011, she was the featured expert invited to the White House to brief President Barak Obama and higher education leaders on issues of college costs. Her research reports and sources developed as part of the Delta Project are widely used and respected by all constituencies in higher education policy deliberations. In 2012, she assumed the role of executive director of the National Association of System Heads, a group for presidents and chancellors of public university and community college systems. She earned her master's degree in higher education from the University of California–Berkeley. She has worked as a policy analyst for the University of California system, served as staff director for the Ways and Means Committee in the California State Assembly, and in the early 1990s served as a lobbyist for the National Association of Independent Colleges and Universities (NAICU). She later served as a consultant to the California State University and Colleges system. Wellman's research was featured in Goldie Blumenstyk's front-page article of the *Chronicle of Higher Education*, "A Policy Wonk Brings Data on College Costs to the Table" (February 5, 2012).

Wilkinson, Rupert

Wilkinson is author of *Aiding Students, Buying Students: Financial Aid in America* (2005), which is the definitive work on historical and contemporary developments in loans, grants, and programs for college students provided by public and private agencies. Wilkinson is retired as Professor of American

Studies and History at the University of Sussex in England. He has also taught in the United States at Brandeis University, Smith College, and Wesleyan University. He is the author or editor of eight other books on elites and on American culture and has published articles on student aid in the *College Board Review*, the *Chronicle of Higher Education*, and the *Journal of Student Financial Aid*.

Zook, George F.

George F. Zook was chair and primary author of the 1947 President Commission Report *Higher Education for American Democracy*. Born in 1885, Zook died in 1951. He served as president of the American Council on Education, he was U.S. commissioner of education, and he was president of the University of Akron.

Key Publications

Discussion of ideas and analysis of data and issues are the life-blood of higher education policy research and deliberations. Within the numerous specialties of public policy and legislative programs, higher education—including the topic of costs of higher education—has attracted an informed, literate, and artic-ulate array of publications and journals. Their formats range from daily electronic delivery updates to weekly and quarterly publications both in hard copy and electronic media. Articles and reports are characterized by strong reliance on data-driven statistical sources combined with insightful writing styles.

Change: The Magazine of Higher Education: http://www.changemag.org

Change magazine addresses contemporary issues in advanced learn-ing. It is issued six times annually and intended for professionals in settings such as institutions of higher education, corporations, and foundations. Its purpose is to inspire and communicate with informed practitioners, utilizing a magazine, rather than academic journal, format. This is part of an effort to emphasize trends, analyze implications of educational programs, policies, and methods. *Change* also looks to provide innovative ideas and understanding by presenting pieces on innovative institutions and individuals, management and finance in higher education, entrepreneurial education, and governance and public policy for accountability in postsecondary education. It is partnered with the Council of Colleges of Arts and Sciences (CCAS). CCAS is an American association of baccalaureate-granting colleges of arts and sciences. Its purpose is to uphold the arts and sciences as the principal influence on U.S. higher education.

Chronicle of Higher Education: http://chronicle.com

The *Chronicle*, based in Washington, DC, is a print and web-based publication. The *Chronicle* has over 70 writers, editors, and international correspondents. The print version is generally published weekly, with 44 issues annually. It is published into two parts. The first section offers job postings and news. The second section is the *Chronicle Review*, an arts and ideas magazine. The *Almanac of Higher Education* (with reports on contemporary topics) is also sent annually to subscribers. Over 64,000 academics subscribe to the *Chronicle*, with a readership of over 315,000. The *Chronicle's* website publishes news stories, advice columns, and academic job postings every weekday. The website offers content from the latest issues (selected content is available strictly to subscribers), job postings, archives, and discussion forums. In addition, there are professional tools such as online curriculum vita management and salary databases. More than 12.8 million of the *Chronicle's* web pages are viewed each month, with an excess of 1.9 million unique visitors. A *Chronicle* columnist was a finalist for the 2005 Pulitzer Prize, and the *Chronicle* is a nine-time finalist for the National Magazine Awards. It has also earned praise from the Education

Writers Association and the Society of News Design. The *Chronicle* has been ranked one of the 10 most credible news sources by Erdos & Morgan (2007), and won Best Political Coverage honors among independent magazines from the *Utne Reader* (2007).

Grapevine: http://grapevine.illinoisstate.edu/

Since 1960, *Grapevine* has published annual collections of data concerning state tax support for higher education (universities, colleges, community colleges), and state higher education agencies. Since 2010, *Grapevine* data (tables that include both tax and nontax support) have been created by Illinois State University's Center for the Study of Education Policy in cooperation with the State Higher Education Executive Officers (SHEEO). *Grapevine* produces an annual survey requesting tax appropriations from states for the current period, as well as any revisions to previously reported data. *Grapevine*'s survey has been merged with SHEEO's annual survey for its State Higher Education Finance (SHEF) project. (See http://www.sheeo.org/finance/shef-home.htm.) The resultant survey requests data that are collected in an updated State Support for Higher Education (SSHE) database. The SSHE data produce a preliminary report for state appropriations (*Grapevine* tables), as well as an in-depth SHEF report, which provides trends in state support, considering inflation and enrollment numbers. As states revise their budgets, the information is updated. The current, combined questionnaire does not include appropriation amounts for individual institutions.

Inside Higher Education: http://www.insidehighered.com

Inside Higher Ed is an online news outlet that provides updates, job postings, and opinions concerning higher education. The publication offers breaking news and feature stories, daily commentary, career columns and tools. Founded in 2004 by executives with experience in higher education journalism and recruitment,

Inside Higher Ed promotes accessibility to all by eliminating or lowering costs for subscribers. All of its web content and job postings are free, while employers pay a nominal fee to advertise positions. *Inside Higher Ed*'s position is that higher education evolves rapidly and radically, and needs a site that provides accurate and reliable information. It considers itself a watchdog, providing investigative reporting. However, it attempts to keep its content spirited by posting cartoons and humor columns, along with its news, commentary, and blogs. *Inside Higher Ed* presents itself as "a gathering place for all of the many constituents and diverse institutions that make up the rich web of higher education."

Journal of Higher Education: https://ohiostatepress.org

The *Journal of Higher Education (JHE)* is published by The Ohio State University Press and edited by Scott Thomas of Claremont Graduate University's School of Educational Studies. *JHE* is published bimonthly. Its articles incorporate disciplinary methods and critical approaches to examine issues within higher education. Founded in 1930, the *Journal of Higher Education* is one of higher education's leading and well-established scholarly journals.

Review of Higher Education: http://www.press.jhu.edu

Published quarterly, the *Review of Higher Education* is considered a leading journal for research in higher education. It is published by Johns Hopkins University Press and edited by Amaury Nora of the University of Texas at San Antonio. The journal's intention is to advance the study of higher education by publishing peer-reviewed research, articles, essays, and reviews. The *Review of Higher Education* is the official journal of the Association for the Study of Higher Education (ASHE) and promotes qualitative and quantitative systematic inquiry that provides implications for practice. The *Review's* audience includes scholars, administrators, and public policymakers with interests in critical issues of higher education.

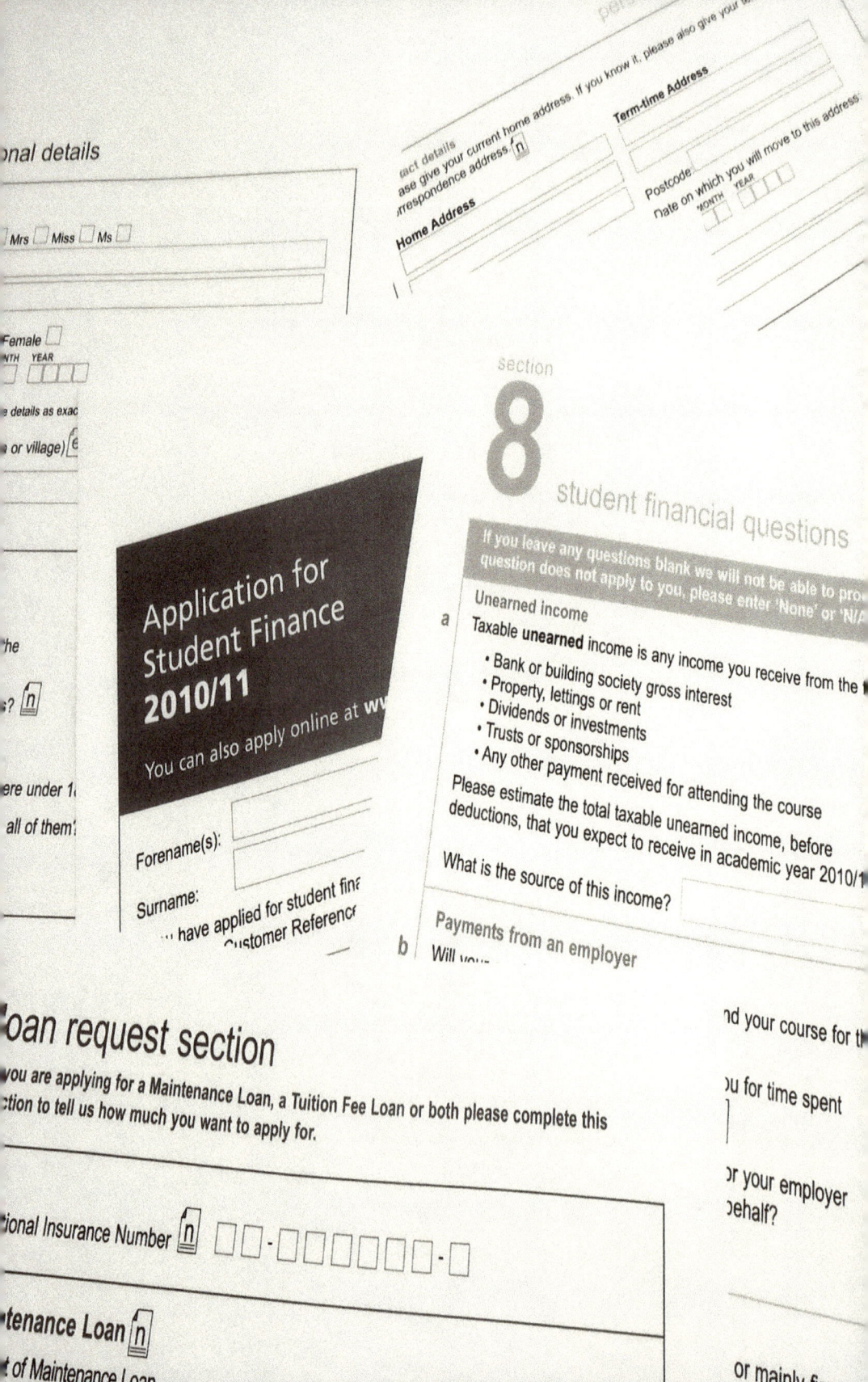

5 Documents

Introduction

Discussions about the cost of higher education are heirs to a rich legacy of historical documents that illustrate an interesting blend of continuity and change over several centuries in American institutions and society.

Constitution of the American Society for Educating Pious Youth for the Gospel Ministry (1815)

Source: Eliphalet Pearson. *Constitution & Address of the American Society for Educating Pious Youth.* Boston, Massachusetts: American Society for Educating Pious Youth for the Gospel Ministry, 1816.

Highly organized, systematic student financial aid has a long history in our nation, starting with the colonial colleges and then flourishing in the early 19th century of the new United States. The impetus came from private, voluntary associations—not from the state or federal government. The American Educational Society's scholarship program, launched in 1815, was both a pioneer and a model in focused, effective student aid. Between 1815 and 1835, the AES funded on average over 1,000 college students per year.

(Ian Jeffery/iStockphoto.com)

Taking into serious consideration the deplorable condition of the inhabitants of these United States, the greater part of whom, as appears from authentic documents and well supported estimates, are either destitute of competent religious instruction, or exposed to the errors and enthusiasm of unlearned men, we, whose names are underwritten, do hereby, in the fear of God and love of man, form ourselves into a Society for the benevolent purposing of adding, and of exciting others to aid, indigent young men of talents and hopeful piety, in acquiring a learned and competent education for the Gospel Ministry, upon the principles and in the manner following, viz. . . .

VII. Qualified candidates for this charity may be aided in each of the several stages of preparatory education for the ministry. But, except in very singular cases, no applicant shall be assisted, even in the first stage, who is not fifteen years of age; nor in either stage, shall any candidate receive assistance, who shall not produce, from serious and respectable characters, unequivocal testimonials of real indigence, promising talents, and hopeful piety; nor shall any person be continued on this foundation, whose Instructor or Instructors shall not annual exhibit to the Directors satisfactory evidence, that in point of genius, diligence, literary progress, morals, and piety, he is a proper character to receive this sacred charity; in addition to which, each beneficiary, after his admission into any College, shall annually exhibit to the Directors a written declaration, that it continues to be his serious purpose, if his life be spared, to devote that life to the gospel ministry. . . .

IX. If any person, who has been assisted by the Society, with a view to the gospel ministry, shall not devote himself to that work; he shall within a reasonable time refund the sum, expended for his education, with lawful interest for the same, whenever required by the Directors.

The Morrill Land Grant Act (1862)

Source: Public Law 37-108, which established land grant colleges, July 2, 1862; Enrolled Acts and Resolutions of

Congress, 1789–1996; Record Group 11; General Records of the U.S. Government; National Archives.

2012 marks the sesquicentennial of this historic, influential legislation that has been integral to extending public higher education—and to broadening the curricula associated with state universities. Named in honor of Vermont legislator Justin Morrill, who served both in the House of Representatives and, later, as U.S. Senator, the Morrill Land Grant Act also illustrates how higher education in the United States often has been enhanced due to its role as a secondary character in some larger national drama of public policies. In this case, the primary concern of the U.S. Congress was how to promote the settlement and sale of vast amounts of land in the territories of the West.

Chap. CXXX.—AN ACT Donating Public Lands to the several States and Territories which may provide Colleges for the Benefit of Agriculture and Mechanic Arts. Be it enacted by the Senate and House of Representatives of the United States of America in Congress assembled, That there be granted to the several States, for the purposes hereinafter mentioned, an amount of public land, to be apportioned to each State a quantity equal to thirty thousand acres for each senator and representative in Congress to which the States are respectively entitled by the apportionment under the census of eighteen hundred and sixty: *Provided,* That no mineral lands shall be selected or purchased under the provisions of this Act.

SEC. 2. *And be it further enacted,* That the land aforesaid, after being surveyed, shall be apportioned to the several States in sections or subdivisions of sections, not less than one quarter of a section; and whenever there are public lands in a State subject to sale at private entry at one dollar and twenty-five cents per acre, the quantity to which said State shall be entitled shall be selected from such lands within the limits of such State, and the Secretary of the Interior is hereby directed to issue to each of the States in which there is not the quantity of public lands subject to sale at private entry at one dollar and twenty-five cents per acre, to which said State may be entitled under the provisions of this act, land scrip to the amount in acres for the deficiency of its distributive share: said scrip to be sold by said States and the proceeds thereof applied to the uses and purposes prescribed in this act, and for no other use or purpose whatsoever:

SEC. 4. And be it further enacted, That all moneys derived from the sale of the lands aforesaid by the States to which the lands are apportioned, and from the sales of land scrip hereinbefore provided for, shall be invested in stocks of the United States, or of the States, or some other safe stocks, yielding not less than five per centum upon the par value of said stocks; and that the moneys so invested shall constitute a perpetual fund, the capital of which shall remain forever undiminished (except so far as may be provided in section fifth of this act), and the interest of which shall be inviolably appropriated, by each State which may take and claim the benefit of this act, to the endowment, support, and maintenance of at least one college where the leading object shall be, without excluding other scientific and classical studies, and including military tactics, to teach such branches of learning as are related to agriculture and the mechanic arts, in such manner as the legislatures of the States may respectively prescribe, in order to promote the liberal and practical education of the industrial classes in the several pursuits and professions in life.

Sixth. No State while in a condition of rebellion or insurrection against the government of the United States shall be entitled to the benefit of this Act.

Seventh. No State shall be entitled to the benefits of this act unless it shall express its acceptance thereof by its legislature within three years from July 23, 1866

Foundations and the Privately Endowed University as a New Type (1922)

By Jesse Barnard Sears

Source: Jesse Barnard Sears, *Philanthropy in the History of American Higher Education.* Washington, DC: U.S. Government Printing Office, 1922, pp. 67–83.

Indicative of the unprecedented growth, wealth, and popularity of colleges and universities in American life was the federal government's sponsorship of Jesse Brundage Sears's 1922 study of donors, donations, and endowments in U.S. higher education. The following excerpt deals with what author Sears called the Late National Period, 1865–1918.

Philanthropy in the Colleges of This Period [1865–1918]

Down to 1865 practically every college begun its existence with very small funds, usually with little or no real endowment, and had had to pass through a long financial struggle before it had won a clientage sufficient to guarantee its future. During the period under discussion colleges continued to be founded on that same basis. Drury College began in poverty in 1873 and remained poor until 1892, when a gift of $50,000 laid the foundation of her present endowment of over a quarter of a million. Carleton College, chartered in 1867, began with $20,000 received from the citizens of Northfield and $10,000 received from Congregational Churches of the State. In 1915 this college possessed endowment funds of almost a million dollars. Washburn College, chartered in 1865, was started by small gifts from the Congregational Churches, but by 1915 had developed an endowment of over $360,000. These are but three from the many well-known illustrations of this type.

The Privately Endowed University: A New Type

In addition to this type, however, we see the beginning of a new era in educational philanthropy—an era in which a great and independently endowed university could spring into existence almost at once from the gifts of a single benefactor.

Such schools did not have to go to the public and beg for funds, nor await any sort of social sanction. They secured their charters as corporations, erected their buildings, called together their faculties, organized their curricula, and opened their doors to students. They start, therefore, as educational and philanthropic, and we might also say, social experiments. Can such financially powerful corporations be trusted to keep the faith with America's educational, economic, religious, and social ideals was the question in many minds at that time . . .

Summary and Conclusions

We may characterize this period in the growth of higher education in America as follows:

The question of State versus private endowments of higher education has been fought through and settled favorably to both methods: the church has continued its work of founding small colleges; several very large institutions (in a sense, a new type) have been founded by the fortunes of single individuals and have not looked to the church for support; a number of large foundations, the aim of which is research and general educational stimulus and supervision, have been created; a new philosophy of education, which has found expression in the organization, administration and management of our institutions of higher learning has been worked out.

In opening up new territory to higher education during this period, the State has for the most part done the pioneering, thus reversing the custom of pre–Civil War days when the church school led the way.

From a general view of the work of philanthropy in higher education, as gathered from the Reports of the United States Commissioner of Education, we have seen that philanthropy has gradually built up a vast fund for the permanent endowment of higher learning; that from this source, together with annual gifts, philanthropy is still bearing decidedly the larger part of the burden of higher education, though the State is assuming a relatively larger portion of this burden each year; and, that tuition has covered practically the same percentage of the total annual cost from 1872 to the present.

Serviceman's Readjustment Act (1944)

Source: An act to provide Federal Government aid for the readjustment in civilian life of returning World War II veterans, June 22, 1944; Enrolled Acts and Resolutions of Congress, 1789–1996; General Records of the U.S. Government; Record Group 11; National Archives

Well-known by its nickname, the GI Bill, this landmark legislation relied on cooperation of colleges and universities and generous entitlement funding from the federal government to provide student financial aid and institutional choice for veterans of World War II to attend college and other postsecondary education programs.

Chapter IV Education of Veterans Sec. 400. (a) Subsection (f) of section 1, title I, Public Law Numbered 2, Seventy-third Congress, added by the Act of March 24, 1943 (Public Law Numbered 16, Seventy-eighth Congress), is hereby amended to read as follows:(f) Any person who served in the active military or naval forces on or after September 16, 1940, and prior to the termination of hostilities in the present war, shall be entitled to vocational rehabilitation subject to the provisions and limitations of Veterans Regulation Numbered 1 (a), as amended, part VII, or to education or training subject to the provisions and limitations of part VIII.(b) Veterans Regulation Numbered 1 (a), is hereby amended by adding a new part VIII as follows:

Part VIII

1. Any person who served in the active military or naval service on or after September 16, 1940, and prior to the termination of the present war, and who shall have been discharged or released there-from under conditions other than dishonorable, and whose education or training was impeded, delayed, interrupted, or interfered with by reason of his entrance into the service, or who desires a refresher or retraining course, and who either shall have served ninety days or more, exclusive of any period he was assigned for a course of education or training under the Army specialized training program or the Navy college training program, which course was a continuation of his civilian course and was pursued to completion, or as a cadet or midshipman

at one of the service academies, or shall have been discharged or released from active service by reason of an actual service-incurred injury or disability, shall be eligible for and entitled to receive education or training under this part.

2. Any such eligible person shall be entitled to education or training, or a refresher or retraining course, at an approved educational or training institution, for a period of one year (or the equivalent thereof in continuous part-time study), or for such lesser time as may be required for the course of instruction chosen by him. Upon satisfactory completion of such course of education or training, according to the regularly prescribed standards and practices of the institutions, except a refresher or retraining course, such person shall be entitled to an additional period or periods of education or training, not to exceed the time such person was in the active service on or after September 16, 1940, and before the termination of the war, exclusive of any period he was assigned for a course of education or training under the Army specialized training program or the Navy college training program, which course was a continuation of his civilian course and was pursued to completion, or as a cadet or midshipman at one of the service academies, but in no event shall the total period of education or training exceed four years: Provided, That his work continues to be satisfactory throughout the period, according to the regularly prescribed standards and practices of the institution: Provided, however, That wherever the additional period of instruction ends during a quarter or semester and after a major part of such quarter or semester has expired, such period of instruction shall be extended to the termination of such unexpired quarter or semester.

3. Such person shall be eligible for and entitled to such course of education or training as he may elect, and at any approved educational or training institution at which he

chooses to enroll, whether or not located in the State in which he resides, which will accept or retain him as a student or trainee in any field or branch of knowledge which such institution finds him qualified to undertake or pursue: Provided, That, for reasons satisfactory to the Administrator, he may change a course of instruction: And provided further, That any such course of education or training may be discontinued at any time, if it is found by the Administrator that, according to the regularly prescribed standards and practices of the institution, the conduct or progress of such person is unsatisfactory.

5. The Administrator shall pay to the educational or training institution, for each person enrolled in full time or part time course of education or training, the customary cost of tuition, and such laboratory, library, health, infirmary, and other similar fees as are customarily charged, and may pay for books, supplies, equipment, and other necessary expenses, exclusive of board, lodging, other living expenses, and travel, as are generally required for the successful pursuit and completion of the course by other students in the institution: Provided, That in no event shall such payments, with respect to any person, exceed $500 for an ordinary school year: Provided further, That no payments shall be made to institutions, business or other establishments furnishing apprentice training on the job: And provided further, That if any such institution has no established tuition fee, or if its established tuition fee shall be found by the Administrator to be inadequate compensation to such institution for furnishing such education or training, he is authorized to provide for the payment, with respect to any such person, of such fair and reasonable compensation as will not exceed $500 for an ordinary school year.

6. While enrolled in and pursuing a course under this part, such person, upon application to the Administrator, shall be paid a subsistence allowance of $50 per month, if

without a dependent or dependents, or $75 per month, if he has a dependent or dependents, including regular holidays and leave not exceeding thirty days in a calendar year. Such person attending a course on a part-time basis, and such person receiving compensation for productive labor performed as part of their apprentice or other training on the job at institutions, business or other establishments, shall be entitled to receive such lesser sums, if any, as subsistence or dependency allowances, as may be determined by the Administrator: Provided, That any such person eligible under this part, and within the limitations thereof, may pursue such full time or part-time course or courses as he may elect, without subsistence allowance.

President's Commission Report on Higher Education for American Democracy (1947)

Source: George F. Zook, chair. "Toward Equalizing Opportunity." *A Report of the President's Commission on Higher Education: Higher Education for American Democracy: Volume I: Establishing the Goals.* New York: Harper and Brothers, 1947, pp. 36–39.

Whereas the 1944 GI Bill concentrated federal resources to address a specific, pressing problem—accommodating and encouraging military service veterans to enroll in postsecondary education—the 1947 President's Commission provided a long, comprehensive, and visionary report on the potential for an expanded model of higher education to be pursued over several decades

Toward Equalizing Opportunity

The American people should set as their ultimate goal an educational system in which at no level—high school, college, graduate school, or professional school—will a qualified individual in any part of the country encounter an insuperable economic barrier to the attainment of the kind of education suited to his aptitudes and interests.

This means that we shall aim at making higher education equally available to all young people, as we now do education in the elementary and high schools, to the extent that their capacity warrants a further social investment in their training.

Obviously this desirable realization of our ideal of equal educational opportunity cannot be attained immediately. But if we move toward it as fast as our economic resources permit, it should not lie too far in the future. Technological advances, that are already resulting in phenomenal increases in productivity per worker, promise us a degree of economic well-being that would have seemed wholly Utopian to our fathers. With wise management of our economy, we shall almost certainly be able to support education at all levels far more adequately in the future than we could in the past.

The Commission recommends that steps be taken to reach the following objectives without delay:

1. High school education must be improved and should be provided for all normal youth. This is a minimum essential. We cannot safely permit any of our citizens for any reason other than incapacity, to stop short of a high school education or its equivalent. To achieve the purpose of such education, however, it must be improved in facilities and in the diversity of its curriculum. Better high school education is essential, both to raise the caliber of students entering college and to provide the best training possible for those who end their formal education with the twelfth grade.

2. The time has come to make education through the fourteenth grade available in the same way that high school education is now available. This means that tuition-free education should be available in public institutions to all youth for the traditional freshman and sophomore years or for the tradition 2-year junior college course. To achieve this, it will be necessary to develop much more extensively than at present such opportunities as are now provided in

local communities by the 2-year junior college, community institute, community colleges, or institute of arts and sciences. The name used does not matter, though community college seems to describe these schools best; the important thing is that the services they perform be recognized and vastly expanded. Such institutions make post–high school education available to a much larger percentage of young people than otherwise could afford it. Indeed, as discussed in the volume of this Commission's report, "Organizing Higher Education," such community colleges probably will have to carry a large part of the responsibility for expanding opportunities in higher education.

3. The time has come to provide financial assistance to competent students in the tenth through fourteen grades who would not be able to continue without such assistance. Tuition costs are not the major economic barrier to education, especially in college. Costs of supplies, board, and room, and other living needs are great. Even many high school students are unable to continue in school because of these costs. Arrangements must be made, therefore, to provide additional financial assistance for worthy students who need it if they are to remain in school. Only in this way can we counteract the effect of family incomes so low that even tuition-free schooling is a financial impossibility for their children. Only in this way can we make sure that all who are to participate in democracy are adequately prepared to do so.

4. The time has come to reverse the present tendency of increasing tuition and other student fees in the senior college beyond the fourteenth year, and in both graduate and professional schools, by lowering tuition costs in publicly controlled colleges and by aiding deserving students through inaugurating a program of scholarships and fellowships. Only in this way can we be sure that economic and social barriers will not prevent the realization of the promise

that lies in our most gifted youth. Only in this way can we be certain of developing for the common good all the potential leadership our society produces, no matter in what social or economic stratum it appears.

6. The time has come to make public education at all levels equally accessible to all, without regard to race, creed, sex, or national origin. If education is to make the attainment of a more perfect democracy one of its major goals, it is imperative that it extends its benefits to all on equal terms. It must renounce the practices of discrimination and segregation in educational institutions as contrary to the spirit of democracy. Educational leaders and institutions should take positive steps to overcome the conditions which at present obstruct free and equal access to educational opportunities. Educational programs everywhere should be aimed at undermining and eventually eliminating the attitudes that are responsible for discrimination and segregation—at creating instead attitudes that will make education freely available to all.

California Master Plan (The Donahoe Act) (1960)

Source: Senate Bill 33. Section 1. Division 16.5 of the Education Code, Division 16.5. Higher Education Chapter 1. General Provisions. http://www.cpec.ca.gov/Billtrack/ Donahoe_Act.pdf

After World War II, California acquired national and worldwide importance as a state that was large in population, prosperous in its economic development, and committed to implementing the ideals of mass higher education that had been advanced in the 1947 President's Commission on Higher Education for American Democracy. The California Master Plan of 1960 was soon renamed as the Donahoe Act in honor of Assemblywoman Dorothy Donahoe, chair of the Assembly Education Committee, who passed away on April 4, 1960. She had authored the resolution

(ACR 88) calling for the creation of the Master Plan and had been instrumental in the subsequent negotiations leading to its successful adoption. The act was memorable because it demonstrated that the complexity of institutions required planning and coordination if resources were to be used effectively in promoting a state citizenry that was college educated. The resultant Master Plan was shaped in large measure by the influence of Clark Kerr, president of the world-famous multicampus system of the University of California. The California Master Plan gained national attention, including being featured as a cover story for Time *magazine. More than a half-century after its passage into law in California, the California Master Plan persists as the model and inspiration for postsecondary education expansion and planning in numerous nations world-wide. Ironically, celebration of the half-century anniversary coexisted with grave concern as to the efficacy of this distinctive plan for statewide higher education in the 21st century.*

SENATE BILL NO. 33
SECTION 1. Division 16.5 is added to the Education Code, to read:
DIVISION 16.5. HIGHER EDUCATION
CHAPTER 1. GENERAL PROVISIONS
22500. Public higher education consists of (1) all public junior colleges heretofore and hereafter established pursuant to law, (2) all state colleges heretofore and hereafter established pursuant to law, and (3) each campus, branch and function of the University of California heretofore and hereafter established by The Regents of the University of California.
22501. It is hereby declared to be the policy of the Legislature not to authorize or to acquire sites for new institutions of public higher education unless such sites are recommended by the Coordinating Council for Higher Education and not to authorize existing or new institutions of public education, other than those described in subdivisions (2) and (3) of Section 22500, to offer instruction beyond the fourteenth grade level. Nothing in this section shall be construed to require any further

recommendations as a prerequisite to legislative action with respect to state colleges intended to be in operation by 1965 or University of California campuses intended to be under construction by 1962, as set forth in the recommendations contained in the Master Plan for Higher Education printed at page 42, paragraphs 4 and 6, Senate Journal (Regular Session) for February 1, 1960.

22502. Each segment of public higher education shall strive for excellence in its sphere, as assigned in this division.

22503. This division shall not affect the existence or status of the state nautical school.

22504. The provisions of this division shall supersede the provisions of any other law which conflict with the provisions of this division.

CHAPTER 2. UNIVERSITY OF CALIFORNIA

22550. The Legislature hereby finds and declares that the University of California is the primary state-supported academic agency for research.

22551. The university may provide instruction in the liberal arts and sciences and in the professions, including the teaching profession. The university has exclusive jurisdiction in public higher education over instruction in the profession of law, and over graduate instruction in the professions of medicine, dentistry, veterinary medicine and architecture.

22552. The university has the sole authority in public higher education to award the doctoral degree in all fields of learning, except that it may agree with the state colleges to award joint doctoral degrees in selected fields.

22553. The university may make reasonable provision for the use of its library and research facilities by qualified members of the faculties of other institutions of public higher education in this State.

CHAPTER 3. THE STATE COLLEGE SYSTEM

22600. The State College System shall be administered by a board designated as the Trustees of the State College System of California, which is hereby created.

22601. The board shall be composed of the following four ex officio members: the Governor, the Lieutenant Governor, the

Superintendent of Public Instruction, and the person named by the trustees to serve as the chief executive officer of the system; and 16 appointive members appointed by the Governor, except that the members, as of the effective date of this section, of the State Board of Education shall serve ex officio as and among the first appointive trustees. The terms of the appointive members shall be four years, except that the first appointive trustees, including the members of the State Board of Education, shall classify the terms of their offices by lot so that four of the first appointive terms shall expire on the first day of March of each calendar year, commencing in 1961 and ending in 1964. The Speaker of the Assembly shall have the status of a Legislative interim committee on the subject of the State College System and shall meet with the board and participate in its work to the extent that such participation is not incompatible with his position as a Member of the Legislature.

22605. The State College System shall be entirely independent of all political and sectarian influence and kept free therefrom in the appointment of its trustees and in the administration of its affairs, and no person shall be debarred admission to any department of the state colleges on account of sex.

22606. The primary function of the state colleges is the provision of instruction for undergraduate students and graduate students, through the master's degree, in the liberal arts and sciences, in applied fields and in the professions, including the teaching profession. Presently established two-year programs in agriculture are authorized, but other two-year programs shall be authorized only when mutually agreed upon by the Trustees of the State College System and the State Board of Education. The doctoral degree may be awarded jointly with the University of California, as provided in Section 22552. Faculty research is authorized to the extent that it is consistent with the primary function of the state colleges and the facilities provided for that function.

CHAPTER 4. JUNIOR COLLEGES

22650. The public junior colleges shall continue to be a part of the public school system of this State. The State Board of

Education shall prescribe minimum standards for the formation and operation of public junior colleges and exercise general supervision over public junior colleges.

22651. Public junior colleges shall offer instruction through but not beyond the fourteenth grade level, which instruction may include, but shall not be limited to, programs in one or more of the following categories: (1) standard collegiate courses for transfer to higher institutions; (2) vocational and technical fields leading to employment; and (3) general or liberal arts courses. Studies in these fields may lead to the associate in arts or associate in science degree.

CHAPTER 5. CO-ORDINATING COUNCIL FOR HIGHER EDUCATION

22700. There is hereby created an advisory body, the Coordinating Council for Higher Education, to be composed of three representatives each of the University of California, the State College System, the public junior colleges, the private colleges and universities in the State, and the general public. The university shall be represented by three representatives appointed by the regents. The State College System shall be represented by its chief executive officer and two trustees appointed by the trustees. Public junior colleges shall be represented by a member of the State Board of Education or its chief executive officer as the board may from time to time determine, and a member of a local public junior college governing board and a public junior college administrator. The junior college governing board member shall be selected by the State Board of Education from a list or lists of five names submitted for its consideration by any association or associations of state-wide coverage which represent junior college governing boards. The public junior college administrator shall be selected by the State Board of Education from a list of five names submitted for its consideration by the California Junior College Association. The private colleges and universities shall be represented by three persons, each of whom shall be affiliated with a private institution of higher education as a governing board member or as a staff member in an academic or administrative capacity and shall be appointed by the Governor after consultation with an association or associations of such private institutions. The general public shall be represented by three members appointed by the Governor. Appointments and removals made pursuant to this section shall be at the sole discretion of the appointing authority specified herein.

22701. The council shall appoint and may remove a director in the manner hereinafter specified. He shall appoint persons to such staff positions as the council may authorize.

22702. The council shall prescribe rules for the transaction of its own affairs, subject, however, to the following requirements and limitations: (1) the votes of all representatives shall be recorded; (2) effective action shall require the affirmative vote of eight members; and (3) the affirmative votes of 10 members hall be necessary to the appointment or removal of the director.

22703. The coordinating council shall have the following functions, advisory to the governing boards of the institutions of public higher education and to appropriate state officials; (1) review of the annual budget and capital outlay requests of the university and the State College System, and presentation of comments on the general level of support sought; (2) advice as to the application of the provisions of this division delineating the different functions of public higher education and counsel as to the programs appropriate to each segment thereof, and in connection therewith shall submit to the Governor and to the Legislature within five days of the beginning of each general session a report which contains recommendations as to necessary or desirable changes, if any, in the functions and programs of the several segments of public higher education; and (3) development of plans for the orderly growth of public higher education and the making of recommendations on the need for and location of new facilities and programs.

22704. The council shall have power to require the institutions of public higher education to submit data on costs, selection and retention of students, enrollments, plant capacities and other matters pertinent to effective planning and co-ordination, and shall furnish information concerning such matters to the Governor and to the Legislature as requested by them.

22705. This division shall be known and may be cited as the Donahoe Higher Education Act.

SEC. 2. There is hereby appropriated from the General Fund for the support of the state system of higher education the sum of one hundred thirty-one thousand eight hundred sixty dollars ($131,860) or so much thereof as may be necessary, to be expended as follows:

(a) To the Trustees of the State College System of California for expenses incurred by the trustees pursuant to Chapter 3 (commencing at Section 22600)of Division 16.5 of the Education Code, including planning for the uninterrupted performance of the functions and duties transferred to the board—$81,860

(b) To the Co-ordinating Council for Higher Education for expenses incurred by the council pursuant to Chapter 5 (commencing at Section 22700) of Division 16.5 of the Education Code—$50,000

Higher Education Act Reauthorization: Creation of the BEOG (Pell Grants) (1972)

Source: Public Law Higher Education Act of 1965, Title IV, Part A, Subpart 1; 20 U.S.C. 1070a. Amendments: Public Law 92-318-June 23, 1972. Pages 247–251.

Although federal programs for student financial aid had been established through various, sporadic initiatives by the late 1960s, it was the 1972 reauthorization of the Higher Education Act that provided the setting for a large-scale, enduring program. The Basic Educational Opportunity Grants (BEOG) were the linchpin of a multifaceted constellation of scholarship grants, loans, and work-study programs that were generously funded—and focused on making undergraduate education accessible and affordable, especially to young women and men from historically underserved constituencies. The BEOG eventually was renamed Pell Grants in honor of U.S. Senator Claiborne Pell (D, RI), a longtime advocate and the architect of the program. The BEOG was distinctive in that it was a federal grant that did not require repayment by the student; furthermore, it was defined and administered according to a new lexicon of financial aid terminology—and coordination with families, colleges, and state agencies.

PUBLIC LAW 92-318 – June 23, 1972

Part A of title IV of such Act is amended to read as follows:

PART A – GRANTS TO STUDENTS IN ATTENDANCE
AT INSTITUTIONS OF
HIGHER EDUCATION

Statement of Purpose: Program Authorization

Sec. 401. (a) It is the purpose of this part, to assist in making available the benefits of postsecondary education to qualified students in institutions of higher education by –

(1) Providing basic educational opportunity grants (hereinafter referred to as "basic grants") to all eligible students;

(2) Providing supplemental educational opportunity grants (hereinafter referred to as 'supplemental grants') to those students of exceptional need who, for lack of such a grant, would be unable to obtain the benefits of a postsecondary education.

(3) Providing for payments to the States to assist them in making financial aid available to such students; and

(4) Providing for special programs and projects designed (A) to identify and encourage qualified youths with financial or cultural need with a potential for postsecondary education, (B) to prepare students from low-income families for postsecondary education, and (C) to provide remedial (including remedial language study) and other services to students.

Sec. 411. (a) (1) the commissioner shall during the period beginning July 1, 1972 and ending June 30, 1975, pay to each student who has been accepted for enrollment in, or is in good standing at, an institution of higher education (according to the prescribed standards, regulations, and practices of that institution) for each academic year during which that student is in attendance at that an institution, as an undergraduate, a basic grant in the amount for which that student is eligible as determined pursuant to paragraph (2)

(2) (A) (i) The amount of the basic grant for a student eligible under this subpart for any academic year shall be $1,400, less an amount equal to the amount determined under paragraph (3) to be the expected family contribution with respect to that student for that year.

(B) (i) The amount of a basic grant to which a student is entitled under this subpart for any academic year shall not exceed 50 per centum of the actual cost of attendance at the institution at which the student is in attendance.

What Price Egalitarianism? (1981)

Source: Debra Shore. "What Price Egalitarianism?" *Brown Alumni Monthly* 81(February 1981), 12–18. Used by permission.

Whereas most historical documents on the rising costs of higher education show the national or "macro" perspective of legislators, policy analysts, and lobbyists—with emphasis on the conditions and construction of formal financial aid programs, this 1981 article provides a distinctive, underreported point of view: it brings to life how simultaneously university officials (presidents, deans, vice presidents, and board members) deal with severe budget problems as well as how applicants and incumbent students talk with their families to try to plan their educational future—and how decisions by one constituency influence others.

Soaring energy costs and a larger-than-expected enrollment of freshmen and upperclassmen needing financial aid have thrown Brown's balanced budget into a precarious position and the University now faces some difficult questions. Can Brown afford financial aid to students? If so, at what cost? And if not, what does that mean for diversity—racial, geo- graphic, economic—in the student body at Brown?

Craig Jones is a senior at Brown, a history concentrator from Winston-Salem, North Carolina. He is tall, blond, wears boots, and sounds like the country he comes from. Craig is also the first person in his family to go to college (his mother, a National Merit Scholar, dropped out after one semester to marry her high school sweetheart). He had never heard of Brown until his junior year in high school, when an older friend began investigating colleges in the north.

"I went through the catalogues and I narrowed it down to ten schools," Craig says, "and seven of 'em were in the Northeast. Brown, Amherst, Tufts—all had pretty liberal curriculums, no distribution requirements. I had this idea I was going to be a leftist social re-former. I winnowed it down to four schools— Carolina, Duke, and Virginia, and I decided to take one long shot and I picked Brown. I'd never been to any of 'em but I looked at things like minority students and geographic mix what most people concentrated in and those kind of demographic things. I figured that because Brown was an Ivy League school it probably had a classy looking diploma.

"My mother was really opposed to the idea of my going away to school. And during the year I started planting seeds in my mother's head. I didn't get in at Virginia; I was waitlisted at Duke, and got in to Brown and Carolina. I called my mom from the post office and I said 'Guess what? I'm going to Brown.' and she said, 'Well, boy, I hope you find th' money.' "

Hope You Find the Money

No phrase more succinctly describes the central problem at Brown University. Indeed, many of the crises in Brown's history have centered on finding the money. One has only to recall the effort in 1769 to find a permanent home for the fledgling Rhode Island College—with Bristol County, Newport, and Providence entering into the bidding (Providence won, the chief reasons being the large sum of money subscribed by the community—nearly $9,000, the central location, and easy communication)—or ever attempt to attract a patron by offering to name the College for any-one who donated $5,000 (Nicholas Brown made the offer, in 1804). More recently, one may recall the severe financial crisis at own in the early 1970s—a period when the University spent nearly $15 million from its endowment to meet budget deficits—and the occupation of University Hall by minority students in 1975 to dem-onstrate their concern that the University was not living up to its commitments to minority affairs, this occurring in a larger net of student concern over budget cuts.

Today, though the situation is much improved over the early 1970s and indeed no subsequent offer has been issued for a donor to name the college, and though the University has id a balanced budget for the last two years, Brown is struggling still. The question is, as always, how much can be done with too lit-tle? This year the problem centers on financial aid.

With annual charges totaling over $10,000 next year, Brown is indisputably one of the most expensive colleges in the country. As costs of attending Brown have risen, Brown has attempted to ease some of this burden to students and their families by also increas-ing financial aid, but resources of the University have not kept pace with the costs. "While our sources of revenue are growing," says Senior Vice President Richard Ramsden '59, "they're not growing much as or in excess of inflation." Tuition is Brown's largest source of income and it has risen approximately 60 per cent in the last five years. Other sources of revenues are income from endowment, indirect cost recovery from grants and contracts, and gifts from alumni through the Brown Fund.

Two things happened this year that put special pressure on the always pinched budget process: it now appears that Brown's energy costs, primarily its electric bill, will run approximately $600,000 to $700,000 over budget; and financial aid at the undergraduate and graduate levels is also running about $600,000 over budget. Fortunately, Brown's balanced budget for the current year can absorb those overruns. "We can cover those costs with increased revenues," Dick Ramsden explains. "We have more students, short-term investment income, indirect cost recovery and a contingency fund. We built the budget on an enrollment of 5,175 undergraduate students, but we now have about 5,350, so we will be balanced for this year. On the other hand," Ramsden says, "for the next year, in spite of all the money and efforts for conservation, our electricity costs are going through the roof." Since 1973, Brown's electricity costs have risen 202 percent, though consumption has dropped approximately 10 percent. Cost per kilowatt hour almost tripled from 1973 to 1979—from one and a half cents to four cents—and rose rapidly again last year. In the year ended June 30, 1980, Brown spent approximately five cents per kilowatt hour; the rate had reached about six and a half cents per kWh by last fall and was expected to reach eight cents on January 1. "That could conceivably go to nine or ten cents in the next fiscal year," Ramsden says. "New England is the highest cost area in the country for electric power, and Rhode Island is the only state that has no nuclear or hydroelectric power, so we're having to build considerably more money into the energy budget than we first thought."

The second part of this year's struggle has to do with financial aid. From 1974 to 1979, approximately 30 percent of the undergraduate students at Brown received some form of financial aid from the University, be it in the form of an outright grant of money, a loan, a campus job (known as work/study), or a combination of all three. During that same period, federal aid for college students grew rapidly (in the form of Basic

Educational Opportunity Grants [BEOGs] and Supplemental Education Opportunity Grants [SEOGs]). This permitted the University's total awards to students to grow considerably, though the total amount required from its unrestricted income was actually modest. Most observers of the federal scene feel that rapid growth has now ended, and some worry about the extent to which even the present aid programs will receive funding. Both prospects place a greater burden on universities to meet the needs of their students. Moreover, says Dick Ramsden, "because of inflation, which has resulted in high increases in our own charges, the need of our students has been growing even more rapidly than our fees."

Each year in February, March and April, the Brown admission office accepts applicants for the freshman class without regard to any student's ability to pay. (This is firm policy.) The names of these accepted students are then sent to the financial-aid office, where Director Alan Maynard '47 and his staff calculate an aid package for those applying for financial aid—usually a combination of grant, loan, and job—based on the student's need as assessed by the standards of the College Scholarship Service. When an offer of admission to Brown University then goes out in mid-April, an offer of financial aid accompanies it. (In the latter half of the 1950s the Ivy League schools agreed to offer basically similar aid packages to mutually accepted candidates so that no school could effectively "buy" a student, be she an athlete or he a physicist, with a substantially larger offer of aid. Hence, in early April, Alan Maynard meets with the financial- aid directors of the other Ivy schools to adjust, up or down, the awards to be offered to these overlapping students.)

The admission office extends offers of admission to a certain number of students based on an estimate of how many will matriculate: for a freshman class of 1,300 students, the admission office accepts 2,600 students, anticipating that 50 percent will decide to enroll at Brown. (This 50 percent is known as the yield and predicting the yield is a delicate business. If the yield is up, that is, if more students decide to come to Brown than the University counted on, there may not be enough dormitory space to accommodate all the students who want it, and so on.) The financial-aid office bases its budget for freshman financial aid on the same anticipated yield as the admission office. They expect that about 50 percent of those students offered aid will decide to enroll at Brown and thus require the aid money. So, with a freshman financial-aid budget of $1.5 million, the financial-aid office can "go out" with offers of $3 million.

This year, more freshmen requiring aid enrolled at Brown than anyone expected. The yield was up. Thirty-seven percent of this year's freshmen received financial aid (485 students, compared to 400 in last year's freshman class). This rise of 4 or 5 percent in the number of freshmen requiring aid meant that the financial-aid office needed about $315,000 more than was originally projected. This year, too, more upper-class students qualified for and needed aid; both these factors, the considerable increase in the number of financial-aid students at the freshman and at upper class levels, have caused financial-aid expenditures for 1980–81 to run approximately $600,000 over the budget.

In some ways the University's budget is not much different from one's own household budget. Let's say you've set aside a certain amount each month for rent and your landlord suddenly raises it—or, if you own your own home, your property taxes are increased. Well, chances are you dig in deeper and find the money somewhere. You spend less on food or clothes; you defer maintenance (a traditional university budget ploy); you buy fewer books; you live a pinched existence, hoping your salary will increase enough to cover the increase in costs (as the University hopes contributions to the alumni fund will increase and investments will prosper). Sometimes you have to borrow money or dip into your savings, as Brown borrowed heavily from its endowment—its savings—in the early 1970s. Sometimes you float a check, essentially paving this month's rent with next month's paycheck (you know that one?). A rent increase, unfortunately, is not a one-time expenditure; you face the higher bill each month. Similarly, an increase in financial aid is not a one-time expenditure. "When you make an offer to a freshman," Dick Ramsden explains, "you're not making a one-year obligation. You're really making a four-year obligation." So when Brown signed a new lease with the increased number of freshmen requiring financial aid this year, the University knew it was facing what is essentially a four-year rent increase. And while Brown was able to cover the $600,000 increase this year, it had essentially used next year's paycheck to do so.

Take a look at the books. In the 1980–81 budget, Brown set aside $5,030,000 for undergraduate financial aid, an increase of 13.4 percent over the previous year. But that wasn't enough money. More freshmen came requiring aid—once an offer is made Brown is bound to make good on it—and more upperclassmen needed it, too. Apparently Brown's increase in fees for 1980–81 of $1,140, or 13.1 percent, exceeded after-tax family income increases for the calendar year 1979, on which 1980–81 awards are based. Hence Brown's actual expenditures for undergraduate financial aid will probably be around $5,650,000 for 1980–81.

This year, as Dick Ramsden says, Brown can cover; the confrontation concerns next year's budget. The problem is that actual expenditures this year are now at the level which Brown might normally have expected to reach next year. A general rule of thumb followed by the University is that any increase in tuition requires a concomitant increase in the financial-aid budget. Substantial increases in tuition and fees—beyond, say, 11 or 12 percent—require even larger increases in the financial-aid budget because more students will then qualify for aid. The 1980–81 financial-aid budget represented a 13.4 percent increase over 1979–80, accompanying the 13.1 percent increase in fees. Had things followed according to plan, a 10- to 12-percent increase in the 1981–82 budget over the 1980–81 budget of $5,030,000 would result in a 1981–82 budget of between $5.5 and $5.6 million, slightly less than the $5,650,000 the University now expects to spend this year. Thus to build a "normal" increase for next year's budget on top of the actual figures spent this year would require a 1981–82 budget of $6.2

to S6.3 million, approximately a 25-percent increase over the 1980–81 budget. So, if Brown hopes to continue to make good on its commitment to the financial-aid students now here, and if the University wishes to maintain its commitment to a diverse student body, then it will have to come up with more money for financial aid next year. How can this be done?

Where Will the Money Come From?

Brown is a people-intensive proposition: most of its money comes from people and most of its expenses go for people. Tuition and fees provide about 65 percent of Brown's revenues; salaries, benefits, and student aid comprise 63 percent of Brown's expenses. So when more money is needed, it come; from people, too. The question, of course, is . . . who?

From the Students?

(1) Brown can increase tuition. Because the University does not have many endowment funds restrict) solely to scholarship grants, unlike some other Ivy League schools, most (the money devoted to financial aid comes from tuition. In essence, the 70 percent of Brown's students who do n receive outright grant aid subsidize the 30 percent who do. If tuition, room, and board for 1981–82 were increased more than the now-projected $1,350, or 14 percent, some of that additional income could be used for financial aid.

(2) Brown can increase the amount of "self-help" required of financial-aid students in the form of jobs and loans. Financial aid students at Brown receive anywhere from $100 to $7,500 depending on their need. All these students have as a part of their aid package a self-help requirement; students are expected to contribute to the costs of their education by working during the summer and school year and by taking out loans under a variety of federal programs. (The University guarantees these students employment during the academic year; financial-aid

recipients are not expected to work more than ten hours a week.) In 80–81, students were expected to save between $750 and $950 from their summer jobs (depending on their class; seniors are expected to earn more than freshmen) and to contribute $2,400 in term-time self-help—an average of $1,450 in loans and $950 in a job. (This total comes from working ten hours per week at minimum wage.) Each $100 increase in the term-time self-help expectation decreases the necessary financial-aid grant budget by $166,000. (By the same token, each $100 increase in resident fees, in the absence of other sources of aid, results in increased student need of $166,000. This is based on 60 grant aid recipients.) So, the University could increase its self-help expectations—between $400 and $700—have been proposed—and thus decrease the burden on the University budget to come up with more grant money.

(3) Brown could limit the number of students on financial aid.

Since the University has already ride commitments to support current students, this approach would have to start with the freshman class. This could be done by placing a limit on the freshman financial-aid budget and by assuming that only 375 to 400 freshmen receive aid in 1981–82, compared to 450 this year. Placing a limit on the freshman-aid budget will require rejection of otherwise qualified candidates.

What guarantee does Brown have that the same miscalculation that occurred last year won't occur this year? Once the offers go out, Brown has no choice but to comply— and since pre-wiring the yield is a risky endeavor, there is no real guarantee that next year's yield of financial-aid applicants doesn't also surpass expectations. But the Brown admission office does have a procedure to reduce the number of financial-aid students before the offers go out if the total aid offers go over the Budget (Brown Alumni Monthly, April 1979).

The process, devised by the Committee on Admission and Financial Aid (a group of students, faculty members, and administrators that advises the university on admission and financial-aid policies), works this way: As the Board of Admission makes its decisions throughout February, March, and April to admit or reject applicants to Brown, it varies across some candidates who are coined "marginal." Whether for reasons of academic ability or personality, these students do not receive a clear vote for admission—but neither are they rejected out of hand. In a way, they constitute a working wait list and these candidates receive a special designation as such.

If Admission Director Jim Rogers '56 discovers in early April that he has accepted too many applicants—remember he can go out with only a certain number of offers, too—these specially designated students are the first to be dropped to the standard waiting list. If, on the other hand, he discovers that he has accepted too few students, he takes from this group for the "A-1 Admit" pile. The names of these candidates are sent to the financial-aid office along with the other accepted applicants, and Alan Maynard and his staff construct aid packages for those who have applied for financial aid. When all the tallying is done, if Alan Maynard finds that he has awarded too much—that the amount of aid he proposes to offer to accepted freshmen exceeds the amount he has in his budget for freshman financial aid—then a special procedure is invoked.

"We print out a list of all financial-aid students by the amount of scholarship they were awarded, in descending order by amount," Rogers explains. "We are charged to look at that list and pick out those students who are academically most marginal, which we have already done by giving them a special designation when we accepted them in the committee. We look at everyone and then pull those with the highest aid awards. We have to take students off to meet a certain monetary figure," Rogers stresses, "not a certain number of students." So far, this procedure has been used twice: in 1975, when seventy-two students were removed from the accepted pool in order to correct a potential aid deficit; and in 1978, when eighteen students were removed from the accepted pool because freshman financial-aid offers were $100,000 over budget. "Generally we put these students on the waiting list," Rogers says, "but we usually have no money for people on the waiting list." It is this procedure that would be used to meet a dollar limit on the freshman financial-aid budget.

(4) Brown could accept more students. More students would mean additional tuition income—and, proportionately, additional financial-aid recipients.

From the Faculty and Staff?

(1) Brown could reduce the increases in compensation it has pledged to faculty members and staff.
(2) It could cut some members of the faculty and staff, thereby saving money.

From Other Sources?

(1) Brown could reduce the amount of money budgeted for library acquisitions.
(2) It could further defer maintenance to its buildings and machinery.
(3) It could board up its new athletic center, which will cost some money to open and maintain.

The dilemma, re-phrased:
Go back and think for just a moment about that household budget and that rent increase. Clearly you had several choices—to look for more money, to reduce your style of living, to sell some assets, take in a roommate, whatever. But there is another

possibility. You could move. You know, reassess the situation and decide it wasn't worth it. You can decide to get out.

In surveying its own household and regarding its contract with financial-aid students, Brown too could reassess the situation—and Brown could decide to move. Faced with increasing budgetary pressures and not enough money to go round, Brown is now at the cusp of a major debate concerning financial aid and the very mission of the University. And Brown may or may not decide to shift its position. For instance, what is Brown's commitment to financial aid? Can Brown afford to support students who cannot pay their own way—or as many as it has in the past? Does the University want to? Does Brown really need a diverse student body? (What is diversity in a student body anyway?) What obligation does Brown have to ensure that every student who wants to come here and whose application is accepted is indeed able to come? Why? What price egalitarianism?

Fifty-three percent of the students who receive financial aid at Brown are either athletes or minority students and 69 percent of all minority students at Brown last year—Hispanics, Asians, blacks and American Indians—received financial aid. So any reduction in the number of students receiving aid may mean—though not necessarily—fewer athletes and minority students at Brown. Is the University reneging on its commitments to minority students? To a diverse student body? This is the heart of the present confrontation.

In November and December, when Brown's administrators were attempting to finish constructing next year's budget, Dick Ramsden told the members of the Committee on Admission and Financial Aid (CAFA) that Brown could probably not afford a financial-aid budget of more than $5.6 to $5.8 million in 1981–82 and that to meet even this figure would require substantial increases in self-help and a limit placed on the freshman financial-aid budget (to approximately $1,500,000). This prompted a flurry of objections. At an open forum sponsored by CAFA, two primary concerns emerged from the crowd of students attending: first, Where am I going to get the money for these new assessments in self-help? And second, Is Brown going to suffer in its heterogeneity if changes are made?

Impressed by the severe strain many students on financial aid already feel, the members of CAFA voted to reconsider their initial $5.8-million budget recommendation. (CAFA recommends a financial-aid figure to the Advisory Committee on University Planning which makes its final recommendations to the president, who submits the budget to the Corporation for approval.) A CAFA subcommittee returned with a $6.1-million figure which, if adopted, would reduce to some extent the increase in self-help expected of each student. This figure of $6.1 million was recommended to ACUP in December. That committee has yet to make its final decision. (CAFA's recommendation was based on an assumed $1,000 increase in tuition and a $400 increase in self-help. It now seems that tuition and fees will increase by $1,350 and the self-help requirement by as much as $700.)

The question, however, remains: Where will the money come from? If Brown is to absorb a greater percentage of the financial-aid budget—that is, if the additional money is intended to come from scholarship grants rather than from self-help or fewer freshmen financial-aid recipients—where will the money come from? The tradeoffs, too, remain: the money must come from increased tuition or decreased salaries.

Mixed Voices

Carolyn-Michelle Vernon '83, a member of CAFA and an international relations concentrator from Ossining, New York; Jennifer Freeman '81, an applied math and sociology concentrator from Atlanta, Georgia; Falomni Prescott '82, a sociology of education concentrator from Brooklyn, New York:

Jennifer: "If we do get the $6.1 million or if we don't, either way we're hurting."

Falomni: "It's not even the incoming freshmen, but a lot of us just won't be here next year. I already have the maximum amount of loans each year. I've never been able to save the amount that they want you to save over the summer and I have never made the $900 throughout the year that they say you should make."

Carolyn: "A lot of financial-aid students live in areas where unemployment is fantastic and if they live at home they can't make the kind of money the University says they should."

Jennifer: "Because of extra loans fewer financial-aid students will be going on to graduate school because they come out of here with $7,000 in loans. Between forty-five and fifty-five seniors are going to graduate this year When they entered, there were eighty or ninety. So many of them left after freshman year because of financial difficulties."

Falomni: "Don't be fooled by the seemingly large package you get as a freshman because they will be decreased. My mother and I have talked about it. I have the maximum loans an even she has loans and we're just debted out."

Carolyn: "The whole attitude or lack of concern on the part of the administration is what really disturbs me 'Well, this is the way life is—some of us make it, some of us don't.' 'This is how the school is; if you can't afford it well. ... ' 'It's unfortunate that you can't pay—well, goodbye. ... ' That's the attitude to me."

Jennifer: "With the more affluent blacks now being recruited by Brown, it's just like different heights, different weights, you have different colors, am people believe there is diversity and interaction among people of all these diverse backgrounds but that's not true, they're gonna do that, they shouldn't even bother with window dressing."

Carolyn: "They say the leaders of tomorrow come from places like Brown but if all the students are upper-class white people, who are you just clearly saying our leaders are going to be? If you're not allowed in certain circles, you know what that means."

Jennifer: "Brown will become more and more dependent on those who can pay and who can afford it. It won't be able to grow the way it wants to."

Richard J. Ramsden '59, senior vice president: "Eighteen months ago we found that our main electrical feeder line from

Prince Lab to Walter Wilson was not only overloaded but in a dangerous condition, and so very quickly we had to dig it up and put in a new line. That had to be done and it was an expense of $250,000 to $300,000.

"The compressors at Meehan Rink now have to be replaced; they are delicate machines and Meehan is twenty years old. We need to paint the interior ad to do it properly is probably a $40,000 to $50,000 job. The costs of doing many of these things rise so much every year that it's better to get them done now, so we're balancing between current needs and future needs. What you do when you run a deficit you're over consuming for *that* generation, which simply means you're early leaving less for future generations. Students understand this with respect to the environment, but it's exactly the same with the budget. Why are we so special that we can afford take more than our fair share in consuming Brown's physical and financial resources in what is designed to be a perpetual institution? We want to leave this a stronger place."

Ed Kornhauser, professor of engineering, present member and former chairman of CAFA: "We may eventually have to re-think the philosophy of our financial-aid program. That's not being done now. We're getting by year by year with a little squeezing, a little pushing. Eventually we'll have to make some kind of decision whether to allocate a larger fraction of money to financial aid or to limit the number of students who can receive aid.

"Ideally we should admit a class without respect to financial need at all. In practice we can't do that. Our resources are limited and we have to strike some balance. If you spend more on financial, you have less to spend on the things which make this college worth coming to in the first place.

"I don't think we should be ashamed of the fact that this is not a public institution and we don't have resources to provide a free education to everybody. I think we have a reasonable compromise—30 percent on aid and 70 percent cash customers. That's about as far as we can go.

"In order to get more money, they would raise tuition another couple of hundred dollars, which is effectively putting the burden on the larger portion of students and removing it from the aid students, or they could take it from salaries and reduce the increase in compensation that the faculty had been hoping for. Those are really the only two areas you can get money from.

"If you make tuition too high, you begin to lose students to your competition. If you cut salaries, you begin to lose faculty."

Harriet Sheridan, dean of the College since 1979 and a member of CAFA: "It is important to stress that financial aid is not an end in itself but a means to an end and that end is the student body. Who comes to Brown and why do we strive for a certain mix? Financial aid is not a charity, but it is in fact to the advantage of those who subsidize them to have a financially aided population here. One gets a mix of contributions. Without this mix, Brown would be a very homogeneous place. Yet the world is not a very homogeneous place and those who will thrive are those who can get along with people regardless of their financial status. Part of Brown's mission is to provide for all of its students the complexity of populations in this country and on the globe.

"But it is also true that we cannot continue supporting students at the rate we have been without coming awfully close to killing the goose that lays the golden egg. Where is the point at which you begin to create a withering effect on the University, by draining funds for innovative programs, buildings, and faculty?

"This is not an us-and-them problem. We are in a national context and this is happening all around us. We are having a confrontation with the realities of the economy. It can't be the same as it was in the past, yet you want to maintain a decent course. . . .

"Maybe the single best thing to leave your child as a legacy is a good education. The one legacy that one gives that can only be a beneficial one is education."

David Gold '81, a political science concentrator and member of ACUP from Brookline, Massachusetts: "Where can we come out with a balanced budget? We'll have to throw out add-ons.

We're going to be pushing tuition as far as we can and faculty salaries down as far as we can just to make our basic needs for next year. ... I'm beginning to think that we can't accept the current-state budget concept. We're going to have a damn hard time just paying for our faculty and heating this place.

"The reason that Brown has such problems is because it's an impoverished institution compared to its neighbors. All the places with which we compete effectively have much larger endowments. That Brown is able to do so much is incredible.

"When you ask whether we can come up with more money [for financial aid], the answer is, Tell me where? There are not millions wasted here and as a practical matter it's a fairly efficiently run university. We're not going to get it from waste, so we're going to have to get it from programs. "As financial need grows and grows, our capacity to meet that need will not grow, and that's important. I think our policy has been and will continue to be: we'll do what we can but we can't do it all.

"Let's talk about priorities. There are no easy answers. Why should this institution have a diverse student body? If our commitment is to education, we can educate the 5,000 whitest, WASP-iest people in the country and do very well. Do we have a moral obligation? We have to define what that is. There are strong counter-arguments to the traditional approach to financial aid. That will be a very bitter debate.

"We don't know what we mean when we say 'diversity.' It may come down to financial aid being only a matter of philanthropy and we should just decide how much philanthropy we can afford and what we want to get for that philanthropy.

"What is our relationship to society and why doesn't society in the form of the federal government pay? If education is a social good, why doesn't society pay for it?"

Howard R. Swearer, president of Brown University:

"What can we control? Salaries, tuition, library purchases, numbers of people (students and faculty). We can't control energy. Trying to keep all those in some kind of balance in an increasingly contentious society is a pretty neat trick. I think what we're aiming for is some kind of balance. There will be disagreements among some constituencies, but that's what we're aiming for.

"I think we want to have a diversified student body, diversified in every sense—racially, geographically, income. We're looking for academic talent, but also for that mix which makes for an interesting student body. We will try to minimize how much the pinch on financial aid will impinge on that.

"Above all else, we have to maintain the academic quality, the quality of the educational experience of the students that are here. That just has to be our main concern. It would be a poor effort to increase the financial-aid budget and bring more students to Brown, but then give them a second-rate experience.

In a way, Craig Jones is one of the lucky ones. He did find the money, and he is due to graduate in June. For most of the rest of us, however—students, faculty, and administrators alike—the problems and the pinch linger on.

Delta Cost Project Report Summary (2009)

Source: Trends in College Spending Where Does the Money Come From? Where Does It Go? Washington, DC: Delta Cost Project, 2009. Available at http://www.deltacost project.org/resources/pdf/trends_in_spending-summary.pdf. Used by permission.

This Executive Summary of the 2009 Delta Cost Project Report is one in a succession of systematic, thoughtful analyses of college and university spending and revenues that has shaped the nationwide discourse on the financing of higher education.

Executive Summary of January 2009

About Trends in College Spending

The report, the second from the Delta Project on Postsecondary Costs, Productivity, and Accountability, examines revenue and expenditure data for nearly 2,000 public and private non-profit colleges and universities (representing more than 75 percent of higher education enrollment) and analyzes recent trends, focusing on the period from 2002 to 2006. It is the most up-to-date and comprehensive assessment of higher education finance in the nation.

Highlights

Trends in College Spending analyzes recent patterns in higher education finance by looking at six primary metrics:

Revenue

The shift away from public funding of institutions continues, with most of the new money in higher education coming from tuition and fees, private gifts, and grants and contracts. Much of the new revenue is restricted by the donor, and is not available to pay for core educational programs. At public institutions, state appropriations per student declined from 2002 to 2005 and rebounded slightly in 2006, but did not rebound to earlier levels.

Spending

From 2002 to 2006, total spending on education and related services declined for all types of institutions except research universities. Additionally, the share of educational spending dedicated to classroom instruction declined at all types of institutions from 2002 to 2006. By contrast, spending on academic support, student services, administration, and maintenance increased as a share of total educational costs over the same period.

Student Share of Educational Cost

Students are paying more of the total cost of their education at all institutions except private research universities. From 2002 to 2006, the share of educational costs represented by student tuition rose from just over one-third to nearly one-half at public four-year institutions. At private master's and bachelor's institutions, students are paying between 75 and 85 percent of the full cost of their education.

Spending and Enrollment

The fastest enrollment growth is occurring at the institutions that spend the least per student and have seen little or no total spending growth over the most recent five-year period.

Spending and Tuition

At public research universities, nearly all of the revenues from student tuition increases from 2002 to 2006 (92 percent) were used to offset revenue losses from other sources, primarily state appropriations. At public master's institutions and community colleges, all of the revenues from increased tuition during this period replaced losses from other sources.

At private colleges and universities, tuition increases fueled increased spending. Nearly three-quarters of educational spending increases at private research universities from 2002 to 2006 can be linked to increased tuition.

Spending and Results

Over the past decade, spending per completion (certificates or degrees) has remained fairly steady at public colleges and universities, despite modest year-to-year fluctuations. From 2002 to 2006, spending per completion rose at private research universities, and declined or remained stable at private master's and bachelor's institutions.

Why Metrics Matter

The story told by the metrics in *Trends in College Spending* is relevant and urgent because:

Tough choices loom, and these choices should be guided by data. Campus and university system boards and state policymakers face difficult decisions about spending and priorities in light of the economic meltdown. If institutions are to restrain tuition hikes without sacrificing the quality of their educational programs, they need to use data to target resources to priorities that will pay off in getting students to and through college. Yet very few institutions or states actually look at spending data as part of the budget process.

The call for financial transparency in higher education is growing louder. Policymakers and the public are showing increasing skepticism about spending in higher education, questioning whether tuition increases are helping to expand access and improve quality. The data in this report show that this is a valid question. If colleges and universities want to successfully compete for increasingly scarce public dollars, they must be more transparent about where the money comes from, where it goes, and what it buys—in language that makes sense to consumers and policymakers.

Students are paying for more—and arguably getting less. The economic downturn is likely to bring another round of above-average tuition increases, which means that students will be paying for a larger share of the total educational bill even as less goes to pay for classroom instruction. This will raise new questions about the appropriate role for tuition as a funding source for research, graduate, and professional education, or for high-cost programs that are no longer being subsidized by the state or the federal government.

Print Resources

Historical Context of Higher Education

Books

Altbach, Philip G., Berdahl, Robert O., and Gumport, Patricia J., eds. *American Higher Education in the Twenty-First Century: Social, Political, and Economic Challenges*. Baltimore and London: Johns Hopkins University Press, 1999.

> The editors are three senior, established, and widely published researchers on higher education in the United States in areas of state and federal relations, institutional governance, historical development, legal issues, and public policies. They in turn enlisted specialists with expertise in specific themes and subtopics, with the cumulative result of a readable, informed anthology on central topics in the conduct and character of higher education in the 21st century.

Douglass, John Aubrey. *The California Idea and American Higher Education: 1850 to the 1960 Master Plan*. Stanford, CA: Stanford University Press, 2000.

> California represents an important case study of how a state over time made innovative, substantive investments

---

(Kieran Mithani/iStockphoto.com)

in statewide access to higher education. Culminating with the 1960 Master Plan (see Chapter 5, "Documents"), Douglass's comprehensive survey presents the complex story of influential policies in which generous tax support was combined with thoughtful planning to create a model of universal access to affordable higher education at the end of the 20th century. It is a state profile that set a standard nationwide and internationally.

Flexner, Abraham. *Universities: American, English, German.* New York, London, and Toronto: Oxford University Press, 1930.

The author, influential for decades as a primary investigator for the Carnegie Foundation for the Advancement of Education, turned his attention from policy reforms in such areas as medical education, legal education, and general education at colleges and universities in the United States to consider the international context of higher education. Based on a series of lectures he delivered at Oxford University in 1929, the resultant volume presents one of the first detailed analyses of how the distinctive American approach to the mission and character of universities fared in comparison with prestigious, historic universities in Germany and England. The American campus differed from its European and English counterparts in its emphasis on commercialized intercollegiate athletics, vast array of student extracurricular activities, and uneven academic standards.

Horowitz, Helen Lefkowitz. *Campus Life: Undergraduate Cultures from the End of the Eighteenth Century to the Present.* New York: Alfred A. Knopf, 1987.

Whereas many higher education analyses rely on a "top-down" perspective written by and for institutional administrators such as presidents and board members, historian Helen Horowitz provides a grassroots history of higher education from the point of view of undergraduate students. Contemporary college applicants and students will find this account illuminating because it provides narrative and context for understanding the taxonomy of student life, including the distinctive groupings and clusters into which undergraduates coagulate so as to create a world of their own. Horowitz advances the typology of "insiders," "outsiders," and "rebels" as three enduring, principle groups within the student body. Central to this interpretation is identifying and tracking the importance of socioeconomic class and (lack of) money for paying college expenses as a determinant in a student's prospects for stature and prestige within a campus culture.

Jencks, Christopher, and Riesman, David. *The Academic Revolution*. Garden City, NY: Doubleday Anchor, 1968.

Sociologists Jencks and Riesman connect the rising stature of higher education, including faculty and alumni, within American life during the 20th century. One of their key insights is that the major purposes of going to college are to provide certification and socialization—passports into the upper middle class. These benefits of going to college have included both prospects of upward mobility for newcomers to college and a hedge against downward mobility for daughters and sons of established, educated families.

Kerr, Clark. *The Uses of the University*. Cambridge, MA: Harvard University Press, 1963.

The editors of *Change* magazine relied on a survey of higher education leaders in 1980 to reach the conclusion that this book was the most influential work on higher education published during the latter part of the 20th century. Based on Kerr's talks at Harvard's Godkin Lectures in 1960, it provides a concise, fluid account of the expansion of higher education, with particular attention to the rise in funding and influence of the prestigious research university, fueled by sponsored grants from federal agencies.

Kerr, Clark. *The Great Transformation in Higher Education, 1960 to 1980*. Albany: State University of New York Press, 1991.

> Kerr, who served as president of the University of California and chair of the Carnegie Commission on Higher Education, used this valedictory work to provide an anthology of crucial documents and articles that defined the expansion and improvement of American higher education during the crucial two-decade period from 1960 to 1980.

Rudolph, Frederick. *The American College and University: A History*. Athens: University of Georgia Press, 1990 (re-release of original 1962 edition).

> Historian Frederick Rudolph of Williams College contributed the definitive historical account of American colleges and universities with this 1962 book. Particularly pertinent for those interested in the costs of higher education is his Chapter 9, "Financing the Colleges," which provides an original, thorough account of the distinctive American hybrid model of reliance on tuition payments and other sources to operate colleges year-by-year.

Thelin, John R. *A History of American Higher Education* (2nd ed.). Baltimore and London: Johns Hopkins University Press, 2011.

> This comprehensive interpretation of American higher education over 400 years presents for each era an analysis of access, equity, affordability, and social justice in the complex ritual of "going to college." Each chapter includes distinct attention to the profiles and contours of students as consumers and participants in higher education. Originally published in 2004, the second edition (published in 2011) includes a new concluding chapter on

higher education developments during the first decade of the 21st century.

Veysey, Laurence. *The Emergence of the American University*. Chicago: University of Chicago Press, 1964.

How did the ideal of a great university reach fruition in the United States between 1870 and 1910? That is the question that historian Veysey explains in great detail, with attention to the rivalries among heroic university presidents in their respective campaigns for donors, students, and community support. The historical narrative includes a provocative account of the organizational transformation of the 20th-century American university into a complex bureaucracy that included a discernible institutional culture of academics and administrators.

Articles

Delbanco, Andrew. "The Universities in Trouble," *New York Review of Books* 56 (May 14, 2009). http://www.nybooks.com/articles/archives/2009/may/14/the-universities-in-trouble/?pagination=false

Author Delbanco, a distinguished professor of English at Columbia University, brings together in a lucid essay review the distilled insights of several recently published works about the path and problems of the American campus in the early 21st century. In sum, an embarrassment of riches combined with commercialization and sophistication have left colleges and universities at risk, following years of affluence fueled by donations and high tuition charges—and matched by equally great spending.

Goldin, Claudia, and Katz, Lawrence F. "The Shaping of Higher Education: The Formative Years in the United States, 1890 to 1940." *Journal of Economic Perspectives* 13(Winter 1999), 37–62.

The authors, both economists at Harvard, draw from historical census data and institutional records to support their argument that the creation and development of the dominant features of contemporary higher education in the United States took place in the late 19th century and in the decades prior to World War II. The interpretation is significant because it counters much of the conventional wisdom that sees post–World War II innovations such as the GI Bill, federally sponsored research, federally sponsored student financial aid, and growth of state higher education systems as most influential.

Levine, Arthur. "Higher Education's New Status as a Mature Industry." *Chronicle of Higher Education* 31 (January 1997), A48.

Arthur Levine, whose leadership and research roles include the Carnegie Foundation for the Advancement of Teaching and president of Columbia University Teachers College, provides a snapshot of colleges and universities in what may be termed middle age. No longer a curiosity or infant enterprise in American society, the campus of the late 20th century had acquired both the strengths and liabilities characteristic of an established institution. The caveat is that this new status has often been ignored or overlooked by higher education leaders—an oversight that tends to gloss over the need for new approaches to government relations and public policies—and deliberations on setting goals and attracting necessary resources.

Stoke, Stuart M. "What Price Tuition?" *Journal of Higher Education* (June 1937), 297–303.

This article represents an early, excellent systematic analysis of how and why some colleges drastically increased their tuition charges during the Great Depression of the 1930s. Tuition at most colleges, including prestigious and historic institutions, had been relatively stable and low over several decades. The historic change that by 1937, a small number of highly visible, influential institutions opted to raise tuition substantially year after year, counting on their ability to attract an affluent constituency of applicants and enrolling students.

College Costs and Prices

Books

Archibald, Robert, and Feldman, David. *Why Does College Cost So Much?* New York: Oxford University Press, 2010.

> Economists Archibald and Feldman rely on comprehensive economic data over several years to substantiate their findings that the alleged rising costs of higher education in the late 20th century may have been exaggerated, especially when characterized as a crisis in affordability. As part of their explanation, the authors present readable summaries of major theories of college costs—namely, the "revenue theory" and the "disease theory." On balance, they endorse William Baumol's disease theory as a sound, persuasive explanation for the increasing price and costs of higher education in the United States.

Bowen, Howard R. et al. *Investment in Learning: The Individual and Social Value of American Higher Education.* San Francisco: Jossey-Bass, 1977.

> Bowen provided an alternative to the conventional emphasis of economists on measuring educational outcomes in terms of income and earnings. His research showed demonstrable gains in citizenship, civic engagement, philanthropy, voting records, and community involvement as consequences of a college education. This work was integral to recognition of the importance of the concept of "human capital."

Bowen, Howard. R. *The Costs of Higher Education: How Much Do Colleges and Universities Spend Per Student and How Much Should They Spend?* San Francisco: Jossey-Bass, 1980.

> Economist Howard R. Bowen presented in detail his Revenue Theory of Costs for higher education in the United States. The essential tenet was that colleges raise all they can and then spend all they can.

Cheit, Earl F. *The New Depression in Higher Education: A Study of the Financial Condition of 41 Colleges and Universities*. New York: McGraw-Hill for the Carnegie Commission on Higher Education, 1971.

> Economist Earl Cheit, dean of the Business School at the University of California–Berkeley compiled systematic data on over 20 colleges and universities in 1970. The data showed deep erosion of endowments and revenue streams. The statistical profile of problems contrasted markedly with the images of stability and strength conveyed by campus architecture and public relations news releases. Cheit's warnings were warranted, as all colleges and universities from 1971 to 1985 faced budget problems due to a decade of annual double-digit increases in inflation, especially in such areas as energy expenses.

Clotfelter, Charles. *Buying the Best: Cost Escalation and Elite Higher Education*. Princeton, NJ: Princeton University Press for the National Board of Economic Research, 1996.

> Starting in 1985, a small number of academically selective and financially well-endowed private (independent) colleges and universities initiated deliberate, systematic plans both to raise money and to recruit highly talented undergraduates, graduate students, and faculty. Clotfelder's cumulative case studies illustrate how resources came to be viewed as a means to an end (acquiring and retaining talent) as distinguished from being ends in themselves. This analysis marks, in part, the growing gap between the outstanding private universities and the prestigious flagship state universities, as the latter group tended to lag behind during the period 1985 to the present.

Desrochers, Donna M., and Wellman, Jane V. *Trends in College Spending, 1999–2009: Where Does the Money Come From? Where Does It Go? What Does It Buy?* Washington, DC: Delta Cost Project, 2010.

One of the landmark comprehensive analyses of institutional and state data nationwide, this report from the Delta Cost Project provides invaluable data and interpretation on revenues and expenses at American colleges and universities. The accompanying appendices and databases are especially useful because they allow for valid comparisons across institutional categories and states. One important finding is that within many colleges and universities, year-by-year trends indicate a decrease in spending on educational and instructional activities, with a commensurate increase in administrative and noninstructional costs.

Ehrenberg, Ronald G. *Tuition Rising: Why College Costs So Much.* Cambridge, MA: Harvard University Press, 2001.

Author Ehrenberg brings to the topic credentials as a distinguished professor of labor economics at Cornell University, experience as a vice president for Business and Finance, and director of Cornell's Higher Education Research Institute. The result is a detailed, good-natured explanation about how and why academically selective, prestigious universities have acquired a dynamic that prompts them to spend increasing amounts in the high-stakes competition for talented students and faculty. The various profiles of decision making and organizational behavior provide readers an initiation into the interesting logic used by presidents, professors, and deans—with the shared characteristic that improvement usually requires investment.

Riesman, David. *On Higher Education: The Academic Enterprise in an Era of Student Consumerism.* San Francisco: Jossey-Bass, 1981.

Harvard sociologist David Riesman focused on the simultaneous rise of sophisticated student consumerism in college applications and choice along with the proliferation of deliberate recruitment strategies by college and university admissions offices. By 1980, the diversity and large number of colleges and universities combined with several years of economic recession had complicated traditional routes of access and selection. Attention to brand-name imagery as well as fluctuations in ratings and reputation ascended in importance in individual and institutional strategies.

Schneider, Mark, and de Alva, Jorge Klor. *Cheap for Whom? How Much Higher Education Costs Taxpayers*. Washington, DC: American Enterprise Institute, 2011.

The authors, both experienced higher education policy analysts, are concerned that public awareness of the actual *costs* to taxpayers for the education of college students often is muted because most attention goes to the *price* of college, such as tuition charges. As long as price is kept relatively low or reasonable, the temptation is to presume that expenses for higher education are reasonable. The blind spot in such thinking is that it overlooks taxes paid for student financial aid programs and also the tax benefits many colleges and universities (both public and private) receive in the form of tax exemptions on income and real estate. The authors construct a statistical profile that shows how academically selective colleges—again, both public and private—gain disproportionately in direct and indirect student subsidies from the existing tax system. Also, institutions with high dropout rates and low degree completion drive up taxpayer expenditures because attrition is expensive as a relatively wasted or incomplete effort. Paying more attention to these kinds of relatively low-profile syndromes identified by the authors would mean that eventually citizens would be paying less in tax dollars for support of higher education.

Vedder, Richard. *Going Broke by Degree: Why College Costs Too Much*. Washington, DC: American Enterprise Institute, 2004.

Economist Richard Vedder's book documents in detail sources of waste and inefficiency in American higher education, including practices by students, faculty, and administrators. Central to the excesses, Vedder argues, is that institutions charge increasingly high tuitions and use too few of the revenues for actual educational expenses. One corollary of the situation is that too many students now are encouraged to go to college for inappropriate or peripheral reasons, with poor prospects for jobs and adult opportunities that warrant their college expenditures. A net result of the wasteful practices is that the costs of operating colleges and universities increases year after year at a rate far higher than the general inflationary rate.

Articles

Baumol, William J., and Blackman, Sue Anne. "How to Think about Rising College Costs." *Planning for Higher Education* 23 (Summer 1995), 1–7.

Economist William Baumol joins with Sue Anne Blackman, a senior research assistant in the department of economics at Princeton, to present an interpretation of his "disease theory" of rising costs to explain revenues and expenditures at colleges and universities. Baumol, along with William Bowen, originally developed the disease theory explanation for hiring and spending trends in such activities as performing arts that relied on highly skilled and highly paid experts and professionals.

Blumenstyk, Goldie. "Data Show Wider Gaps in Spending on Students." *Chronicle of Higher Education* (September 23, 2011), A1, A12.

Blumenstyk, award-winning writer for the *Chronicle of Higher Education*, summarizes the comprehensive reports released by the Delta Cost Project, with particular attention to decreased spending per student at community colleges in contrast to other higher education segments.

O'Keefe, Michael. "Where Does the Money Really Go?: Case Studies of Six Institutions." *Change* (November/December 1987), 12–34.

Economist Michael O'Keefe uses statistical records compiled in the federal HEGIS (Higher Education General Information Systems) database to reconstruct patterns of financial behavior at six institutions: Western State University of Colorado, the University of South Carolina, Seattle University, the University of Chicago, Williams College, and Lynchburg College in Virginia. The selected case studies are useful because they represent a range of institutional types such as a large flagship state university, a selective liberal arts college, a tuition-dependent urban Catholic university, a prestigious yet cash-strapped private research university, and a struggling regional state college located in a sparsely populated region. This lengthy article provides a model of how to disaggregate data from the large-scale national data bases such as the Higher Education General Information Survey (HEGIS) and the Integrated Postsecondary Education Data System (IPEDS).

Shore, Debra. "What Price Egalitarianism?" *Brown Alumni Monthly* (February 1981), 12–19.

A detailed case study of how an academically selective, historic university had to deal with budget shortfalls and financial crises in the early 1980s. The full article is presented in Chapter 5, "Documents." Most useful is its juxtaposition of perspectives of undergraduate students, applicants, faculty, and senior administrators.

Student Financial Aid Policies and Programs

Books

Archibald, Robert B. *Redesigning the Financial Aid System: Why Colleges and Universities Should Switch Roles with the Federal Government.* Baltimore and London: Johns Hopkins University Press, 2002.

> Economist Archibald advanced a novel, pragmatic reform proposal for how students and their families ought to pay for college. Drawing from a detailed analysis of conventional practices in which the federal government tends to provide student loans while colleges provide scholarship grants, the author concludes that that a sound policy would be for colleges and federal government to reverse their practices. For Archibald, colleges and universities should be untethered from being primary sources of grants, switching to lending to student aid recipients. Federal student aid programs, in turn, would be reshaped from their accumulated overwhelming emphasis on student loans, toward providing undergraduates with more grants that do not require student repayment. There is little sign yet that this sound, thoughtful proposal has influenced reforms in federal student financial aid programs.

Hess, Frederick M., ed. *Footing the Tuition Bill: The New Student Loan Sector.* Washington, DC: American Enterprise Institute, 2007.

> Editor Frederick Hess, director of the American Enterprise Institute's education policy research initiative, assembled original invited essays which were first to be presented as papers by leading representatives from policy institutes, the banking industry, and colleges and universities to compile a detailed update on the complex student loan enterprise in the United States. Timing of the paper presentations and subsequent publication as an anthology was prescient, as congressional elections in November 2006 signaled redirections in federal

policies, reducing opportunities for private lenders while restoring some of the role of federal agencies as direct lenders.

Wilkinson, Rupert. *Attracting Students, Buying Students: Financial Aid in America*. Nashville, TN: Vanderbilt University Press, 2005.

Historian Rupert Wilkinson, long established as an expert in the study of higher education and the preparation of elites and leadership, devoted several years to the close inspection of the unique, complex American tradition of mixed student aid programs. The resulting publication includes an interesting account of the 19th-century foundations and associations that provided widespread student aid, both in loans and scholarships, in an era prior to federal programs. Wilkinson underscores the uniqueness of the United States' reliance on student consumerism combined with tuition payments as a major source of institutional revenues as the influential factor in fostering elaborate, large-scale student aid operations inside and outside the American campus.

Articles

Baum, Sandy. "College Education: Who Can Afford It?" In Michael B. Paulsen, and John C. Smart, eds., *The Finance of Higher Education: Theory, Research, Policy and Practice*. New York: Agathon Press, 2001, 39–52.

Baum, professor of economics at Skidmore College and highly respected for her studies on college affordability for such groups as the College Board, provided an early warning on marked declines in access and affordability for underserved and lower income student constituencies.

Hearn, James C. "The Paradox of Growth in Federal Aid for College Students, 1965–1990." In Michael B. Paulsen, and John C. Smart, eds., *The Finance of Higher Education: Theory, Research, Policy and Practice*. New York: Agathon Press, 2001, 267–320.

Hearn, drawing from policy analysis based on sociology and economics, traces the historical shift from federal emphasis on grants and access for modest income students, persistently toward an increase on federal loan programs— and student loan indebtedness. The historical implication is systematic documentation of a qualitative change in which affordability and access to college have not been enhanced, representing a departure from the original goals of landmark student financial aid program legislation and design.

Kiester, Edwin, Jr. "The G.I. Bill May Have Been the Best Deal Ever Made by Uncle Sam." *Smithsonian* 25(November 1994), 128–139.

Relying on extensive oral histories and memoirs of World War II veterans who made use of the GI Bill, author Kiester brings to life the transformation of the American campus—and the opportunities for going to college— brought about by the Serviceman's Readjustment Act of 1944 (the GI Bill). One interesting finding is that the appeal and success of the legislation was relatively unexpected by both its advocates and critics.

Access, Equity, and Social Justice

Books

Gardner, John W. *Excellence: Can We Be Equal and Excellent Too?* New York: Norton, 1961.

John Gardner, long influential as a leader in American educational and philanthropic foundations, used this essay to set forth the prospects and problems facing Americans and their institutions in simultaneously accommodating merit with established programs and elites. Written at a time of national prosperity and optimism, this short book provided analysis of the complex, often contradictory values about education and mobility espoused in American culture.

Gerald, Danette, and Haycock, Katie. *Engines of Inequality: Diminishing Equity in the Nation's Premier Public Universities.* Washington, DC: Education Trust, 2006.

> Although flagship state universities have long occupied a prominent place in our national imagination as a source of opportunity for talent from diverse origins, this systematic analysis documented causes for concern about the gap between our ideals and realities. In sum, the socioeconomic profile of undergraduates at the most distinguished state universities showed a small and declining percentage of Pell Grant recipients, with a commensurate sustained drift toward student bodies drawn from relatively affluent, highly educated families. The policy implication was that these public universities, far from promoting opportunities across a wide span of the population, were showing signs of fostering growing inequalities.

Karabel, Jerome. *The Chosen: The Hidden History of Admission and Exclusion at Harvard, Yale, and Princeton.* Boston and New York: Houghton Mifflin, 2005.

> Berkeley sociologist Jerome Karabel analyzes undergraduate "selective admissions" over more than a half-century at the prestigious "Big Three" of Harvard, Yale, and Princeton. A repeated finding is that more often than not, "selectivity" leaned toward nonmerit factors in which exclusion or quotas were imposed, based on such indices as religion, race, and ethnicity.

Levine, David O. *The American College and the Culture of Aspiration, 1915–1940.* Ithaca, NY: Cornell University Press. 1986.

> Historian David O. Levine shows how during the period between World War I and World War II, the expansion of American higher education was characterized by crystallization and clustering into enclaves of privilege. In sum, one sees the rudiments of a "sorting machine" based on family income and privilege emerge in the complex

network of junior colleges, state universities, regional colleges, and private colleges—a new configuration of academic institutions that was in large part a function of the expansion of the public high school and its role as a source of a new, expanding cohort of future college students in an era of mass higher education.

Synnott, Marcia Graham. *The Half-Opened Door: Discrimination and Admissions at Harvard, Yale, and Princeton, 1900–1970.* Westport, CT: Greenwood Press, 1979.

Synnott's research in the archives of Harvard, Yale, and Princeton for the first seven decades of the 20th century represents highly original and insightful analyses of the partial gains of meritocracy in America's historic, elite institutions. Her work provides much of the foundation and data from which subsequent works, such as Jerome Karabel's *The Chosen*, build their subsequent interpretations of access and exclusion in American higher education.

Zook, George, chair, *Higher Education for American Democracy: A Report of the President's Commission.* New York: Harper and Brothers, 1947.

Zook, who was president of the University of Akron and later president of the American Council on Education, was selected by the president of the United States, Harry Truman, to serve as director and editor of this detailed inventory and analysis. Zook led a blue ribbon presidential commission of higher education officials on this massive project. Although the six-volume study included numerous sections on the financing of higher education, its emphasis was on the need for Americans and their legislators to pursue goals of equity, access, affordability, and social justice in the post–World War II period. In sum, higher education was characterized as a national "good" and also as central to the pursuit of equity and social mobility in American life.

Articles

Carey, Kevin. "The End of College Admissions as We Know It." *Washington Monthly* (August–September 2011). http://www.washingtonmonthly.com/magazine/septemberoctober_2011/features/the_end_of_college_admissions031636.php

> Kevin Carey, policy director for Education Sector, a non-profit think tank based in Washington, D.C., examines in detail the strategies and principles of ConnectEDU, a Boston-based innovative organization committed to transforming how elementary school and high school students learn about colleges and student options.

Kramer, Martin. "The Unsmart Choices of Smart Students." *Change* (March/April 2000), 50.

> Martin Kramer, a longtime senior editor at *Change* magazine, contributes a sad-but-true account of the flaws and fallacies to which many college applicants succumb in trying to navigate the options and complexities of the college admissions pursuits that are distinctive to the United States.

Trow, Martin. "Reflections on the Transition from Elite to Mass to Universal Higher Education." *Daedalus* 99(Winter 1970), 1–42.

> The late Martin Trow, sociologist at the University of California–Berkeley, captured the essence of the qualitative changes in American higher education that were being driven by the quantitative changes in the move toward attempting to provide mass and even universal access to formal studies beyond high school. Trow's concluding observation was that this laudable goal would eventually face structural stress, perhaps collapse, in attempting to accommodate virtually all late adolescents in pursuit of postsecondary education.

Public Policy and the Financing of Higher Education

Books

Breneman, David W., Leslie, Larry L., and Anderson, Richard E., eds. *ASHE Reader on Finance in Higher Education*. Needham

Heights, MA: Simon and Schuster for the Association for the Study of Higher Education, 1996.

The editors—all prominent economists of higher education with administrative experience—bring together over 500 pages of primary sources, original articles, and key documents that have shaped discussions about the financing of higher education over three centuries, with particular attention to issues and trends in the last half of the 20th century.

Callan, Patrick M., and Finney, Joni E., eds. *Public and Private Financing of Higher Education: Shaping Public Policy for the Future.* Phoenix, AZ: American Council on Education and Oryx Press, 1997.

This anthology surveys the condition of higher education between 1990 and 1995. Its introductory section on national trends is followed by detailed case studies of public higher education in five important states: New York, Florida, Minnesota, Michigan, and California. The concluding theme is that higher education faces uncertainty in an extended period of resource constraints.

Carnegie Council on Policy Studies in Higher Education. *Three Thousand Futures: The Next Twenty Years for Higher Education.* San Francisco: Jossey-Bass, 1980.

This series of essays and recommendations by a blue ribbon panel of higher education experts represents an earnest effort by academic officials to take stock of the situations which faced 3,000 colleges and universities in the United States who are in the midst of a decade of financial strain. Both a finding and a warning, the study notes that an estimated one fourth to one third of American colleges and universities were at risk of being closed down if they failed to heed concerns about declining revenues and endowments as well as haphazard institutional management.

Ehrenberg, Ronald, ed. *What's Happening to Public Higher Education?: The Shifting Financial Burden*. Baltimore: Johns Hopkins University Press, 2006.

> Prompted by the growing imbalance between the vitality of leading independent colleges and universities and the relative decline of state universities, this anthology probes why the public decline has been taking place—and how it might be alleviated with new strategies and policies at state and federal levels.

Gladieux, Lawrence E., and Wolanin, Thomas R. *Congress and the Colleges: The National Politics of Higher Education*. Boston: Lexington Books of D.C. Heath, 1976.

> This study provides a detailed account of how a bill becomes a law, namely, the machinations and deliberations associated with the landmark student financial aid legislation in the 1972 reauthorization of the Higher Education Act. It is an especially significant case study because the reauthorization included creation of the Basic Educational Opportunity Grant (BEOG), later renamed Pell Grants in honor of the program's architect and advocate, Senator Claiborne Pell (D-RI.) The heart of the story is in the process, as negotiations across both houses of Congress brought to the fore a range of philosophical differences and options in the means and ends of federal financial aid programs.

Heller, Donald E., ed. *The States and Public Higher Education Policy: Affordability, Access, and Accountability*. Baltimore and London: Johns Hopkins University Press, 2001.

> Heller, longtime professor and director of the Center for the Study of Higher Education at Pennsylvania State University, is now dean of the College of Education at Michigan State University. His anthology, published in 2001, brings together original analyses by higher education scholars who consider the problems that state

universities are facing in the early 21st century in terms of maintaining commitments to affordability, access, and accountability. Chapters include such timely topics as the mixed consequences of technological change on state universities.

Finn, Chester E., Jr. *Scholars, Dollars and Bureaucrats.* Washington, DC: Brookings Institution, 1978.

Author Finn uses the disciplines of political science and history to explore the significant question of how the federal government became heavily involved in funding and regulating higher education, even though there was little evidence that the U.S. Constitution allowed for such involvement. His findings are that federal presence in colleges and universities is now established in two major areas: (1) student financial aid programs and (2) research and development sponsored by numerous and disparate federal agencies.

McPherson, Michael. Schapiro, Morton Owen, and Winston, Gordon C. *Paying the Piper: Productivity, Incentives, and Financing in U.S. Higher Education.* Ann Arbor: University of Michigan Press, 1993.

This anthology, published in 1993, considers how concepts such as "quality" in higher education coincided with and complicated economic measures of institutional productivity and effectiveness. The urgency of the book was prompted by signs of sustained annual tuition increases combined with declines in the rate and often the actual dollars of public support for institutions of higher education. These fiscal and structural developments were taking place in a context of what the authors describe as an era in which higher education had come "under assault." Its concluding chapters emphasize the need for changes in higher education budgeting formats and practices—and serious reconsiderations of institutional operations and missions.

Paulsen, Michael B., and Smart, John C., eds. *The Finance of Higher Education: Theory, Research, Policy & Practice.* New York: Agathon Press, 2001.

> This anthology is part of the annual series of comprehensive volumes published by Agathon Press dealing with the theory, research, policy, and practices that shape higher education in the United States. Overarching theories of the economics of higher education are followed by policy analyses of college affordability, federal and state policies toward higher education, and consideration of prospects for budgeting reforms in colleges and universities.

St. John, Edward, and Parsons, Michael D., eds. *Public Funding of Higher Education: Changing Contexts and New Rationales.* Baltimore and London: Johns Hopkins University Press, 2004).

> The coeditors enlist original essays by established scholars to address a dramatic change in the customary widespread support of generous public funding for higher education. By the start of the 21st century, state university presidents could no longer presume their institutions would receive adequate, let alone generous, support from state legislatures – a source of support that had been in place nationwide since the end of World War II. Evidently, the bipartisan consensus among conservatives and liberals who had long endorsed ample funding had eroded—policy planners, along with institutional leaders, began to face a renegotiation of the fundamental compacts about the funding and mission of higher education in the United States.

Articles

Wallace, Thomas. "The Age of the Dinosaur Persists." *Change* 25(July–August 1992), 56–63.

> Author Wallace, writing from the perspective of his role as president of Illinois State University, examines the origins

of a staple of state government relations with state colleges and universities: enrollment-driven per capita subsidies for students. The problem with this once effective policy (that was first established in the 1950s) is that by 1990, state legislatures were hampering public campuses by simultaneously failing to increase per student subsidies to account for inflation and rising costs, and prohibiting public institutions from raising tuition charges to bridge this growing gap that was leaving public institutions malnourished due to what was an artificially low and inaccurate calculation of what it truly cost to educate an undergraduate student in a given academic year. Wallace proposed as a solution that public institutions be allowed to follow a model characteristic of private (independent) colleges: a "high tuition, high financial aid model." According to this model, tuition charges are sufficiently high to reflect the actual costs of providing an education, yet still affordable and equitable when accompanied by increased need-based student financial aid.

College Student Enrollment and Retention

Books

Adelman, Clifford. *Answers in the Tool Box: Academic Intensity, Attendance Patterns and Bachelor's Degree Attainment.* Washington, DC: U.S. Department of Education, 2004.

> Adelman's thoughtful use of large-scale United States Department of Education's Integrated Postsecondary Education Systems (USDOE IPEDS) databases allows him to revise and complicate conventional profiles and patterns of how students go to college, choose courses and programs, and graduate. Thanks in large part to the diversity of institutions, including community colleges, and allowances for stopping out and transferring, as well as dropping out, Adelman's research suggests that going to college patterns are not linear and often are shaped by priorities and perspectives of students that are overlooked

or dismissed by higher education officials and administrators as the basis for informed decisions. One implication is that many data collection templates are not well suited for tracking the kinds of decisions and changes that undergraduates now make as a matter of course in their extended higher education journeys.

Bowen, William G., Chingos, Matthew, and McPherson, Michael. *Crossing the Finish Line: Completing College at America's Universities.* Princeton, NJ: Princeton University Press, 2009.

One source of inefficiency and frustration in American public higher education is the chronically low graduation rates of undergraduates. Economists Bowen, Chingos, and McPherson rely on a nationwide sample of student retention, attrition, and degree completion data to document the finding that for many state universities, there is less than a 63 percent bachelor's degree completion rate after six years of study. The authors look at trends in college choice along lines of socioeconomic level and high school transcripts to identify sources of low achievement. One interesting finding for policy reconsideration is the relative effectiveness of transfer programs and student financial aid in promoting degree completion.

Hess, Frederick M., Schneider, Mark, Carey, Kevin, and Kelly, Andrew. *Diplomas and Dropouts: Which Colleges Actually Graduate Their Students (And Which Don't.* Washington, DC: American Enterprise Institute, 2009.

This monograph, sponsored by the American Enterprise Institute, provides a useful reference work for documenting retention and graduation rates according to the contours of institutional types and clusters. It is a good companion work with *Crossing the Finish Line*, the 2009 study by Bowen, Chingos and McPherson.

Hossler, Donald, Schmit, Jack, and Vesper, Nick. Going *to College: How Social, Economic, and Educational Factors Influence the Decisions Students Make.* Baltimore and London: Johns Hopkins University Press, 1998.

Going to College tells how high school students make choices about postsecondary education. Drawing on their nine-year study of high school students, the authors explore how students and their parents negotiate these important decisions. Family background, finances, education, information—all influence students' plans after high school and the career paths they pursue, as do the more subtle messages delivered by parents and counselors that shape adolescents' self-expectations. For high school guidance counselors, college admissions counselors, parents and teachers, and public policymakers, this book is a valuable resource that explains the decision-making process and helps adults to help students make appropriate choices. The authors identify predisposition, search, and choice as the three stages in the student decision-making process. Predisposition refers to the plans students develop for education or work after they graduate from high school. The search stage involves students discovering and evaluating a variety of colleges and universities. In the choice stage, students choose a school to attend from among a list of institutions that are being seriously considered.

Thelin, John R. *The Attrition Tradition in American Higher Education: Connecting Past and Present.* Washington, DC: American Enterprise Institute, 2009.

Most recent analyses of college student retention and attrition in the United States are limited because they are time bound to statistical databases in which data draw only from recent years. Student enrollment data presented in Integrated Postsecondary Education Systems and (IPEDS) and Higher Education General Information Survey databases, for example, do not extend back further than about 1970. In this study the author, an historian, relies on detailed cohort tracking of undergraduates admitted to selected colleges—Harvard, Brown, Amherst, University of Kentucky, and Transylvania University—around 1910. These statistical findings are then interpreted in light of student and professor memoirs as well as accounts by deans of admission from 1910 to 1960. The finding, contrary to conventional wisdom, is that even prestigious, historically elite colleges a century ago exhibited relatively low graduation rates. The implication is that concern about dropouts and failure to complete degrees is an historic, enduring situation—not merely a recent problem to surface in American higher education. One finding is that at many colleges and universities prior to 1970, some professors and academic administrators took pride in a high dropout rate, following the logic that it was a testimony to the demanding academic standards of that college.

Articles

Hacker, Andrew. "They'd Much Rather Be Rich." *New York Review of Books* (October 11, 2007), 31–34.

"Student consumerism" since the early 1980s has led to an expensive, complex ritual of college application and admission between students and admissions offices. Political scientist Hacker synthesizes several recent works, and the net finding is that the result of this complex ritual is colleges spend increasing amounts on campus life amenities, nonacademic staff, and extracurricular services, and less on hiring faculty and funding academic programs. The residual consequence for undergraduates in recent years is that they seek and expect such campus services, and in their professional and adult aspirations, they place great emphasis on pursuit (and achievement) of wealth. The result is a serious crisis in the essential mission of American colleges and universities.

Lewin, Tamar. "Universities Seeking Out Students of Means." *New York Times* (September 21, 2011), A18.

This news story reinforces the points made by preceding authors such as Andrew Hacker on the tendency of colleges to recruit applicants who have little if any financial need.

Administration and Regulation of Higher Education
Books

Carey, Kevin, and Schneider, Mark, eds. *Accountability in American Higher Education*. New York: Palgrave MacMillan, 2010.

The fundamental premise of this anthology is that higher education in the United States, for all its accomplishments, is disorganized and has not been subject to adequate standards of information gathering and analysis. In sum, accountability in such areas as faculty productivity, student achievement, institutional spending, and measured accomplishment of objectives and goals remains underdeveloped—and sorely needed. Without such essential information and indicators, meaningful discussion of rising costs of higher education remains difficult to achieve.

Mayhew, Lewis B. *Surviving the Eighties*. San Francisco: Jossey-Bass. 1979.

Stanford professor of higher education Lewis B. Mayhew provides case studies of sound and foolish responses a number of colleges and universities were making in response to the extended problems of inflation and declining student demand in the late 1970s and early 1980s.

Rosovsky, Henry. *The University: An Owner's Manual*. New York and London: W. W. Norton, 1990.

Rosovsky, a longtime dean at Harvard College, uses the straightforward prose and perspective of car manuals to create a comparable guide to diagnosing the operations and problems of a modern university. Although many of his specific examples are drawn from Harvard University, they have sufficient general connection and appeal to help the reader understand the structure and culture of most high-powered universities. The heart of Rosovsky's owner's guide to a university is that one must understand the distinctive internal logic of an organization to make sense out of its priorities and decisions.

Tuchman, Gaye. *Wannabe U: Inside the Corporate University.* Chicago and London: University of Chicago Press, 2009.

Sociologist Tuchman provides a guide to the justifications and goals of excessive spending at ambitious universities in the United States during the past two decades. External signs and symbols of stature combined with benchmark adulation represent a 21st-century higher education version of Thorstein Veblen's classic notion of conspicuous consumption.

Wilson, James Q. *Bureaucracy: What Government Agencies Do and Why They Do It.* New York: Basic Books, 1989.

The late James Q. Wilson, long respected for his sociological studies of organizational behavior, looks at a range of state, local, and federal agencies in search of some general insights about how they work. State universities are included in the mix along with prisons, departments of motor vehicles, federal agencies, and the social security administration. One of the more intriguing analyses is Wilson's characterization of the organizational tension between top-down administrative edicts and their potential for conflict with the essential, core professional values of organizational staff.

Articles

Bok, Derek. "The Federal Government and the University." *Public Interest* (Winter 1980), 80–101.

Bok, influential as president of Harvard University, made the case that by 1980, federal regulations affecting colleges and universities had become excessive and intrusive. Writing as an advocate for fellow university presidents, his conclusion was that requirements in terms of record-keeping and regulation compliance had eroded the federal government's long tradition of avoiding interference in the right of colleges and universities for self-determination in such areas as "what shall be taught, who shall teach, and who shall be taught." Furthermore, Bok was concerned that the increase in government regulation had driven up institutional expenses substantially.

Glazer, Nathan. "Regulating Business and the Universities." *Public Interest* (Summer 1979), 42–65.

Sociologist Glazer reviewed changing federal policies toward regulation of both business and higher education, and arrived at an important finding contrary to conventional wisdom: over the course of the 20th century, the federal government had flip-flopped in its regulatory philosophy. The original approach was to apply increasingly strict standards of accountability on commercial corporations, while exempting colleges and universities from myriad regulations. By 1979, the approach had reversed, as colleges and universities were increasingly being subjected to detailed regulation and oversight, whereas federal legislation showed emphasis on reducing government regulation of businesses. The dysfunctional result was increasing expenditures of time and money by universities in order to be in compliance.

Gulland, Eugene D., and Steinbach, Sheldon E. "Antitrust Law and Financial Aid: The MIT Decision." *Chronicle of Higher Education* (October 6, 1993), B3.

Writing from the perspective of national higher education associations, the authors are attorneys who were disappointed in the court ruling that dissolved and prohibited collective discussions by consortia of selective independent colleges. Central to their dissent was the historical reminder that originally, Congress had exempted colleges from such legislation as the Sherman Antitrust Act. Furthermore, the group discussions among presidents and deans of admission had served to make optimal use of need-based student financial aid resources so as to promote, rather than impede, affordability and access.

Healy, Michelle. "Ivy League Settles Price-Fixing Suit on Aid." *USA Today* (May 23, 1991), 1A.

Contemporary news coverage of a landmark case in which Ivy League institutions, joined by Stanford and Massachusetts Institute of Technology (MIT), were the subject of a lawsuit by the federal government on charges of tuition price fixing. This was a legal challenge to a practice that the university presidents had made known for years, suggesting that there was no invidious attempt at collusion or secrecy. MIT would be the one institution among the group to reject the settlement.

Private (Independent) Colleges and Universities

Books

Clark, Burton R. *The Distinctive College: Antioch, Reed & Swarthmore*. Chicago: Aldine, 1970.

Sociologist Clark used historical case studies of three distinctive liberal arts colleges—Antioch, Reed, and Swarthmore—to construct some generalizations about how, slowly over time, some institutions have managed to raise their educational standards and enhance their reputation. Central to his analysis is the notion of "organizational saga"—the heroic events and individuals who at crucial junctures made a difference in transforming an institution.

Koblik, Steven, and Graubard, Stephen R., eds. *Distinctively American: The Residential Liberal Arts College.* New Brunswick, NJ: Transaction Press, 2000.

> In an era when flagship state universities and powerful research campuses have tended to dominate press coverage, editors Koblik and Graubard use original essays by scholars and experts on a diverse range of programs and practices within liberal arts colleges. The anthology includes, for example, detailed accounts of faculty research and student involvement in projects and publications in the sciences. The net result is to make an effective argument that liberal arts colleges are not only a distinctively American institution, but also that they are surviving and thriving in the early 21st century.

Spies, Richard R. *The Future of Private Colleges: The Effect of Rising Costs on College Choice.* Princeton, NJ: Princeton University Industrial Relations Section, 1973.

> Spies, a professor of engineering at Princeton who took on administrative policy and planning projects for the president and the dean of admissions, drafted one of the first and most original systematic analyses of problems facing selective private colleges in their ability to recruit and enroll outstanding students who might have financial need. His study coincided with Earl Cheit's publication that warned of financial problems that would ultimately set constraints even at relatively well-endowed colleges and universities. Spies eventually would serve as Princeton's vice president for Finance and Administration. His Princeton-sponsored study eventually would provide a model for numerous associations and consortia who wanted to make informed decisions about setting tuition levels, allocations of resources among student aid, and other institutional expenditures within a finite annual operating budget.

Philanthropy and Fundraising

Books

Curti, Merle, and Nash, Roderick. *Philanthropy in the Shaping of American Higher Education*. New Brunswick, NJ: Rutgers University Press, 1964.

> Excellent, essential account of philanthropy and fundraising as central parts of American colleges and universities from the colonial era into the mid-20th century. Chapters provide context on how fundraising and major gifts came to be staples of American colleges and universities.

Articles

Arenson, Karen W. "Soaring Endowments Widen a Higher Education Gap." *New York Times* (February 4, 2008), A14.

> News account of how several consecutive years of double-digit interest returns on endowment investments enabled a small number of prosperous colleges and universities to pull further ahead of the higher education pack.

Blumenstyk, Goldie. "Pressure Builds on Wealthy Colleges to Spend More of Their Assets." *Chronicle of Higher Education* 54 (November 2, 2007), A1–A20, A21.

> Timely, forthright news coverage of congressional concerns over a situation in which a small number of universities acquired large endowments, leading to investigation by a congressional subcommittee.

Shepard, Robert S. "How Can a University That Raises a Billion Have a Tight Budget?" *Chronicle of Higher Education* (January 12, 1994), A48.

> The author, who was vice president of development at the University of Pennsylvania, makes a case for understanding by internal and external campus constituencies how even those institutions with effective fundraising campaigns remain pressed to provide funding for all programs.

As such, it is a fitting illustration of Howard Bowen's "revenue theory" of higher education finance in which universities tend to exhibit an ability to spend available resources.

For-Profit Higher Education

Books

Breneman, David W., Pusser, Brian, and Turner, Sally E. *Earnings from Learning: The Rise of For-Profit Universities.* Albany: State University of New York Press, 2006.

Drawing from national Integrated Postsecondary Education Data Systems (IPEDS) 2003 databases and numerous other documents and sources, the three authors—all from the University of Virginia—analyze the growing for-profit universities in terms of student demand, instructional costs, and interrelations with the large, established nonprofit higher education sector in the United States. This data-driven survey is comprehensive and its tone is balanced. It concludes with policy implications for the future of higher education.

Ruch, Richard S. *Higher Ed, Inc.: The Rise of the For-Profit University.* Baltimore: Johns Hopkins University Press, 2001.

This overview of a fast growing sector that consisted of more than 700 institutions in 2001 is largely descriptive. It provides a guide to the development and approaches used, especially by five major for-profit colleges. The author writes from experience, having been an administrator at DeVry University.

Articles

Bartlett, Thomas. "Phoenix Risen: How a History Professor became the Pioneer of the For-Profit Revolution." *Chronicle of Higher Education* (July 10, 2009), A1, A10–A13.

This detailed biographical profile of the founder of the University of Phoenix (UOP) emphasizes how John

Sperling, a history professor at San Jose State University in California identified in the 1970s nontraditional students' (including working adults) growing demand for college courses and degree programs. The origins of UOP programs to meet such needs started long before the advent of Internet technology, even though by 2009 this was the format and medium with which UOP had come to be associated in the public forum.

Wilson, Robin. "Profit Colleges Change Higher Education's Landscape." *Chronicle of Higher Education* (February 12, 2010), A1, A16–A19.

Scrutinizing and analyzing the interdependence of "traditional" degree-granting colleges and universities with a growing number of programs and courses offered by the for-profit sector of colleges is the focus of this thoughtful account of intersegmental relations in the diverse landscape of postsecondary education in the United States.

Intercollegiate Athletics and the Costs of Higher Education

Books

Kirwan, William E., and Turner, Gerald R., co-chairs. *Restoring the Balance: Dollars, Values, and the Future of College Sports.* Miami, FL: Knight Commission on Intercollegiate Athletics, 2010.

The Knight Commission, a voluntary association formed in 1990 of higher education leaders and related groups, released a sobering report in 2010 on the state of campus spending on college sports. Systematic data showed that institutional spending on varsity sports had increased at a substantially higher rate than spending on educational activities. The most alarming finding was that many university presidents readily acknowledged in a survey that they, as presidents, had lost control of athletic department spending.

Sperber, Murray. *Beer and Circus: How Big-Time College Sports Is Crippling Undergraduate Education.* New York: Henry Holt, 2000.

Sperber provides an injunction against the argument that since college sports spending is quarantined to a special, auxiliary enterprise, it is of little consequence or concern to the host university. He counters that the direct and indirect costs of supporting a big-time college sports program include an erosion of the over-all educational character and climate of an academic institution.

Sperber, Murray. *College Sports, Inc.: The Athletic Department vs. The University.* New York: Henry Holt, 1990.

Sperber focuses on the structural unit of intercollegiate sports—the generic athletics department or, in some cases, the separately incorporated university athletic association—to describe and criticize how an activity can be given special status and exemption within a modern university.

Articles

Sander, Libby. "After Big Cuts, Mighty Stanford Sports Long for Sunnier Days." *Chronicle of Higher Education* (November 8, 2009). http://chronicle.com/article/Recession-Clouds-Future-of/49066/?sid=at&utm_source=at&utm_medium=en

Stanford University, long hailed for its frequent annual record as the outstanding intercollegiate athletics program within the National Collegiate Athletic Association (NCAA) Division I and also the alma mater of more Olympic athletes than any other university, demonstrated a strong commitment to provide funding, including athletic grants-in-aid, for a large number of men and women student-athletes. Furthermore, athletic success was in harmony with academic achievement, as Stanford student-athletes consistently showed a graduation rate of about 96 percent in an academically selective environment; this is higher than the graduation rate for the entire Stanford student body. By 2009, however, author Sander documented and interpreted the financial problems that had forced cutbacks in this exemplary program. The findings were problematic for colleges and universities elsewhere because few if any institutions could match the resources and commitment Stanford had provided over decades to ensure a well-funded athletics program.

Suggs, Welch. "How Gears Turn at a Sports Factory: Running Ohio State University's $79 Million Program Is a Major Endeavor, with Huge Payoffs and Costs." *Chronicle of Higher Education* (November 29, 2003), A1, A32–A37.

The Ohio State University's intercollegiate athletics program, characterized as a high-powered, finely tuned, and well-funded "sports factory," offers 36 varsity sports in the highest level of competition, NCAA Division I. Its annual budget of $79 million in 2003 increased to over $100 million in 2011. Award-winning writer Suggs provides a detailed account of revenues and expenses in this high-profile, high-stakes varsity sports program. Important to note is that this profile represents a "best case scenario" characterized by such optimal features as robust revenues from ticket sales and television contracts, cooperation between academic and athletic administrators, a commitment to athletic championships, and the expectation of a strong work ethic among both coaches and student-athletes. Implicit is that most intercollegiate sports programs, including NCAA Division I big-time sports, do not have the resources or capacity to generate revenues as does The Ohio State University.

Draper, Joe, and Thomas, Katie. "As Colleges Compete, Major Money Flows to Minor Sports." *New York Times* (September 2, 2010), A1, A20.

Whereas the American public as well as higher education officials had become used to having high-profile coaches in such revenue sports as football and men's basketball receive salaries in the range of $1 million to $4 million per year, less obvious has been the move by selected universities to increase salaries and resources for "minor" sports that typically do not generate revenues from ticket sales and television broadcasts. This front-page article in the *New York Times* chronicles how an athletics director at a successful, prosperous program (the University of Florida) sought to promote national championships in all sports via incentives, generous salaries, and ample recruitment budgets. The strategy included paying, for example, the head volleyball coach more than $300,000 per year and providing maximum allowable grants-in-aid for all varsity sports. The case study indicates how for some highly competitive universities, the foremost aim is not to bring in money, it is to win conference and national championships in all sports, regardless of the cost of such a goal—even during years when the educational and academic side of the university faced cutbacks and no salary increases for faculty.

Research Universities

Books

Geiger, Roger L. *To Advance Knowledge: The Growth of American Research Universities, 1900–1940.* New York and Oxford: Oxford University Press, 1986.

> Historian Geiger examines the founding of the prestigious Association of American Universities in 1900, as 14 charter member institutions became the guardian of standards in advanced scholarship. This historical account over four decades deals with an era in which the federal government had a limited presence in providing sponsored research and development grants.

Geiger, Roger L. *Research and Relevant Knowledge: American Research Universities since World War II.* New York and London: Oxford University Press, 1993.

This work is a continuation of *To Advance Knowledge* and deals with the origins and growth of large-scale federal agency funding for sponsored research and development conducted by universities. The narrative is punctuated by case studies of institutions that pursued a strategy of "steeples of excellence" in which academic officials designated selected programs and departments that were potentially prestigious to receive extraordinary resources. Case studies also include infamous institutional debacles related to attempts to move into the ranks of federal research grant universities.

Graham, Hugh Davis, and Diamond, Nancy. *The Rise of American Research Universities: Elites and Challengers in the Postwar Era*. Baltimore and London: Johns Hopkins University Press, 1997.

Historians Graham and Diamond chronicle the rise of American universities whose budgets included substantial sponsored research projects. The authors' original contribution is that they provide an alternative to the conventional practice of ranking universities by their gross revenues from external research grants. Instead, they present grant dollars per faculty member as a discerning measure of a university's research stature.

Rosenzweig, Robert M. *The Research Universities and Their Patrons*. Berkeley, Los Angeles, and London: University of California Press, 1982.

Rosenzweig, former vice president of Stanford University, wrote this book during his tenure as president of the American Association of Universities in the 1990s. During the late 1980s and early 1990s, there was an increase in federal regulation and a tapering of federal research funding for higher education, creating concern among the leading research universities that the public and Congress had forgotten the successes and achievements of academic research in a large number of nationally important fields. Rosenzweig's concise, readable book provides a review and a reminder of the success of research universities and their contribution to the national welfare, while making a case for renewed and enhanced federal support.

Professors and Faculty

Books

Baldwin, Roger G., and Chronister, Jay L. *Teaching without Tenure: Policies and Practice for a New Era*. Baltimore: Johns Hopkins University Press, 2001.

> Two senior scholars in the study of higher education document and narrate what they consider to be a dangerous, unfortunate trend: the tendency for college presidents, provosts, and deans to rely increasingly on part-time, non–tenure track adjunct instructors.

Bowen, Howard R., and Schuster, Jack. H. *American Professors: A National Resource Imperiled*. New York and Oxford: Oxford University Press, 1986.

> This volume represents one of the most comprehensive, long-term studies of trends in faculty hiring and compensation over several decades. Its conclusion is that in the past 26 years, professors, especially tenure track professors, have lost ground in their influence and proportional numbers in the college and university.

Ginsberg, Benjamin. *The Fall of the Faculty: The Rise of the All-Administrative University and Why It Matters*. London and New York: Oxford University Press, 2011.

> Ginsberg, a prominent and well-published professor of political science at Johns Hopkins University, argues that "administrative bloat" has transformed university life that is now characterized by a large, well-paid professional staff

that has relatively little involvement with teaching, learning, and other aspects of educational programs.

Hermanowicz, Joseph C., ed. *The American Academic Profession: Transformation in Contemporary Higher Education.* Baltimore: Johns Hopkins University Press, 2011.

> Sociologist Hermanowicz of the University of Georgia has edited an anthology of fresh analyses and data on the problems facing faculty in American colleges and universities in the early 21st century. Contributors are drawn from such varied disciplines as sociology, history, political science, economics, and organizational theory. The general consensus of the contributing authors is that the academic profession in the United States has been successful and a source of prestige, but it is increasingly being placed at risk.

Middaugh, Michael F. *Understanding Faculty Productivity: Standards and Benchmarks for Colleges and Universities.* San Francisco: Jossey-Bass, 2001.

> Michael Middaugh draws on his experience and research from the long-term University of Delaware study of higher education productivity. Among his reported findings is that professors are not a primary source of inefficiency and inordinate expense in the contemporary American college or university.

Articles

Fain, Paul. "Faculty Pay Is Not Part of Academe's Cost Crisis, Expert Tells Trustees' Conference." *Chronicle of Higher Education* (April 4, 2006), A1.

> This is a news account of an informed response to the dramatic claims that high faculty pay and low faculty productivity are largely responsible for financial problems in in colleges and universities.

O'Donnell, Rick. "Why Productivity Data Matter." *Inside Higher Ed* (July 20, 2011). http://www.insidehighered.com/views/2011/07/20/o_donnell_on_faculty_productivity_data

O'Donnell, a major architect of a proposed reform plan for public higher education in Texas, argues that financing higher education will face unbearable costs if customary practices are extended. One strategy for reform—and reducing costs and, perhaps, price—is faculty productivity data. O'Donnell describes five faculty types—"dodgers," "coasters," "sherpas," "pioneers," and "stars." The fundamental premise of the article is that there is substantial underproductivity by professors, especially in the area of undergraduate education. Reforming and reclaiming faculty productivity is ostensibly essential to streamlining the modern university.

International Higher Education

Books

Johnstone, D. Bruce, and Marcucci, Pamela N. *Financing Higher Education Worldwide: Who Pays? Who Should Pay?* Baltimore: Johns Hopkins University Press, 2010.

The authors draw from their extensive research with the International Comparative Higher Education and Finance and Accessibility (ICHEFA) project to study how worldwide expansion of higher education has been funded. Central to their documents and reports is the notion of *cost sharing*—a term that in effect means that rapid higher education expansion has usually been accompanied by a relative decline in government funding and an increased expectation that consumers—students and their families—will pay a growing percentage of costs. This trend, although familiar in the United States, is challenging because it is a relatively new development in many nations.

Wildavsky, Ben. *The Great Brain Race: How Global Universities Are Reshaping the World.* Princeton, NJ: Princeton University Press, 2009.

> Bruce Wildavsky, an award-winning journalist with long experience writing about rankings and reputation in higher education, brings attention to the growing interdependence of American colleges and universities with institutions and innovations in numerous other nations. Central to the movement is the emergence of key players who have the energy and resources to commit to establishing campuses and institutes overseas, far from their historic home base. The account of recent trends also emphasizes cooperative projects that cut across traditional institutional lines and national boundaries.

College Consumerism Tools and Databases

Nonprint Sources

Chronicle of Higher Education's Almanac of Higher Education
http://chronicle.com/section/Almanac-of-Higher-Education/141/

> Each year, the *Chronicle of Higher Education* publishes an Almanac of Higher Education that is a comprehensive compendium of key statistics and information about higher education. Areas typically include profiles of students and faculty, presidential and administrative salaries, enrollment trends, fundraising, philanthropy, endowments, research expenditures, and other demographic and institutional trends. The website, available to subscribers, provides convenient, useful access to an abundance of information covering numerous years.

College Board http://www.collegeboard.org/

> The website for the College Board (known also as the CEEB and the College Entrance Examination Board) is a good home base for acquiring a roadmap of various interrelated resources, programs, and assistance that, together,

provides information and services dealing with the issue of college and paying for college. This includes links to the Scholastic Achievement Test (SAT), the Educational Testing Service (ETS), the Parents Financial Aid Form (PFAF), and numerous other services and planning guides.

College Cost Calculator of the U.S. Department of Education College Affordability and Transparency Center http://collegecost.ed.gov/

Since about 2009, one of the most important, interesting innovations associated with the costs of higher education has been the construction of readily available databases to assist students and their families as they seek to be informed consumers about college choices, costs, and prices. The following articles, presented in chronological order of their publication, provide an overview of innovative databases available to students and their families for informed planning and comparisons in college costs:

Fain, Paul. "New Web Tool Helps Both Experts and Public Grasp Colleges' Costs." *Chronicle of Higher Education* (July 9, 2010). http://chronicle.com/article/New-Web -Tool-Helps-Experts-and/66222/

Lewin, Tamar. "What's the Most Expensive College? The Least? Education Department Puts It All Online." *New York Times* (June 30, 2011), A13.

Anonymous. "Comparison Shopping for College Tuition." *New York Times* (February 26, 2012), SR 10.

College Student Financial Aid Shopping Sheet http://collegecost .ed.gov/shopping_sheet.pdf

Within the broad topic of college costs, an important subset focuses on "shopping" for student financial aid in a complex market of public and private sources. This website, provided by the U.S. Department of Education, assists college applicants by providing comprehensive college student financial aid shopping diagnostic and exploratory guides. One criticism by policy analysis experts is that to obtain comparable, clear data, the site tends to oversimplify and gloss over additional factors and variables that provide a more complete explanation of why and how a particular college has a particular cost and price.

ConnectEDU http://www.connectedu.com/

ConnectEDU, a relatively new start-up organization located in Boston, is described in detail in the preceding chapter's section on organizations. The link noted here introduces prospective students to some diagnostic "buttons" to introduce and guide novices to an array of planning sources and information. It is especially intended to encourage and assist those who heretofore had relatively little familiarity with and information about the complex process and resources associated not only with college planning, but also with long-term considerations about academic and professional options.

Delta Cost Project on Trends in College Spending http://deltacost project.org/index.asp

The home page for the Delta Cost Project of the American Institutes for Research (AIR) gives readers and researchers a convenient menu for reference to a chronological list of full reports, executive summaries, and news releases on the succession of periodic reports that the Delta Cost Project has published on the revenues and expenditure trends of colleges and universities in the United States.

Inflation Calculator http://www.usinflationcalculator.com/

A predictable, pervasive question for a college student to ask is whether it costs more to go to college today than it did for students in an earlier era. A useful tool for starting to answer this question is the inflation calculator that allows a researcher to go back and forth in time on costs and prices that have been indexed for inflation. For example, using the convenient calculator box, one merely inserts data for one year—for example, a tuition charge of $30,000 in 2010—and indicates the year for which one wants a comparison—for example, 1960. The resultant calculation is that $30,000 in 2010 would have been equivalent to a tuition price of a little over $4,000 a half-century ago. Conversely, the price of going to college in 1960 of $3,000 would be equivalent to about $21,834 in 2010. These estimates are neither infallible nor complete, and they need to be interpreted in context with a variety of other sources and information. Despite these limits, they do provide a statistical base from which to see how the price of college may have changed.

IPEDS Data Base http://nces.ed.gov/ipeds/

The Integrated Postsecondary Education Data System (IPEDS) is the annual and cumulative listing of data on finances, enrollment, retention, graduation, and student characteristics. It is supervised and published under the auspices of the U.S. Department of Education's National Center for Educational Statistics. Institutional researchers are able to identify benchmark institutions, groupings, clusters, or specific institutions in calling up comparative and collective data on essential higher education indices. The forerunner to IPEDS was HEGIS (the Higher Education General Information Systems) databases on which compilations were started in the late 1960s.

Knight Commission on Intercollegiate Athletics http://knight commission.org/

The Knight Foundation's Commission on Intercollegiate Athletics website is a user-friendly source of national reports, databases, and current news releases about the policies and programs of college sports. Illustrative of its great didactic contribution is the link to "College Sports 101," a primer on the essential concepts and trends in the funding and priorities of intercollegiate athletics programs.

National Center for Public Policy and Higher Education http://www.highereducation.org/

> The National Center for Public Policy and Higher Education's mission has promoted public policies that enhance Americans' opportunities to pursue and achieve high-quality education and training beyond high school. As an independent, nonprofit, nonpartisan organization, the National Center prepares action-oriented analyses of pressing policy issues facing states and the nation regarding opportunity and achievement in higher education, including two- and four-year, public and private, and for-profit and nonprofit institutions. The National Center communicates performance results and key findings to the public; to civic, business, and higher education leaders; and to state and federal leaders who are poised to improve higher education policy. Established in 1998, the National Center is not affiliated with any institution of higher education, with any political party, or with any government agency. In working to improve higher education through effective public policy, the National Center served both as a resource and catalyst. Its website is set up to provide researchers with a resource for policy development and a catalyst for improving public policy. One of its most attractive resources is its "Measuring Up" interactive feature that provides a report card of periodic state-by-state reports on college affordability.

Policy Direct http://policydirect.org/#

> This innovative Internet resource was developed by the Institute on Higher Education Policy (IHEP) in 2012 with the assistance of the Lumina Foundation. It is intended to be a "one-stop, easy to use resource for quality research that illuminates critical findings and further

challenges around important student outcomes. Its aim is to broaden the reach, relevance and role of research in advancing the critical goals of college preparation, success and productivity." The site is set up with user-friendly buttons to help one explore questions about higher education access and numerous related subthemes.

Introduction

The following list of key events presented in chronological order provides an overview of landmark legislation, public policies, and student financial aid programs that provides a concise guide for following trends and developments in the changing costs of higher education.

1636 First college in the American colonies: Founding of Harvard College in Massachusetts Bay Colony.

1643 First scholarship established at an American college: Ann Radcliff of London, the widowed Lady Mowlson, gives 100 pounds to Harvard College. The annual income was to be used for the "yearly maintenance [of a] poor scholar . . . "

1815 Incorporation and charter for the American Education Society, with headquarters in Boston, Massachusetts, to create a philanthropic foundation to support the collegiate education of a learned, evangelical clergy.

1862 The Morrill Act for the establishment of land grant colleges approved by Congress.

1890 The second Land Grant Act is approved by Congress, extending the creation and funding of land grant colleges to formerly seceded states—and with provision for funding of historically black land grant colleges.

1900 College Entrance Examination Board is founded: "designed to ensure comparability in the standards and quality of higher education qualifications."

1922 Publication of Jesse Barnard Sears's *Philanthropy in the History of American Higher Education* by the U.S. Government Printing Office.

1944 Serviceman's Readjustment Act (the GI Bill) passed by Congress.

1944 United Negro College Fund founded.

1947 Report of the President's Commission on Higher Education, *Higher Education for American Democracy* published.

1958 National Defense Education Act (NDEA) passed. Provisions included the National Defense Student Loan (NDSL) Program, later known as the Federal Perkins Loan Program.

1960 California Master Plan for Higher Education (also known as the Donahoe Act) is adopted by the California Legislature and signed into law by Governor Edmund G. Brown.

1964 Scholastic Aptitude Test (SAT) high point for both record number of students taking the test and all-time high marks for mean scores.

1965 Higher Education Act (HEA) signed into law as part of the War on Poverty.

1971 Earl Cheit's *The New Depression in Higher Education* published.

1972 First reauthorization of the HEA. This included creation of the Basic Educational Opportunity Grants (BEOG) (later renamed as Pell Grants), the Supplementary Educational Opportunity Grants (SEOG), and the Student Loan Marketing Association ("Sallie Mae").

1976 Second reauthorization of the HEA by Congress.

1978 Middle Income Student Assistance Act (MISAA) signed into federal law.

1980 Third reauthorization of the HEA. This included creation of supplemental Parents Loans for Undergraduate Students (PLUS).

1986 Fourth reauthorization of the HEA.

1992 Fifth reauthorization of the HEA. This included creation of a pilot program for federal-direct loans.

1993 Student Loan Reform Act signed into law.

1999 The Bologna Process agreement is signed by European nations. Its purpose is to ensure comparability in the standards and quality of higher education qualifications among the 47 nations who were signatories.

2000 Lumina Foundation created with the mission of expanding student access to and success in education beyond high school, including the goal of having 60 percent of Americans complete college degrees or advanced educational certification by 2025.

2008 Higher Education Opportunity Act includes creation of the College Affordability and Transparency Center website for college cost and price comparisons and calculator.

2009 Delta Cost Project Report, *Trends in College Spending Where Does the Money Come From? Where Does It Go?* published.

2010 College Navigator website is launched by the U.S. Department of Education, in fulfillment of a provision in the Higher Education Opportunity Act of 2008.

2012 Consumer Financial Protection Bureau reports that college student loan debt surpasses $1 trillion, an amount that exceeds the amount owed on all credit cards in the United States.

Introduction

Discussions of issues associated with the rising costs of higher education frequently involve technical terms. This glossary is offered to provide a better understanding of some of the definitions and distinctions in this lexicon because these are crucial both in constructing and implementing policies and programs. These terms are also important to college applicants, college students, and their families when they are considering higher education options.

Academic Medical Center   Known by the acronym of AMC, this refers to designated configurations of an accredited degree-granting institution of higher education that consists of a medical college and at least one allied health program or department and works in cooperation and conjunction with a teaching hospital. AMCs typically have external grants for research and development awarded by a federal agency such as the National Institutes of Health, along with grants and projects sponsored by private philanthropic foundations.

Appropriation   Monies collected by a government agency and dedicated for a particular program, such as for student financial aid grants or loans.

Attrition   College student dropout or failure to return for enrollment.

Budget   An organization's *proposed* annual revenues and expenses—as distinguished from its *actual* record.

Community College   A two-year state (public)-supported institution offering associate's degrees and a variety of other educational and academic courses and programs.

Comprehensive College or University   A degree-granting academic institution characterized by bachelor's and master's programs in a range of fields; does not have doctoral programs.

Consumer Price Index (CPI)   A collective measure published annually in terms of percentage increases. Calculated on the basis of prices consumers pay for a selected "basket of goods." It does not typically include large-expense items such as homes or college tuition.

Cost   The amount of money as an expenditure paid by a *provider* (such as a college) for specified goods and services. The term is often used in conjunction with the term *price*; the two terms are not synonymous, although they may be equal in dollar amounts.

Cost of Attendance   Known by the acronym COA, this is a construct devised by the federal government to calculate and convey the complete expenditures by all parties to provide undergraduate education for a student for one academic year.

Cross-Subsidy   An internal resource allocation practice within a college or university in which revenues acquired by one unit may be deliberately and knowingly diverted to provide resources used by another unit.

Degree Completion   Student success at completing all requirements of courses, grades, and credits of a bona fide program that culminates in conferring an academic degree such as the bachelor of arts (BA) or bachelor of science (BS). This formal, official achievement is an important indicator of goal completion in higher education. Aggregated compilations of individual student's degree completion provide one proxy for an institution's patterns of educational effectiveness.

Disease Theory   The explanation for rising costs at a college, university, or other organization due in large part to increased necessary expenses due to reliance on high-skilled, high-paid professionals, experts, and specialists. The theory was advanced by economist William Baumol, in conjunction with William Bowen.

Effectiveness   In higher education this term refers to the relative ability of a college or university to achieve results or success, often measured by some percentage of degree completion. It is often used in conjunction with the term *efficiency*, although the two terms are not synonymous.

Efficiency   In higher education, the relative ability of a college or university to achieve a goal or provide an educational service at relatively low cost.

Endowment   A legally defined and constrained fund of monies that a college, university, or other educational institution acquires and manages over time.

Entitlement   A government program that is committed to providing resources, subsidies, payments, or awards to any and all individuals who qualify by meeting officially published eligibility conditions.

Expenditure   Money paid out by an institution or organization for goods and services.

Fees   For college and university students, this term refers to institutional charges that a student must pay to receive certain specified services. Examples include a library fee, an academic support fee, an intercollegiate athletics fee, and a student fee. The general category of fees sometimes is parsed to specify fees that are are mandatory or obligatory, whether or not a student wishes to partake of those services.

For Profit Institution   An institution— for purposes of this book, specifically an educational institution—that pays dividends to investors and shareholders. The Internal Revenue Service (IRS) provides specific conditions and criteria for an institution to be incorporated with this legal status.

Free Application for Federal Student Aid   Known by its abbreviation as the FAFSA, this form provided by the U.S.

Department of Education is used to determine student eligibility and financial need for a wide range of federal, state, and institutional awards for student financial aid. See also the earlier document, the PFAF.

Grants   Outright awards of monies to applicants, ranging from individual students, faculty as principal investigators, or as scholarly recipients based on application, review, and selection by the funding agency.

Higher Education Act (HEA)   Large-scale, comprehensive federal legislation dealing primarily with student financial aid and programs to enhance access to and affordability of going to college. The original HEA legislation was passed by Congress in 1965 and has been subject to periodic reauthorization several times.

Higher Education General Information Systems   Known among higher education professionals by the abbreviation HEGIS, this was a federal government data collection and data presentation system by and for colleges and universities in such categories as enrollment, retention, degree completion, and institutional finances. HEGIS, started in 1968, was eventually replaced by the Integrated Postsecondary Education Data Systems. Institutions failing to file timely HEGIS reports place at risk their receipt of federal funding from research grants and other sources.

Higher Education Price Index   Known by the abbreviation HEPI, this measure of annual inflation was developed by college and university leaders in the 1980s as an alternative to the familiar inflationary measure the Consumer Price Index (CPI). Its intent is to track increased costs of goods and services typically purchased by colleges and universities—as distinguished from typical U.S. family household purchases.

Liberal Arts College   An academic institution characterized by courses of study in the arts and sciences, leading to conferral of the bachelor of arts (BA) degree. Operationally, liberal arts colleges tend to be private (independent) in their control and board oversight. They also tend to be relatively small in total enrollment, usually less than 3,000 students. Liberal arts colleges may offer some selected graduate and professional degree programs, but the distinguishing characteristic of the genre is undergraduate BA instruction.

Loans Student financial aid from an institution, a foundation, a federal or state agency, or some approved lending agency. It is a form of student financial aid characterized by required student repayment, as distinguished from a student financial aid award in the form of a grant.

Merit-Based Student Financial Aid Usually in the form of a grant that does not require repayment, merit-based aid is based on selection to identify and reward talent—perhaps measured by grade point average, the Scholastic Aptitude Test (SAT) scores, letters of reference, and some demonstration of achievement or performance, without consideration of a student applicant's financial need.

Need-Based Student Financial Aid Student aid for which selection is determined among academically qualified applicants on the basis of measured, documented financial need. This type of aid tends to include such federal programs as Pell Grants.

Nonprofit Institution In the case of postsecondary education, this refers to a legally determined status as an educational, artistic, and charitable organization. Typically, nonprofit institutions do not pay income tax or property tax. Also, donors' gifts often are tax deductible by the donor.

Packaging A term used by financial aid offers at colleges and universities and at government and philanthropic agencies to refer to the mix of grant, loan, and work study awarded to a student as a resultant "financial aid package." A financial aid package consisting largely of a grant is more appealing to a student than is a package that consists predominantly of a loan.

Parent Financial Aid Form (PFAF) Originally known as the Financial Aid Form, a form created by the College Entrance

Examination Board to provide all applicants for undergraduate admission and all college admissions and financial aid officers with a uniform reporting system of student and family income. It is widely used as a basis for making determinations on need-based student aid. *See also* FAFSA.

Pell Grant   Created as part of the 1972 reauthorization of the Higher Education Act, this student financial aid grant originally was known as the Basic Educational Opportunity Grant (BEOG). The designation Pell Grant was adopted in honor of Senator Claiborne Pell (D, RI), champion and architect of the major student financial aid programs in Congress in the late 1960s and early 1970s. Pell Grants typically are intended to provide need-based financial aid to students from modest income families who show good academic standing.

Per Capita   Literally, "for each head." A useful concept or measure for disaggregating an institution's resources to provide a relative estimate of award or achievement per student or research grant per faculty. Its appeal is that it provides one way to guard against the hegemony of a large institution with high student enrollments or with a large number of faculty dominating rankings and ratings based exclusively on large size.

Philanthropy   Voluntary donation of time, service, goods, or money for the public good.

Price   In higher education, this is the amount of money a student as consumer pays for designated goods and services. It is often used in conjunction with the term *costs of higher education* but is distinct, not synonymous.

Private Institution   Also known as an independent institution, this term refers to a legal category of educational and philanthropic organization under the jurisdiction of a self-perpetuating board of trustees or directors—as distinguished from an educational office or institution that has a board appointed by a state or federal office or agency, for example, by a governor.

Public Institution   In higher education, a college or university that has a board of trustees or board of visitors that is appointed by and reports to the state's governor or to some other government officer.

Research University   A university, either public or private, characterized by a mission that devotes substantial time, space, and resources to sponsored research projects, with external funding via government agencies and/or philanthropic foundations. It is a category that usually includes a strong presence of doctoral programs that lead to conferral of the PhD degree.

Retention   A college or university's ability to have a student maintain good academic standing as well as complete coursework and educational programs so as to be "retained" for subsequent progress.

Revenue   Funds or monies from varied sources that provide income for a college, university, or other institution or educational organization.

Revenue Theory   An explanation of how and why college and university expenditures tend to increase substantially each year. The central tenet of the theory, developed by economist Howard R. Bowen, is that colleges "raise all the money they can, and then spend all the money they raise."

Sticker Price   This popular colloquial term, has been borrowed by higher education constituencies from the argot of automobile sales and car lots. The analogy is that whether one is shopping for an affordable car or an affordable college, the publicized price—"the sticker price"—usually is subject to credits, discounts, and buy-downs. When these items are taken into consideration, the implication is that many, perhaps most, students as consumers receive financial aid or other inducements that make their price less than the original conspicuous sticker price.

Subsidy   An appropriation that an institution such as a college or university deliberately allocates to a particular program or activity, especially when that program or activity does not generate sufficient revenues to be self-supporting.

Tuition   The published, official price for academic courses, services, and goods that a college or university charges enrolled students. It is frequently distinguished from other charges a student may encounter in the form of fees, deposits, room, board, books, clothing, travel, and educational supplies during an academic term.

Tuition Assistance Grant   Widely known by its abbreviation of TAG, this term refers primarily to state policies and programs that award a special category of students with a per capita scholarship, usually applied toward tuition payments. One of the most widespread arrangements is for the state government to award a TAG of, for example, $1,500 per year that is portable for a qualified student who is a resident of the state so that he or she can use it at an independent (private) college within the state.

Tuition Gap   An indicator of the difference between the tuition charged by a state (public) college versus that of the tuition charged by an independent (private) college. When a state provides a state college or university with a per student subsidy, the tuition price tends to be reduced. Independent colleges refer to "tuition gap" data to suggest that although a state college may have a tuition charge that is substantially less than that charged by an independent institution, the actual *cost* of educating a student at the two institutions often is similar.

Unmet Need   A calculation to identify the amount of money a student who has applied for financial aid will have to pay for going to college in a given year, after taking into account the amount provided by all sources of scholarship and financial aid as well as individual contributions from savings and jobs.

Index

About the Author

John R. Thelin is a Professor of the History of Higher Education & Public Policy at the University of Kentucky. From 1993 to 1996, he was Professor of Higher Education & Philanthropy at Indiana University. At the College of William & Mary in Virginia from 1981 to 1993, he was Chancellor Professor, received the Phi Beta Kappa Award for Outstanding Faculty Scholarship, and served as President of the Faculty Assembly and Liaison to the Board of Visitors. From 1978 to 1981, he was Research Director for the Association of Independent California Colleges and Universities.

A 1969 alumnus of Brown University, he was a member of Phi Beta Kappa, concentrated in European History, and was a letterman on the varsity wrestling team. At the University of California–Berkeley he received an MA in American History, a PhD in the History of Education, and was named a Regents Fellow.

John is author of *A History of American Higher Education*. His 1994 book *Games Colleges Play*, a history of intercollegiate sports scandals, received the American Research Library Association's Pen Award. His articles have been published in *The Encyclopedia of American Social History, Review of Higher Education, Journal of Higher Education, History of Education Quarterly, Wall Street Journal, Washington Post, Chronicle of Higher Education,* and *Inside Higher Ed.*

John served as President of the Association for the Study of Higher Education in 2000. At the University of Kentucky, he was named a University Research Professor in 2001 and received the Provost's Award for Outstanding Teaching in 2006. In 2007, he received the American Educational Research Associations Award for Outstanding Research on Higher Education. In 2008, the National Education Association conferred on him their Excellence in the Academy award. He received the Association for the Study of Higher Education's Outstanding Research Achievement Award in 2011.

John has received two major research grants from the Spencer Foundation. In 2009, the Aspen Institute awarded him a research grant to study higher education endowment policies. He has been a member of the American Enterprise Institute's working group on the future of higher education since 2006.